PEN and INK TECHNIQUES

Paulette Fedarb

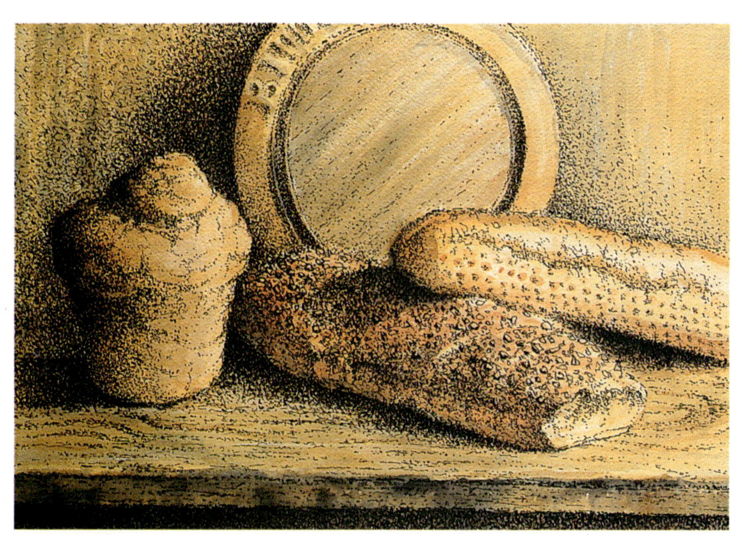

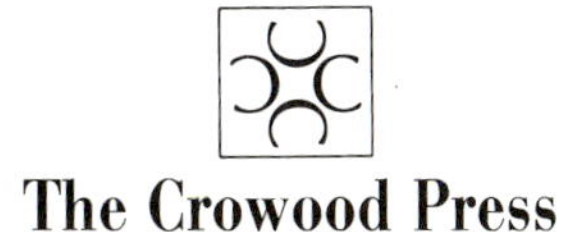

The Crowood Press

CONTENTS

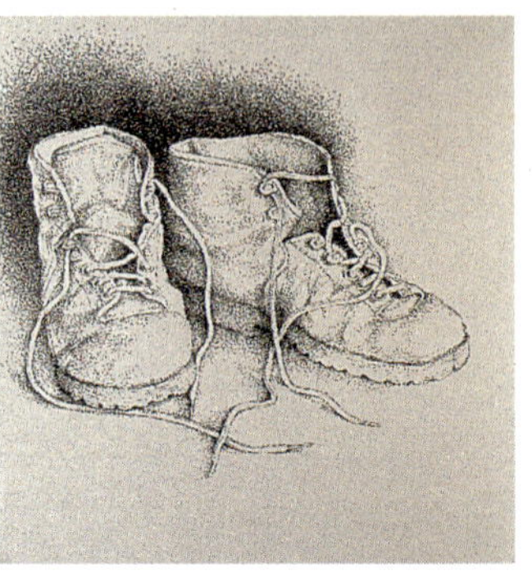

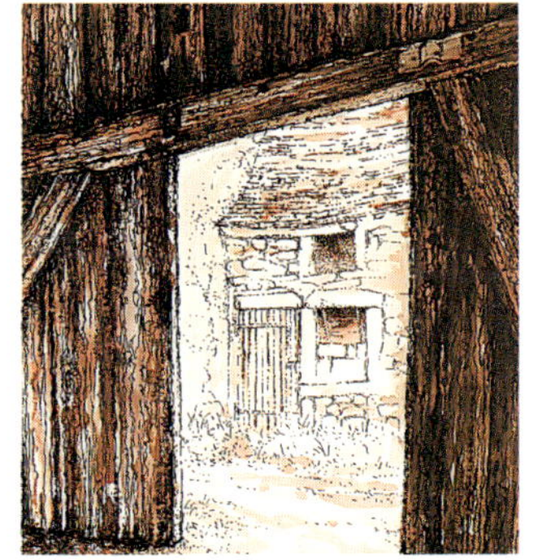

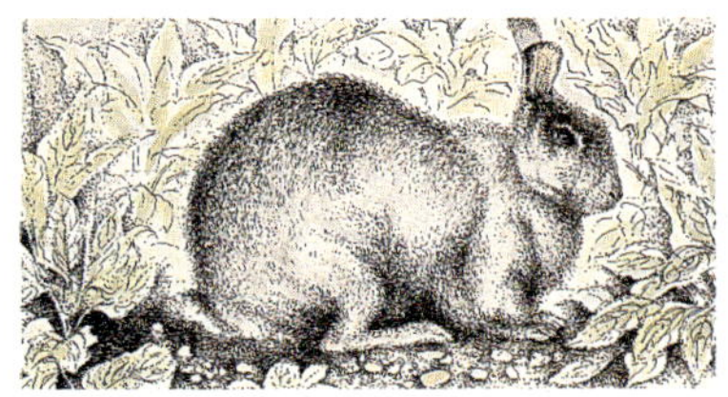

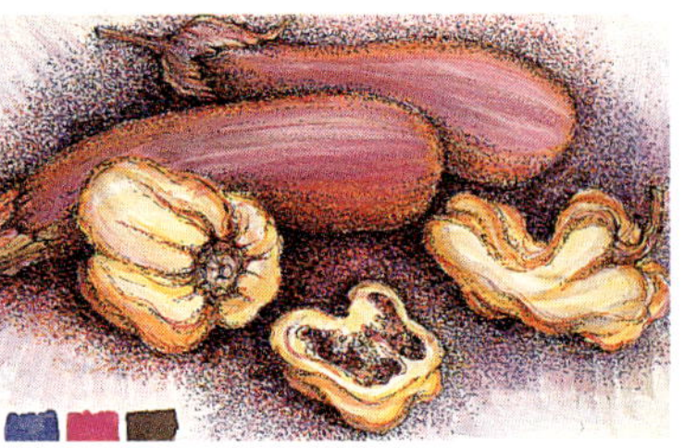

Contents

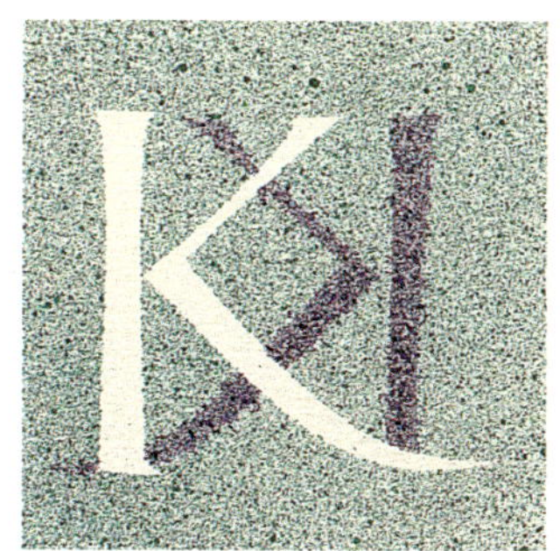

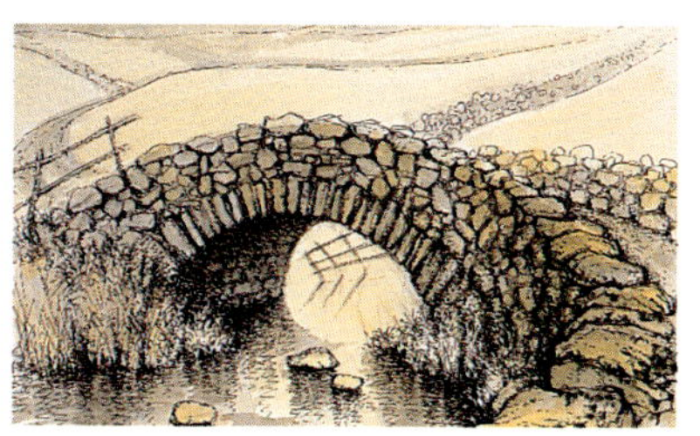

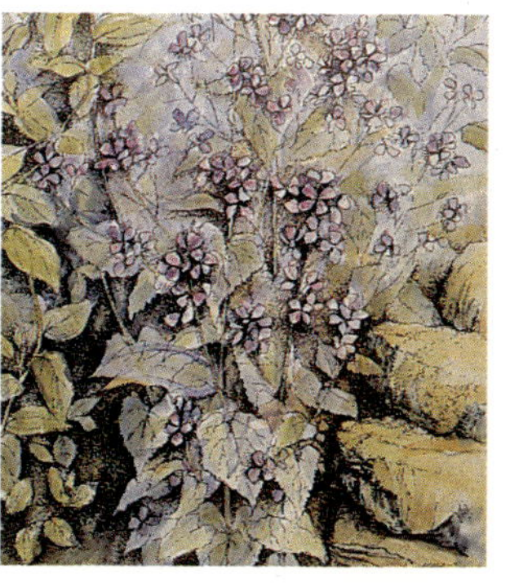

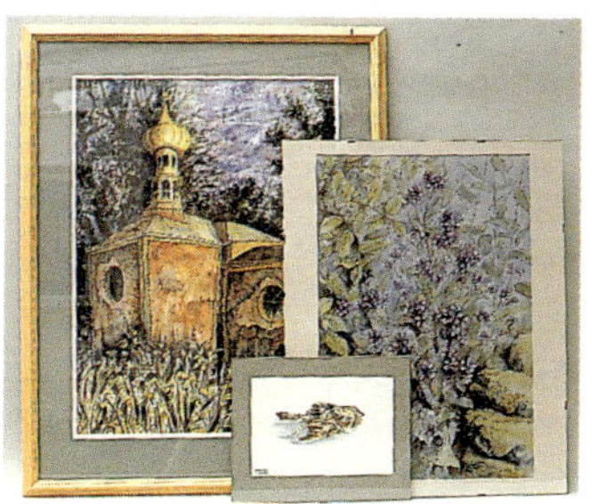

INTRODUCTION

Cheeseplant *Pen drawing on top of freely brushed-on watercolour gives a bold impact.*

The linear pen strokes were made with medium and thick nibs, the pen being held high up the holder to give a loose and fluid line. Most detail has been omitted as it would detract from the spontaneity of the approach.

Anything that can be dipped in a pot of ink – a stick, quill, pen or brush, or even a finger – will make a blob or line that is the first step towards making a drawing. The purpose of this book is to help you develop the skill to direct and control these marks, and to demonstrate some of the creative possibilities of a fascinating branch of drawing. My aim throughout is to give guidance and instruction, not dictation, and to encourage you to build your own personal style.

The fear of not being able to 'rub out' has often held people back from using pen and ink, thus denying themselves access to one of the most enjoyable graphic forms. In practice, it is not such an indelible medium once you know a few 'tricks of the trade'!

The history of pen and ink goes back a long way. Early varieties of ink, made from mixtures of gum, soot and water, were known in prehistoric times and there is evidence that the Chinese and the Egyptians were using this medium as early as 2,500BC. The Romans, too, were familiar with it and even used a form of metal nib.

The types of pen most commonly in use before 1822, when the metal nib came into popular use through mass production, were the quill and the reed pen. The quill was made from the pinion feathers of the goose, crow or raven, and the reed pen was made from a type of stiff, dried grass.

Many of the old masters' drawings were done with a reed pen and a brown ink called bistre, made from charred wood. Rembrandt often used this method to produce the vigorous and lively strokes that are so much admired in his remarkable drawings. A similar vitality is seen in the sketches of Van Gogh, who also liked the reed pen and the bold lines it made.

Today there is a much wider choice of pen, from the traditional dip-pen to the fountain, cartridge, ball-point and fibre-tip. There are also technical and watercolour pens, providing a variety of drawing points both thick and fine, an enormous range for the professional and amateur artist.

Pen and ink is one of the most rewarding and versatile of all drawing media. It can be free and spontaneous or meticulously detailed, with many variants in between. The impact on the page is positive and it is no coincidence that many of the finest drawings have been done in this way. To the artists already mentioned can be added Michelangelo, Hieronymus Bosch, Goya, Picasso and Henry Moore; they are just a few among many others who have used the medium in their own inimitable and powerful style. Study some of these works and you will see for yourself.

The line produced with a dip-pen is possibly more expressive than any other: thick, thin; fluid and continuous, or short and stabbing; sweeping, bold strokes or tentative, searching ones. The mark can be a tiny dot or a spreading flourish across the paper. In addition to these attributes there are practical advantages too. A pen is small and can be slipped into a pocket with a sketchbook for working outside; there is no need to take a lot of other equipment. It dries quickly and will not rub off like pencil or pastel, so avoiding any need for fixative.

The book is divided into sections, each dealing with a specific topic. To help you build up your confidence, it begins with simple, basic instructions, showing how to make different strokes, and progresses to more elaborate and complex methods as your ability grows. The techniques demonstrated involve those that are well known and traditional, like pen and wash, but also other less orthodox ones, as you will discover in the section on Experimental Work. This has been included to provide some fun with the medium and to stimulate fresh, alternative approaches.

The many illustrations include both drawn examples and photographs. Some of these are straightforward pictures demonstrating a particular method, while others are more analytical and show how the picture progresses from start to finish. There are also step-by-step guides which you can try out for yourself, although in general, I would encourage you to follow the *principle* of the technique shown rather than copy the drawings too closely. The danger is that while you may become adept at copying, it may not help you very much with your own creative work. If you are doing a still life, for instance, set up your own group and work from that. It could be a similar group if you like, but the important point is that you would be working from *life* and not the flat page. Always work from what you see around you if possible, however simple it is. It will increase your powers of observation and teach you more about drawing.

As you get to grips with the various techniques in this book I hope you will also learn a great deal about the pleasures of drawing: the feel of the pen and the way it moves over the paper; the flow of brush and wash; the excitement of colour. It is all there just waiting for you to begin.

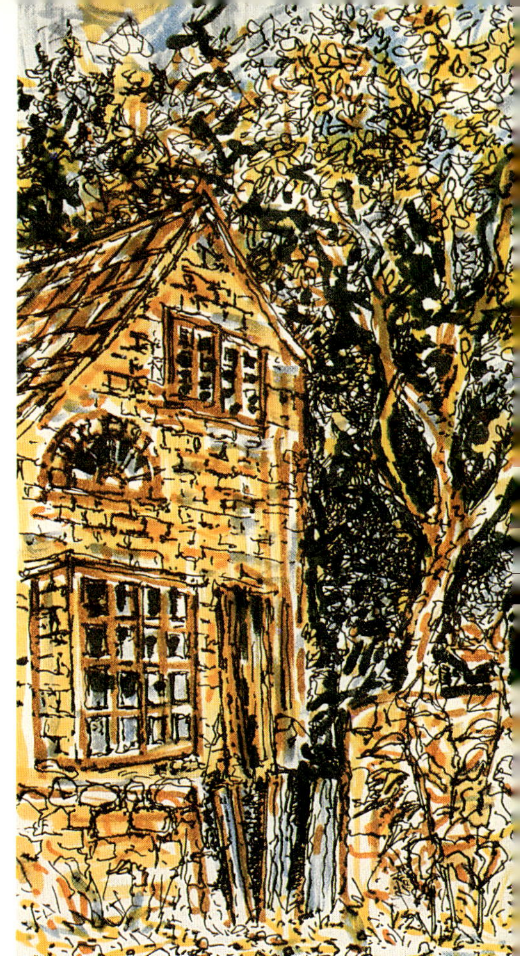

Old Cottage *A quick sketch of an overgrown cottage using water-colour pens and a black ball-point pen. This is an ideal method for making colour sketches on the spot.*

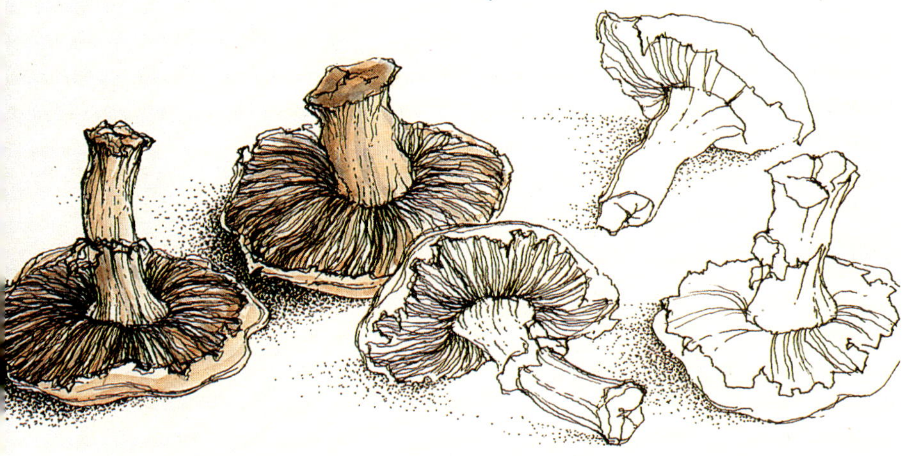

Mushrooms *These studies of mushrooms, using fine and very fine nibs, show how a drawing can change from being spare and economical to more naturalistic.*

The drawings are linear in technique, with tonal stippling on the shadows and added colour washes.

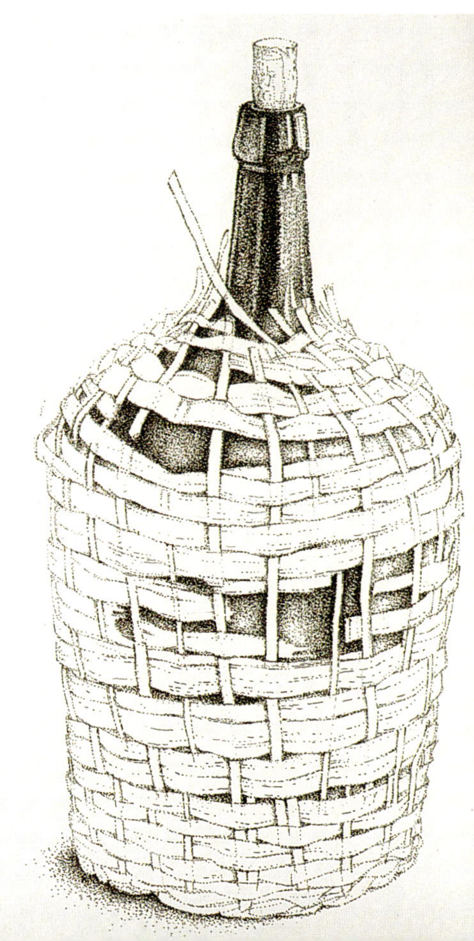

Water Pot *A different approach is shown here in this detailed and careful study of a water jar, using pen and Indian ink. Contrasting textures make an interesting challenge to the artist.*

MATERIALS & EQUIPMENT

MATERIALS & EQUIPMENT

- Pen holders
- Pen nibs
- Brushes
- Quill
- Ball points
- Fibre tips
- Art pens
- Watercolour pens
- Inks
- Papers
- Sketchblocks
- Resists
- Easel
- Drawing board
- Palettes
- Stick
- Toothbrush
- Spray diffuser
- Sponge
- Paper tissue

The pen you draw with, and the paper you draw on, are the most important items of your equipment and will have considerable influence over your handling of the pen and ink technique, and your subsequent development as a draughtsman or woman.

First, the pen itself. You will need a pen holder that feels comfortable in your hand and holds the nib firmly. Try to have more than one so that you have a variety of nibs to choose from and do not have to waste time, or interrupt drawing, to change them.

Second, the nib. Get as wide a selection of these as possible. Different nibs will produce varied strokes, which are essential to the cultivation of lively drawing. How you use and make these strokes will provide the hallmark of your individual style. At the foot of the page is an illustration showing some of the many nibs available, and in the chapter on Basics (*see* page 12), there are examples of lines made with these nibs.

Medium and thick nibs are easier to handle than very fine ones, which can splutter and sometimes cross if pressed too hard; but persevere in mastering the use of the finer nibs because they can produce beautiful and delicate lines. Some nibs are good tempered and will move in any direction, while others are definitely 'one way only'. Practice and trial will determine their potential, and sometimes usage will make them more flexible.

Now the paper. This is available as loose sheets, or in book form, or as a block. Paper is marked by weight, either in grams per square metre (gsm) or pounds. The higher the number, the heavier, or thicker the paper will be. Thus, 96gsm (45lbs) is a thin paper, while 425gsm (200lbs) is a thick paper.

It is important that the paper is appropriate for the work you wish to do. Techniques that require water, as in pen and wash, need a thicker paper than would pen and ink used on its own. You will also have to consider the surface you want; whether it should be smooth and even, or rough and textured.

If you are a beginner, and feel con-

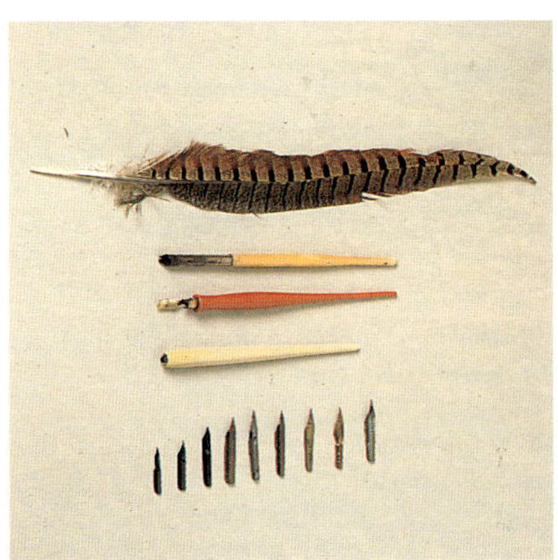

Pens and Nibs *A quill made from a pheasant's feather, pen holders, and an assortment of drawing nibs; thicker ones at the top and finer ones at the bottom.*

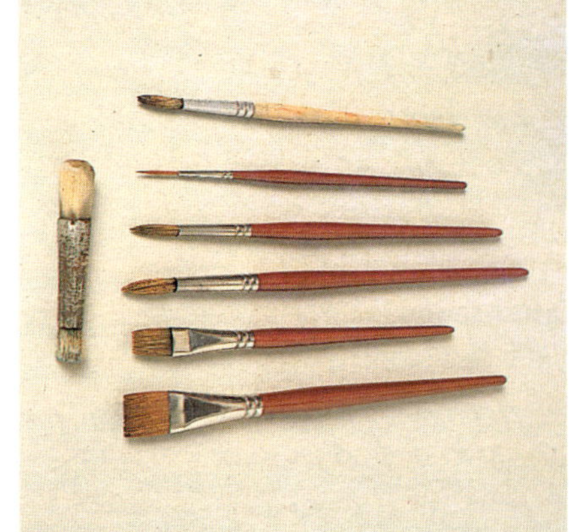

Brushes *Brushes for washes and watercolours. The top four are round, the lower ones are flat, 1 and 2cm (½ and ¾in). The stencil brush at the side will be used in experimental work.*

fused by so much choice, I would advise you to start with a general-purpose cartridge of 150gsm (70lbs). This is a low-cost paper, ideal for someone approaching pen and ink for the first time. It is suitable for stretching, and guidance on this is given in the next section. As your skill develops, you will want to use other qualities and, perhaps, specialist papers.

Towards the end of the book there is a chapter on papers (*see* page 72), which discusses the different types in greater detail than is given here.

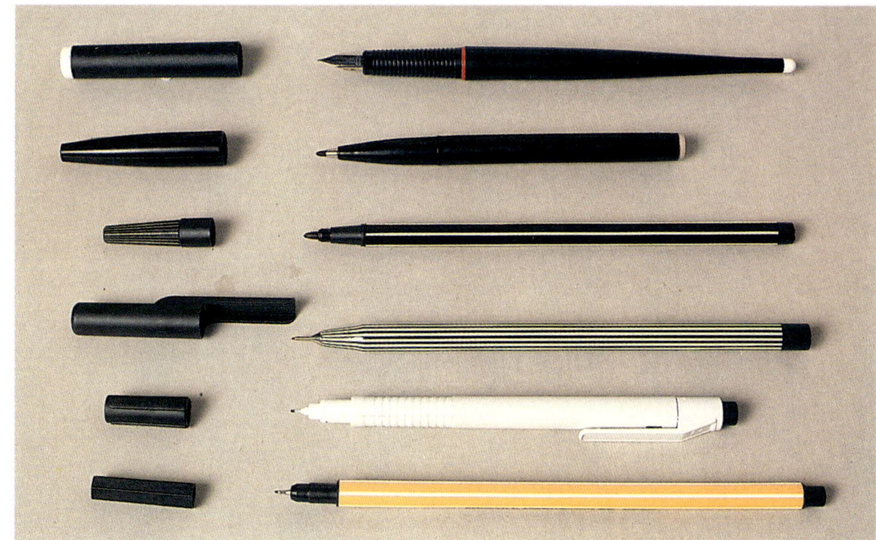

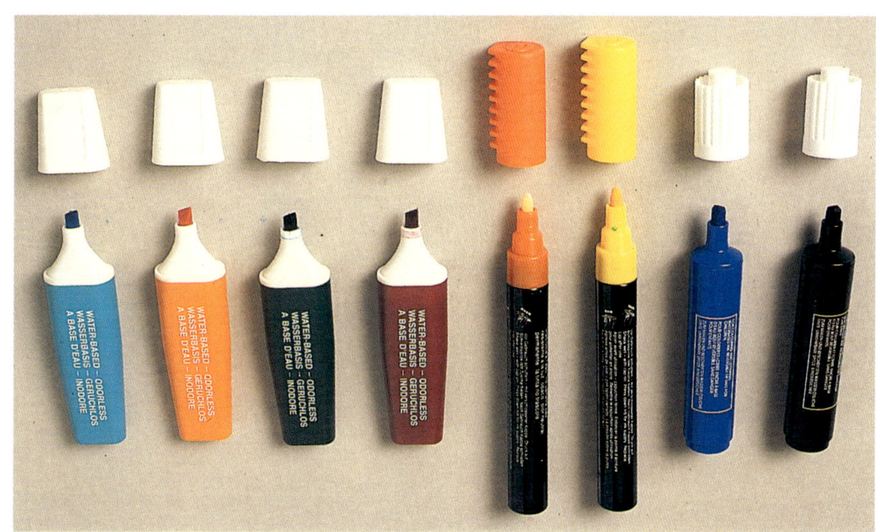

Art Pens/Watercolour Pens *The top illustration shows a collection of pens useful for sketching and making notes, as well as more lengthy studies. Starting from the top they are: art sketching pen and ink cartridges; two fibre-tip pens giving a thick line, good for rapid drawing; three ball-point pens giving a fine, regular line.*

The lower illustration shows watercolour pens. These are also good for sketching and making colour notes. The colours are transparent and can be used together to give colour mixtures. The diagonally shaped points give both thick and thin lines. Keep the tops on when not in use, otherwise they will quickly dry out.

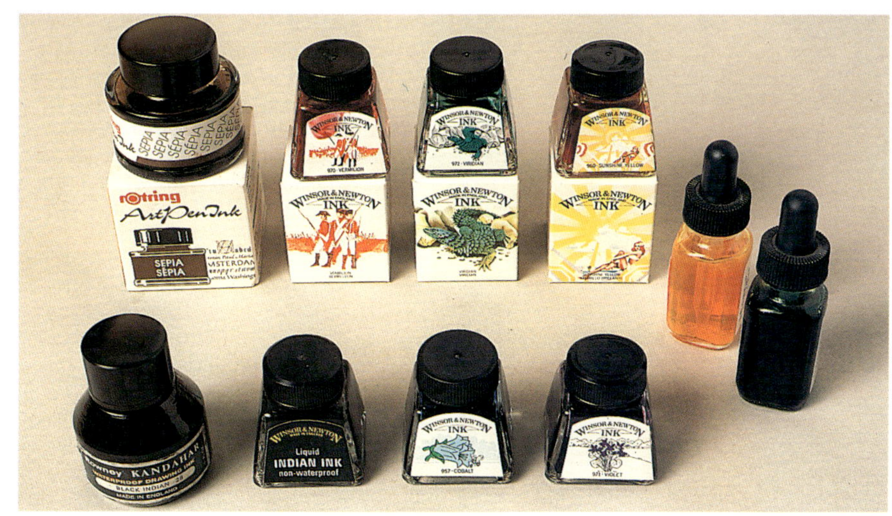

Inks *A picture illustrating coloured inks, both waterproof and non-waterproof. Sepia on the left of the top row: a brown non-waterproof ink; and black Indian (waterproof) and liquid Indian (non-waterproof) on the left of the bottom row.*

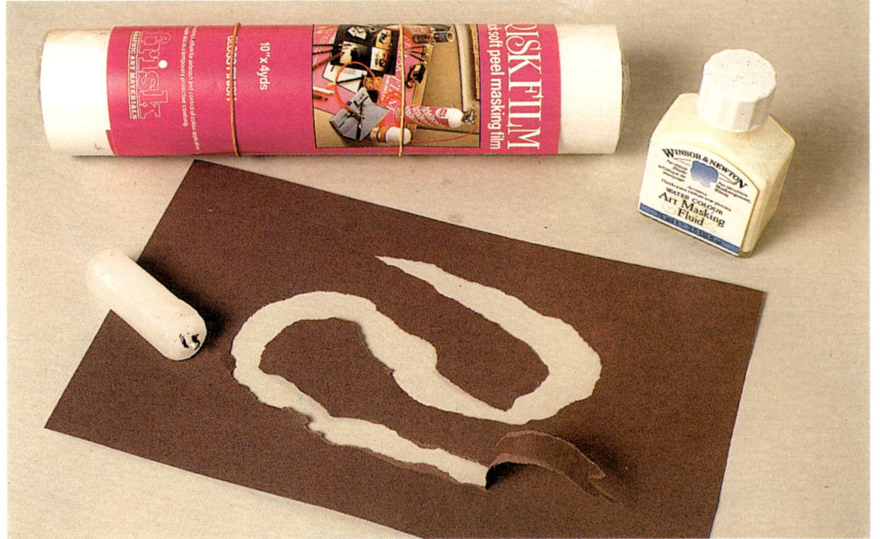

Resists *Resists can be useful in many kinds of art work. Their application in pen and ink techniques will usually be in connection with design and experimental projects, although several artists, including Graham Sutherland and John Piper, have used wax to great effect in their drawings.*

The resists shown in the illustration, working clockwise from the top, are: masking film; masking fluid; torn paper; wax candle.

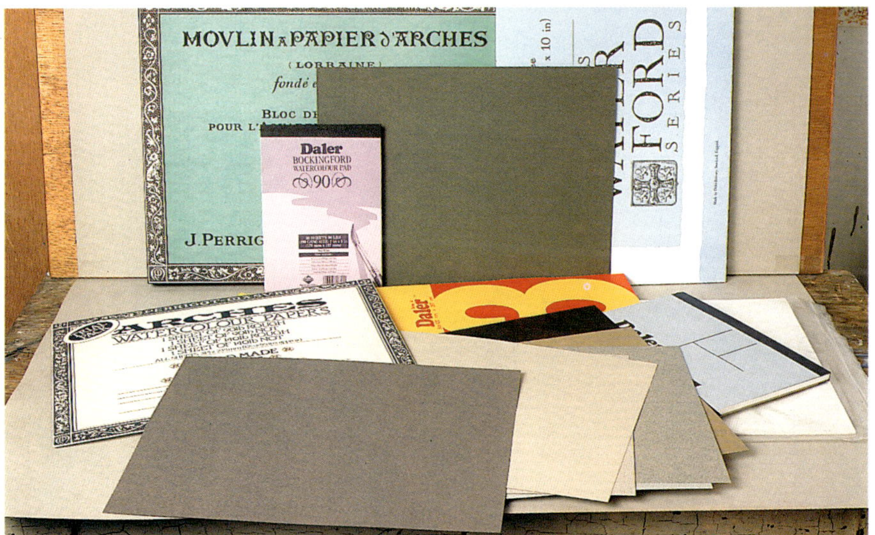

Papers *The picture shows just some of the many papers available, with their assorted sizes and varied formats. Those shown here are blocks, sketchbooks and loose sheets of coloured papers.*

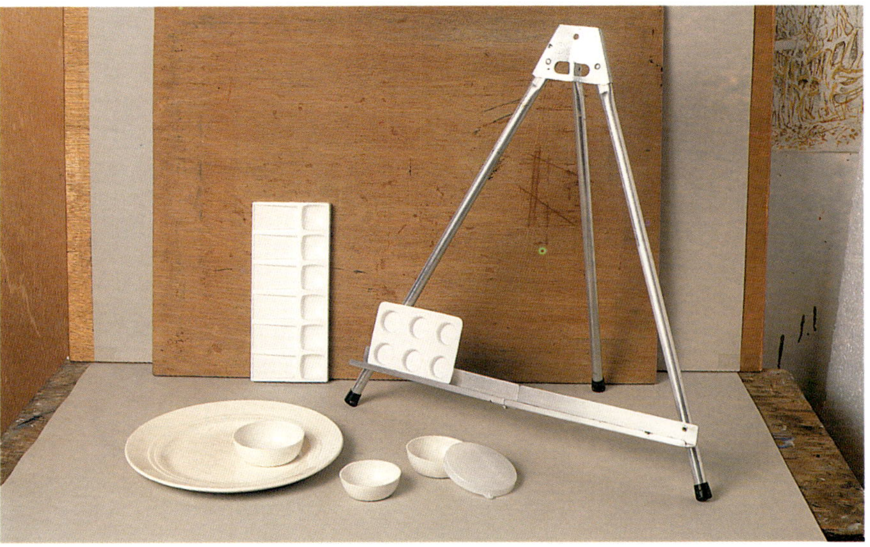

Easels and Palettes *Many people prefer to work on a flat surface for pen drawing, while others find a board propped against a table edge provides sufficient slope. However, if you wish to use an easel there are several suitable ones available.*

The one illustrated is an aluminium table easel and very lightweight. It folds up for convenient storage.

A mixing palette can be anything from an old kitchen plate, preferably white, to purpose-made palettes, usually plastic although china ones are obtainable. An assortment is given in the picture. The circular dishes in the foreground are particularly useful, one fitting inside the other with a lid to keep them together.

Materials & Equipment

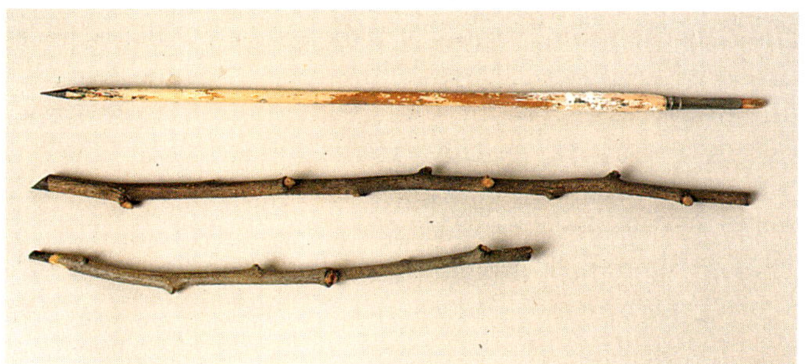

Sticks *Sometimes it is a stimulating change to use an alternative to the conventional pen for drawing. A sharpened stick dipped in ink makes an unusual substitute and can give interesting results.*

The picture shows the sharpened end of a discarded paintbrush, and two sharpened twigs. Try using different kinds of sticks to see whether the hardness or softness of the wood affects the drawn lines.

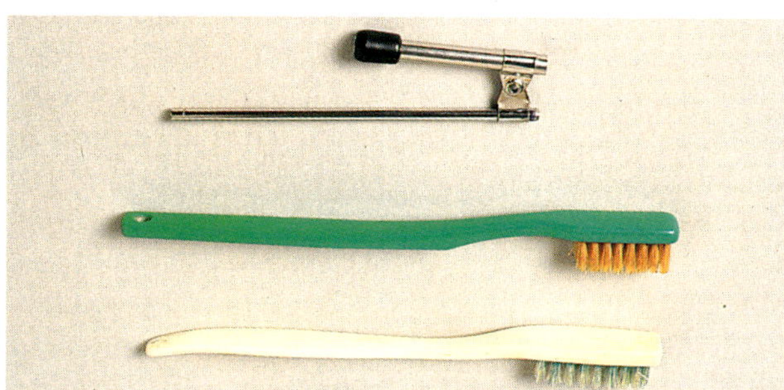

Spray Diffusers and Toothbrushes *Strictly speaking, these are not directly to do with pen and ink drawing techniques, but are included because they will be used with inks in the experimental section of the book.*

Sponges, Tissues and Salt
Sponges can be used for damping paper, lifting parts of the work, or applying inks and paints to make textures.

Tissues can also be used for lifting or applying inks, and are helpful in controlling washes. They are also essential for wiping the pen nib occasionally while drawing to prevent it clogging with ink.

Salt grains are a means of producing a special kind of texture.

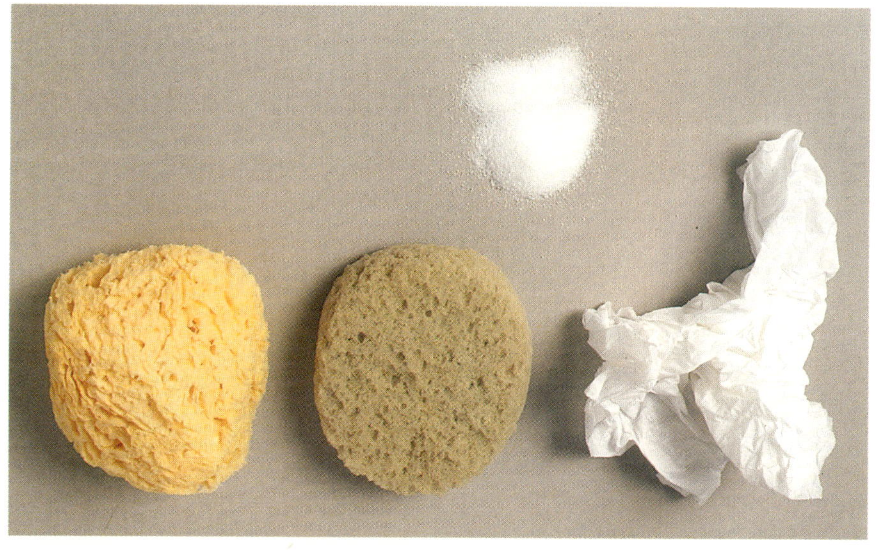

When buying materials always choose the best you can afford – it is better to go for quality rather than quantity. Do not be tempted by elaborate packaging and fancy containers; these can be very costly and you will be paying for the wrapping, not just the contents. A handful of good drawing implements, brushes and carefully chosen colours will be far more useful to you.

Having made your purchase, it is important to look after materials properly to ensure that they last well. They will also be nicer to use and respond more readily to your requirements.

Always clean and dry pens and nibs after use. Rinse brushes in clean water and reshape the hairs. Stand them on their handles in a container; an old mug or jam jar is excellent for this and will prevent the hairs becoming damaged or mis-shapen. Brushes can be subject to moth attack if kept in enclosed containers for long periods.

Have a supply of rough or scrap paper available, ready to try out pen strokes, washes, colours or new ideas and sketches. Rough paper is indispensable for lots of things and can save many a piece of more precious paper.

STRETCHING PAPER

Before starting to stretch your paper, make sure you have all the equipment you will need ready and to hand.

Measure and cut the gumstrip and lay it on the table so that you can see at a glance which are the longer, and which are the shorter pieces. If the gumstrip tends to curl up, roll it up in the opposite direction and it should then lie flat. Wet the sponge and place it on a dish, making sure you have enough space in which to work.

Taking time to ensure everything is prepared before you begin will help to make the task proceed successfully. Trying to cope with gumstrip when your hands are damp can be annoying and difficult to say the least!

As you become proficient at stretching paper, you may find you can reduce the overlap of gumstrip to less than 1cm (½in).

The purpose of stretching paper is to provide a smooth and consistent surface that will not cockle when water is applied to it in the form of watercolour or ink washes. Nothing can be more frustrating to the artist than a lumpy surface where the wash gathers in puddles, thus making it almost impossible to work with any degree of control.

The process involves immersing the paper in water, placing the wet, stretched paper on to a board and fixing all four sides with gumstrip, then letting it dry naturally and completely flat. As the stretched paper dries, it contracts and produces a tight, smooth surface.

Not all paper will need to be stretched. Very thick papers will probably not require stretching and thin papers would be unsuitable for the process because they might disintegrate. In the chapter on different papers (*see* page 72), I will be discussing the different weights of papers that are available.

In general, there seem to be two schools of thought about the necessity of stretching paper. Some artists always do so, in order to ensure a really even and flat surface upon which to work, no matter what technique is to be used; while others only do so when using a technique requiring a lot of water. It is very much a question of personal preference, and whether you feel the extra time needed to prepare the paper is justified.

However, it is important that you know how to do this, and if you study carefully the following step-by-step photographs you should find it a straightforward procedure, though it may require more than one attempt before you produce a perfectly stretched piece of paper.

Occasionally, the gumstrip will pull away from the board. This may be due to uneven drying or because the gumstrip is too narrow to hold the tension of the paper. The gumstrip should not be less than 4–5cm (1½–2in) wide.

Stretching Paper – Step-by-Step

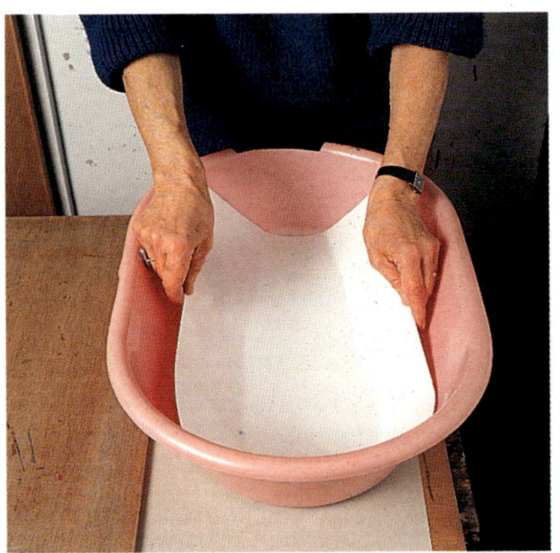

Wetting the Paper *Immerse the paper in cold water for a few seconds. The paper does not need to be saturated. Make sure that the whole surface of the paper is properly wetted.*

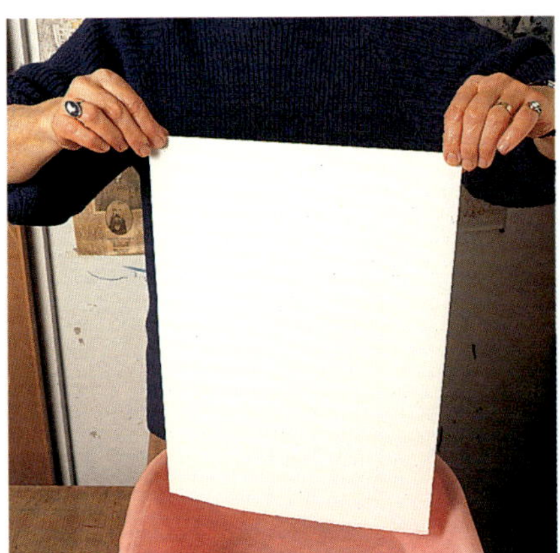

Lift the paper out of the water, holding it by the top two corners. Tilt it slightly towards one corner to allow the surplus water to run off.

MATERIALS
Stretching Paper

- Paper
- Drawing Board
- Gumstrip
- Scissors
- Sponge
- Bowl or sink with water

Place the paper on the board, lining it up with the edges as well as you can, but do not make repeated attempts to do this as it may affect or even tear the paper. It will become easier with time and practice.

Smooth out any creases and air bubbles with your hands, or a sponge if you prefer. Always work from the centre out towards the edges. Sometimes, if there is a large crease, it may be necessary to lift that portion of the paper and then gently smooth it back into position again.

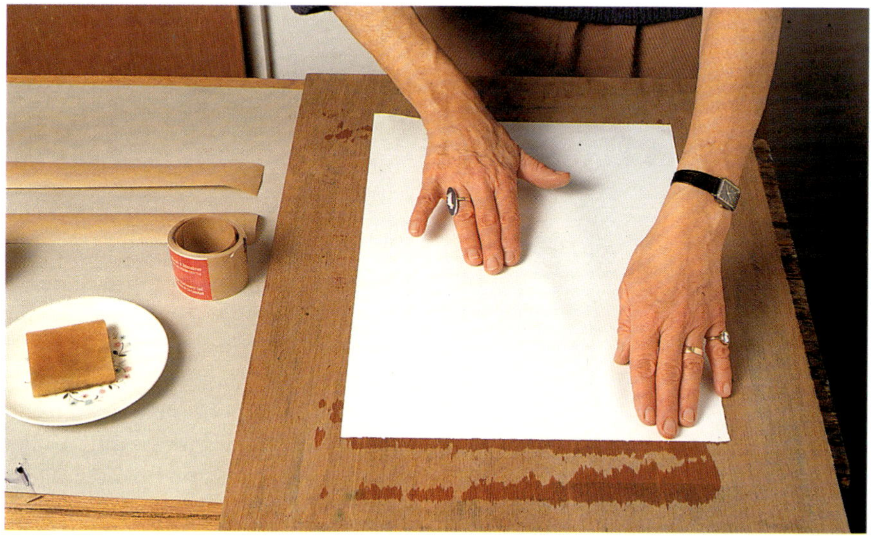

Fix the paper to the board on all four sides with gumstrip. This should be ready to use, having been prepared beforehand. The gumstrip should extend beyond the paper by 4cm (1½in) at each end.

Damp the gumstrip with the sponge, making sure there are no dry spots left. It is sturdy enough for a thorough wetting.

Attach it to the paper, allowing 1cm (½in) overlap. Now the benefit of previously lining up the paper with the board will be felt as it helps in getting the gumstrip straight. Again, this comes with practice so do not worry if it is crooked at first. Press the gumstrip down firmly, working outwards from the centre.

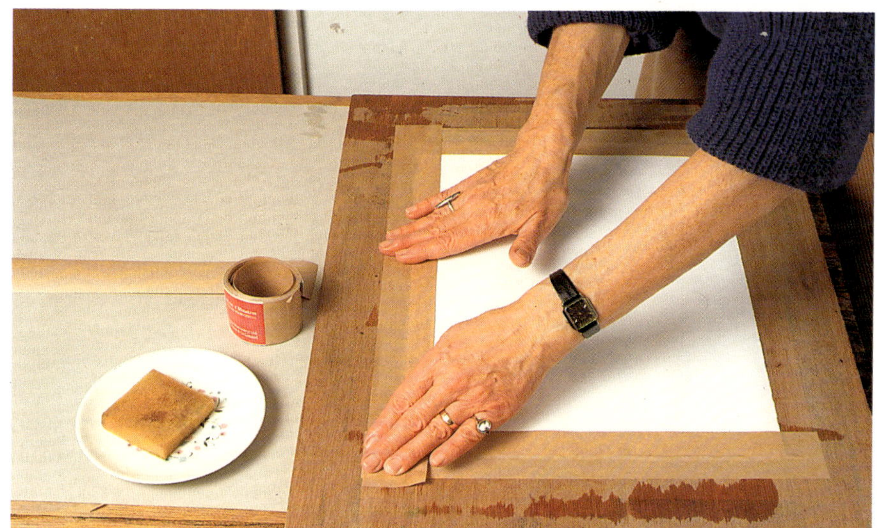

Leave the board in a horizontal position to allow the paper to dry evenly. It should take about an hour to dry although this will naturally depend upon the temperature of the room.

To remove the finished drawing, insert a knife blade under the gumstrip and the paper, and carefully slide it round on all sides. This method will prevent score lines appearing on the board underneath, which will occur if a craft knife is used.

Finally, trim away the gumstrip with a sharp knife and steel rule.

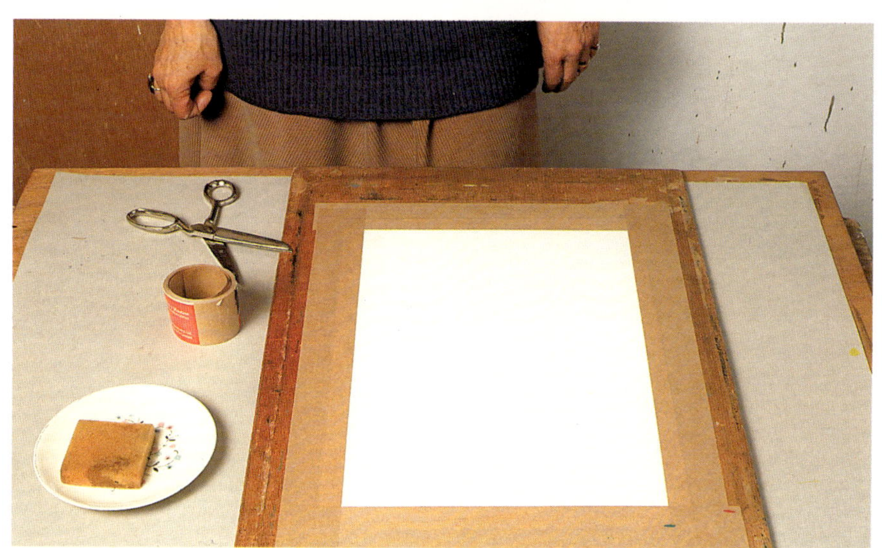

BASICS

MATERIALS & EQUIPMENT

- Paper
- Pen holder
- Nibs
- Black Indian ink
- White chalk
- White watercolour paint
- Drawing board
- Paper tissue

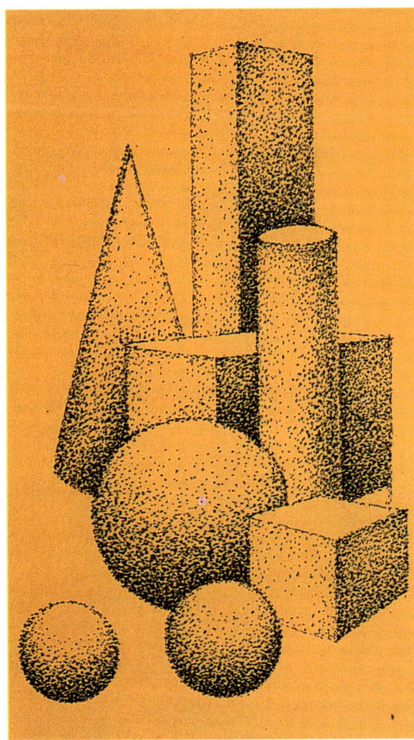

Geometric Shapes *A group of geometric shapes drawn to make them appear solid, using a stippled technique. Notice the graduation of tone from light to dark. It is this subtle change that helps to make them look three-dimensional.*

Lines

Now you are ready to begin. Your paper is in front of you and your pen, nibs and ink beside you.

Having chosen a nib, dip the pen into the ink and make a firm line right across the paper. Now make another one, and yet another, but this time make it wavy. Next, repeat the procedure, holding the pen close to the nib. Notice the difference the position of the hand makes and how this affects the lines.

At the bottom of this page there are examples of marks made with an assortment of implements and nibs. These represent the smallest and, consequently, the most controlled marks that can be made. Try out some for yourself and see how tiny a dot you can produce. Practise the lines shown on the facing page, using different nibs and altering your hand position. By the time the paper is covered you will have begun to familiarize yourself with this technique.

The dot and the line are the foundations upon which pen and ink work is based. The illustrations in this book are all executed using variations of these marks, sometimes in conjunction with other methods.

If you are a beginner, it is important that you get used to the 'feel' of the pen and the type of strokes it will make before you attempt to tackle an actual drawing. There are enough things to get used to: how much ink is needed, how hard to press and which direction to take the pen, without the added complications of drawing a particular shape at this stage.

Having practised these initial stages you should feel confident enough to move on to the next section, using tones.

Lines

The uses for the lines I have given are only suggestions. They can of course be used however you like, and as you become more proficient, you will develop them in your own way. Dogmatism has no place in drawing!

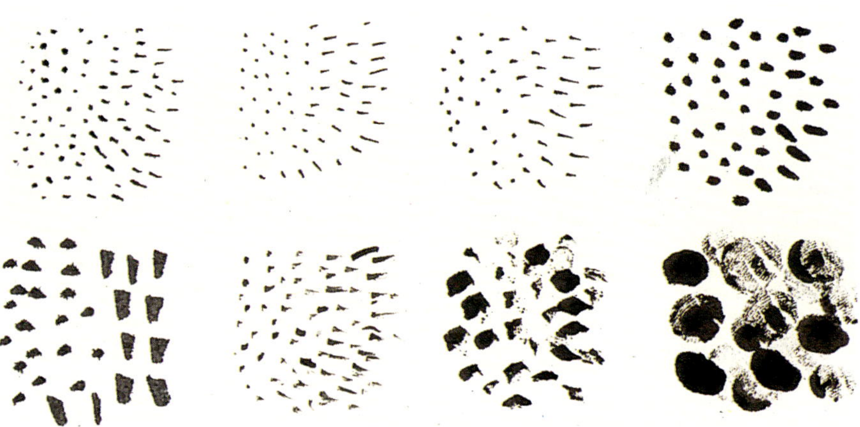

A collection of some of the smallest marks that can be made with various drawing implements and ink. Top row, from the left: dip-pen with medium nib, art pen, ball-point, fibre-tip. Bottom row from the left: watercolour pen, quill, stick, finger.

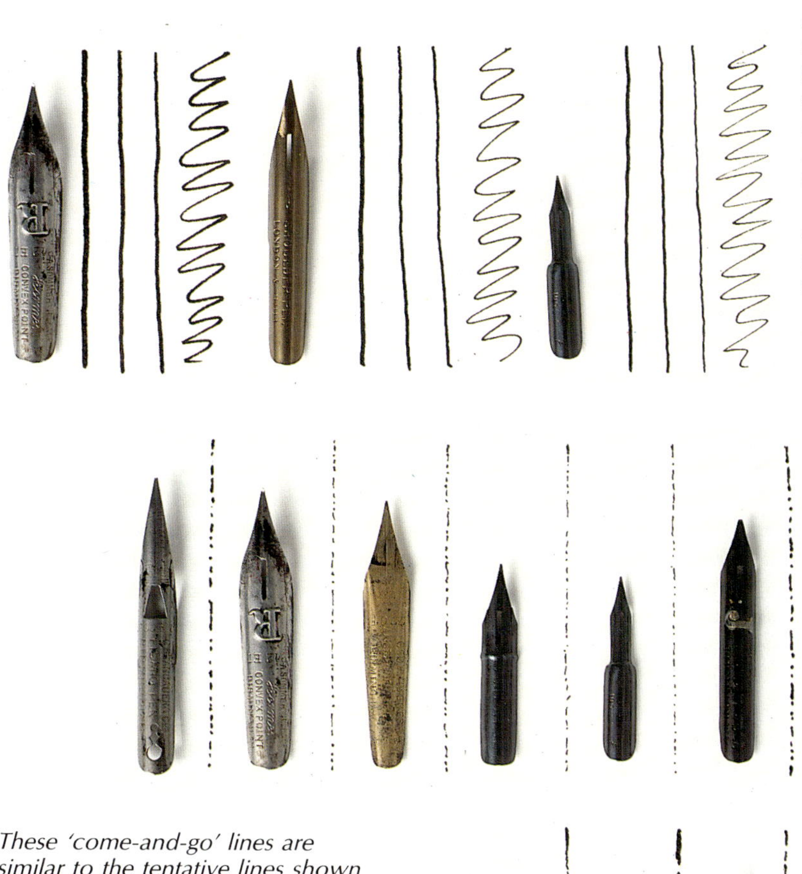

Examples of continuous lines and the nibs they are drawn with: first, thick lines made with Hermes convex point nib; second, medium lines made with a Shoulder pen nib; third, fine lines made with an Artist's pen nib.

The width that a particular pen nib makes will also be determined by the amount of hand pressure that is used when drawing.

Examples of tentative lines, with their nibs. From the left: Figaro nib; Hermes convex point; Pen painting nib; Warranted nib; Artist's pen nib; Elongated JM nib.

This type of line will most likely be used at the beginning of a drawing when you are planning the composition and assessing proportions and do not want to make too firm a commitment at this stage. It is a line admirably suited to searching out the special and unique qualities of a particular form.

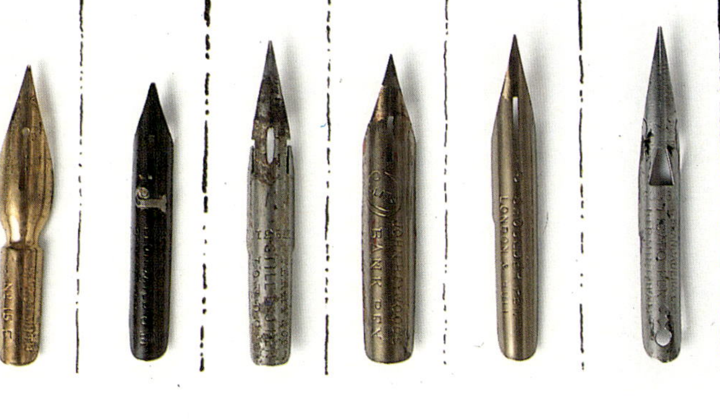

These 'come-and-go' lines are similar to the tentative lines shown above, and would be suitable for the same purpose. The nibs used to make them are, from the left: Hardtmuth 15F; Elongated JM; Stiletto; Bank pen; Shoulder pen; Figaro.

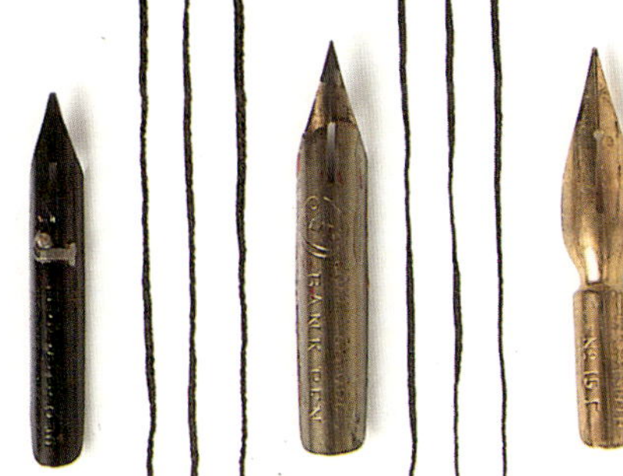

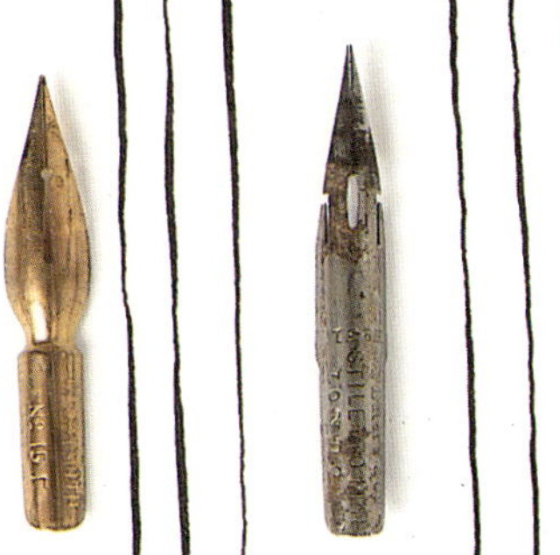

Examples of thick and thin lines, with their nibs. From the left: Elongated JM; Bank; Hardtmuth 15F; Stiletto.

The use of this line encourages flexibility and prevents too rigid and set a movement of the drawing hand. The variation of the stroke is produced by variation of pressure on the nib.

Basics

A drawing done on grey-tinted paper, using black Indian ink and a Shoulder nib.

The tonal techniques used here show the stippled and scribbled methods demonstrated on the opposite page. You will see how the size of the stroke varies according to the degree of control required. Compare the drawing around the fastening holes with the tonal drawing of the background.

The density of pen work in the background helps to push the boots forward, making them stand out in the picture, so that tone is used both to describe the actual form of the boots themselves and also the surrounding space.

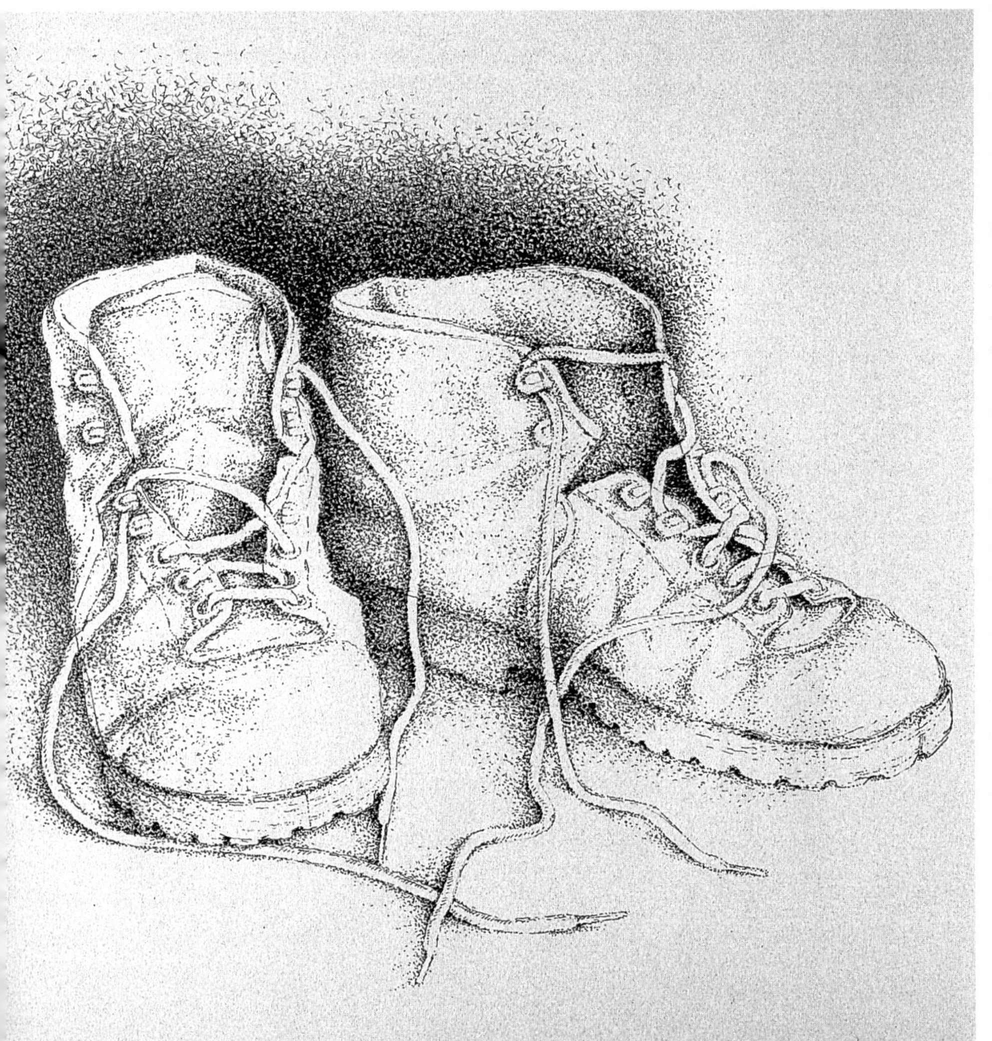

Tones

Tone is the word used to describe the use of light and dark in a picture. It will help to give your drawings substance and make them appear three-dimensional. It can also add to the atmosphere and the mood of your work.

When you draw, you are making an image on a flat piece of paper, unlike the sculptor who works 'in the round', so if you want to make your objects look solid, with space between them, a technique which will do this must be devised. You are in effect seeking to create an illusion. There are many ways of doing this, but here we are concerned only with the pen.

On the opposite page, there are four examples showing techniques for building up tone in drawing. As you will notice, they all consist of either dots or lines used in a special way: the denser or closer together you make these marks, the darker they will appear. Thus you have a range of tone from light, with the dots and lines spaced well apart, to dark, with the dots and lines close together, and a middle range of tones somewhere between the two. Practise these different methods and see how gradual you can make the transition from light to dark, and from dark to light.

These simple exercises will help you to gain control over the pen and the marks it can make. They will also encourage sensitivity, so that your drawing will have movement, and not look too rigid.

If you turn over the page you will find two step-by-step guides showing how to construct a sphere and a box. These two shapes form the basis of many forms you will encounter constantly in picture-making. Your shapes may be wobbly to begin with, but they will improve and you will learn to draw with greater confidence than you would do if you always relied upon drawing aids. A house drawn with a ruler will appear stiff and unnatural. The natural action of your own hand will produce a far more convincing and interesting image. Study and make drawings from them and always try to draw freehand.

Which kind of technique to choose for tonal drawing will largely depend upon personal choice but also upon suitability for a particular subject. For example, if you wish to cover large areas, scribbled and hatched strokes would be appropriate, but for fine, detailed work, stippling may be more suitable. You will usually find that a mixture of strokes works best and prevents monotony of style.

Four examples of stippled tones using different nibs, producing a range of dots from thick to fine. This stippled technique is the one that gives the greatest amount of control in a tonal drawing, owing to the small size of the marks and the subtle gradation it is possible to achieve from dark to light.

The drawback is that it takes time to build up the dots, particularly when covering a large area, and you may prefer a technique that covers the ground more swiftly.

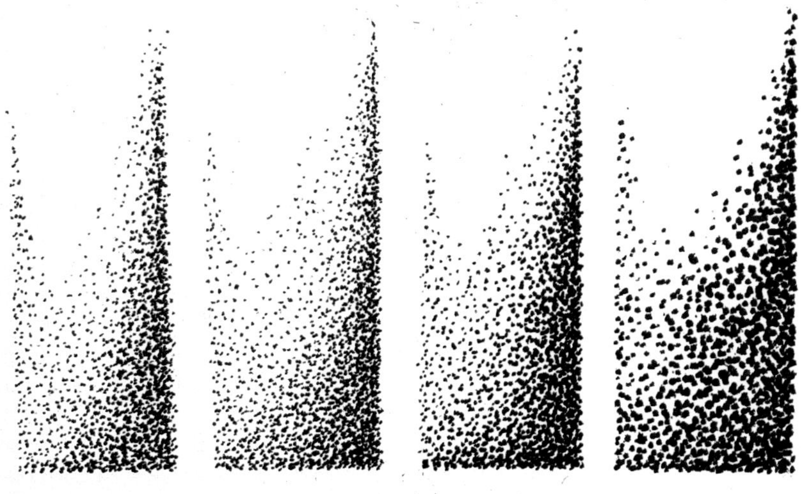

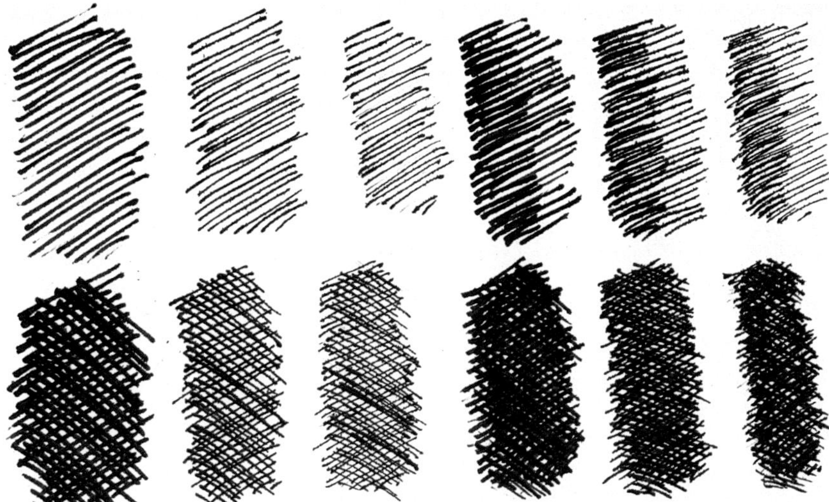

Examples showing various kinds of hatching and cross-hatching. The top row shows hatching, made with a single stroke, and double hatching with a second stroke imposed on the first, resulting in a darker tone.

The bottom row shows cross-hatching and double cross-hatching. A second layer of strokes is drawn over the first, in the opposite direction. In double cross-hatching, the process is repeated, giving a dense tone.

This traditional technique blocks in areas of tone quickly, and was favoured by the old masters, including Michelangelo and Leonardo da Vinci.

Examples of scribbled tones made with different thicknesses of nib. This technique is related to stippling but is freer and better for covering large areas. It is made by scribbling the pen randomly in all directions. Be careful when doing this with fine nibs as they might splutter; a lighter touch of the hand may be needed. Thick or medium nibs should present no problem.

In all the illustrations, notice how thicker nibs produce darker tones, finer nibs producing lighter tones. These techniques can all be mixed and combined, to make a foundation for your individual style.

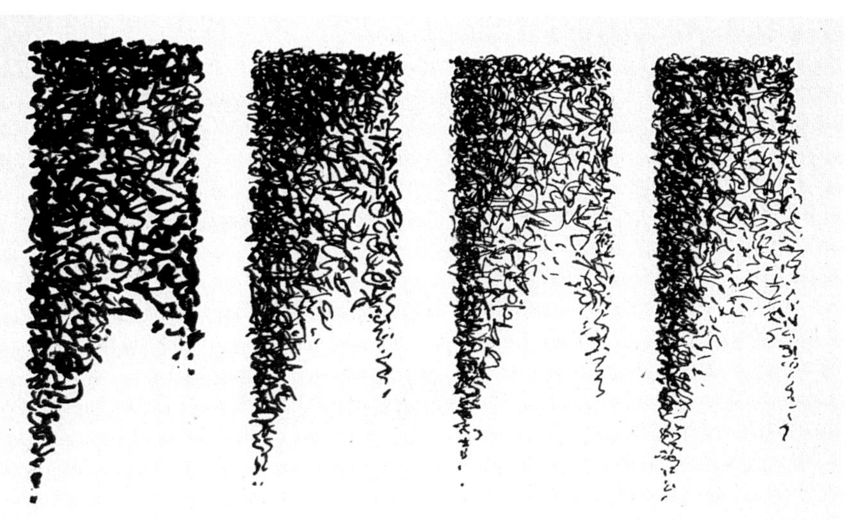

Sphere – Step-by-Step

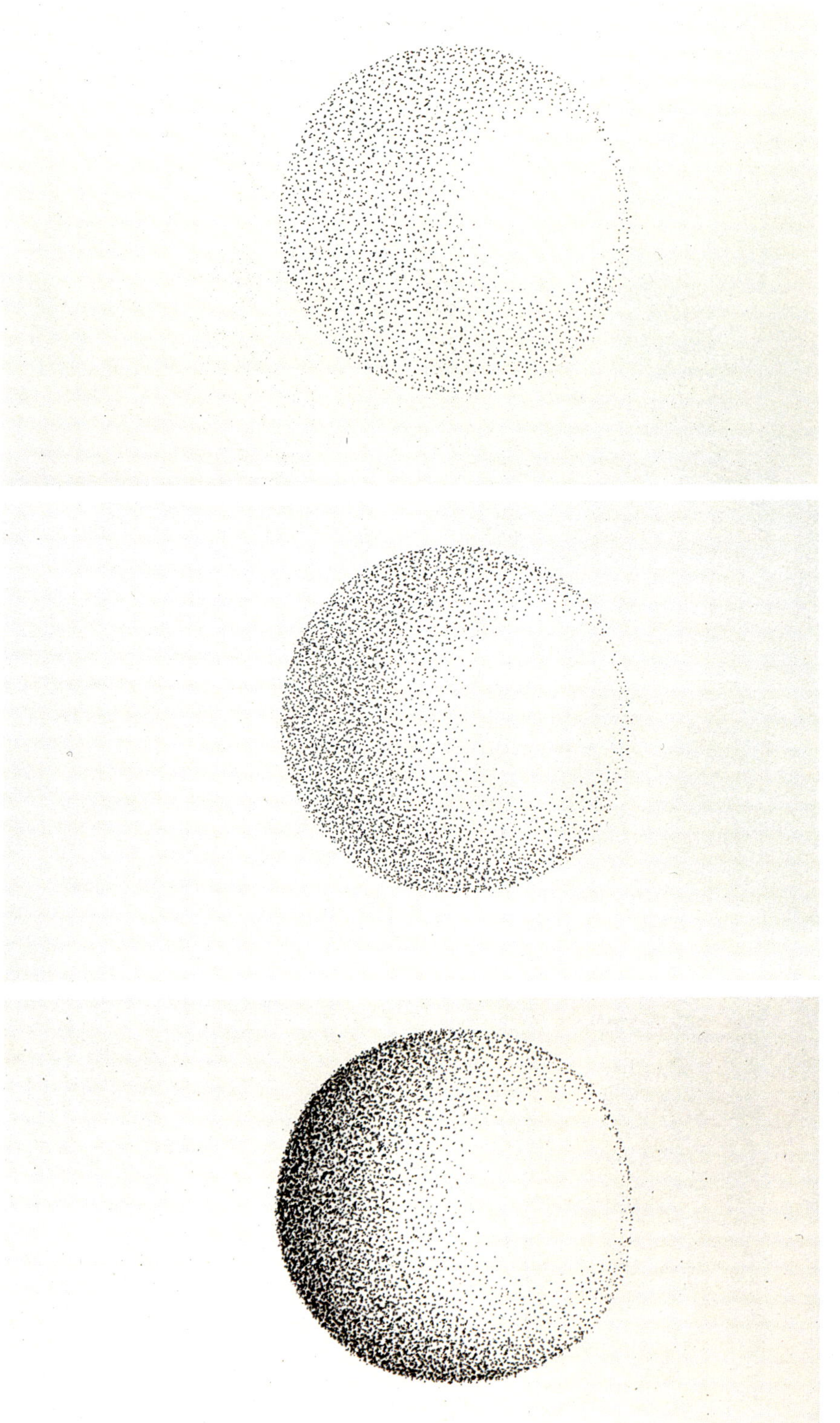

MATERIALS
Sphere

- Drawing paper
- Black Indian ink
- Pen with nib

Make a light outline of a sphere, drawing freehand if possible. This will encourage you to develop a good eye and a confident way of drawing.

The light is coming from the right, so shade in the left-hand side with small dots or lines and the sphere will begin to stand out from the paper. The smaller the mark you make, the more control you will have over the drawing.

Add a second layer of dots, starting a little further towards the left than before and work towards the outer edge away from the light.

The closer the dots are to each other, the darker the tone will appear, so start with them spaced well apart and gradually bring them nearer together. Make the change from light to dark as smooth as you can.

The sphere is now becoming more solid in appearance.

In the final stage, build up the dots to make a really dark tone on the left-hand side. Now the sphere should look as though you could pick it up from the page.

This exercise demonstrates how to depict a three-dimensional object on a flat piece of paper in terms of pen and ink drawing.

Having practised this technique, try drawing from real objects, such as apples, or other round shapes, and see how solid you can make them appear.

MATERIALS
Box

- Drawing paper
- Black Indian ink
- Pen with nib

This exercise involves not only tone but also simple perspective.

Lightly draw in the lines of the box, observing how the lines going away from you get closer together as they recede.

In the three vertical lines, the middle line which is nearest to you, is the longest; the line on the right is shorter, and the line on the left, which is furthest from you, is the shortest of all.

The light is coming from the right, so the end nearest to you will be the lightest part.

Fill in the top and the side of the box with dots, bringing them gradually closer together to darken the tone, as you work towards the far end.

Unlike the sphere with its continuous surface, the box has clearly defined facets, or planes, which divide the tones into separate areas.

Increase the density of the dots on the side of the box, making the tone darker as you work away from the light.

There are now three planes with three distinct tones: the near end (light tone), the top (middle tone), and the side (dark tone).

Try setting this exercise up for yourself by placing a small box near the window and noting the different tones.

Both these guides show ways in which light affects various forms, and how a three-dimensional effect can be achieved.

Once you have mastered this technique, put it into practice using real objects and see how solid you can make them.

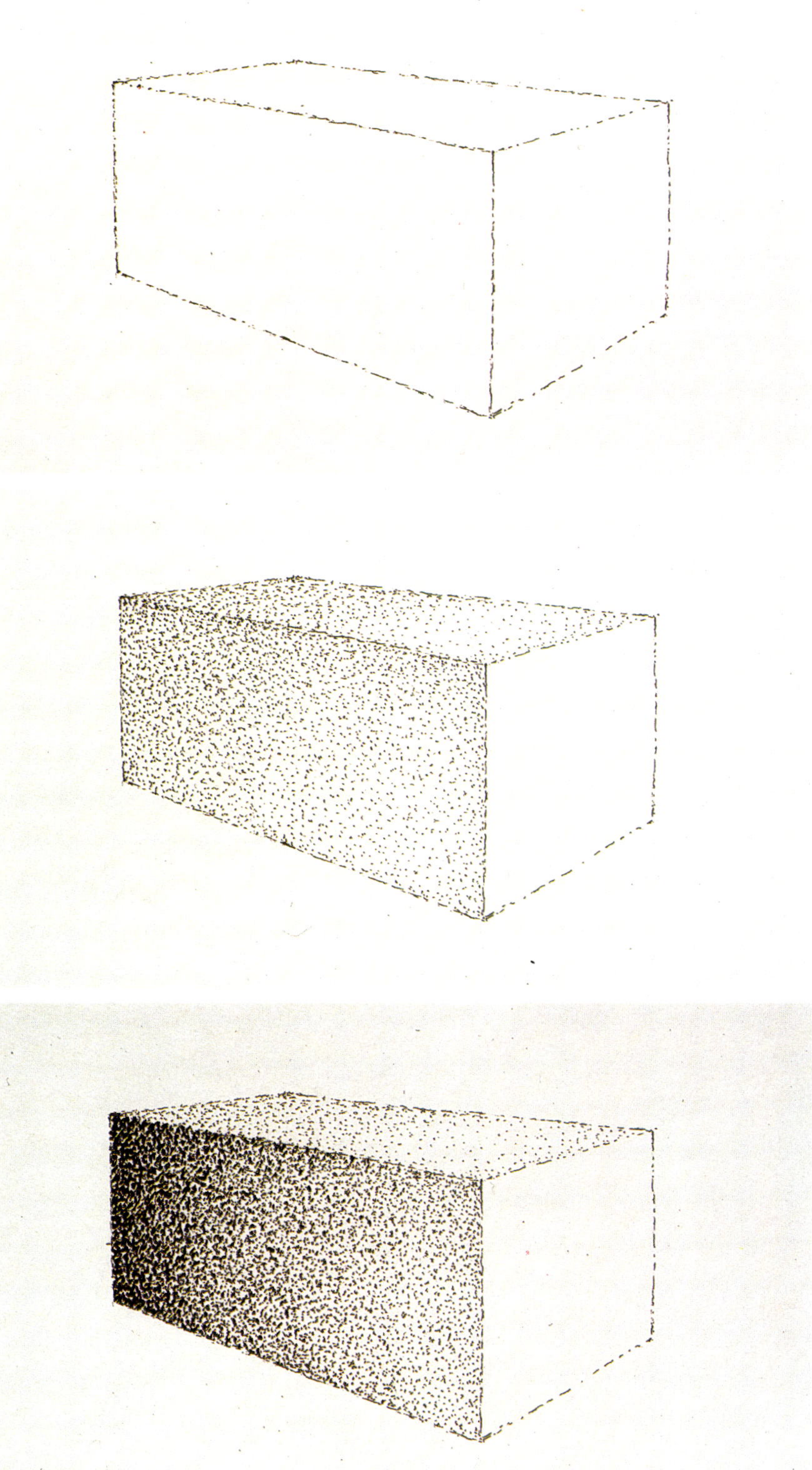

Eradicating Mistakes

One fear commonly associated with pen and ink drawing is not being able to rub out; thinking that any mark you make is irrevocable.

Most of us make blots and misplaced lines from time to time, usually managing to accommodate them during the course of the drawing. If this is not possible, try not to let it bother you too much.

Drawing is creative: never be afraid to show 'working lines', the thought processes that lead to the final result, even with an extra splodge or two. These can add to the uniqueness of a picture. Take Leonardo's drawings of horses; some have eight legs, but what impresses us most is the excitement of action, not the extra limbs.

However, if you do find it necessary to remove mistakes, two remedies are illustrated here. Another is to scrape carefully with a sharp knife and buff the area with a thumb nail.

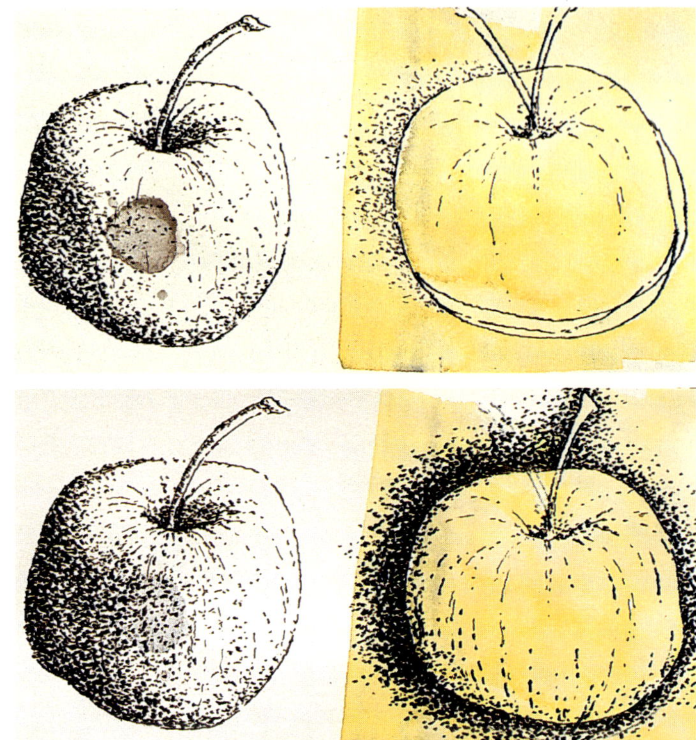

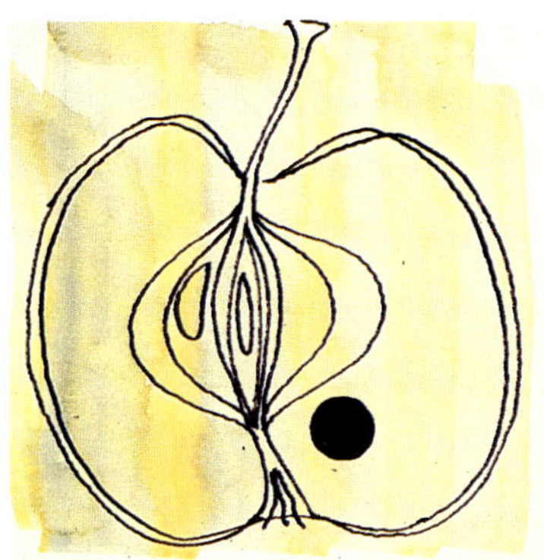

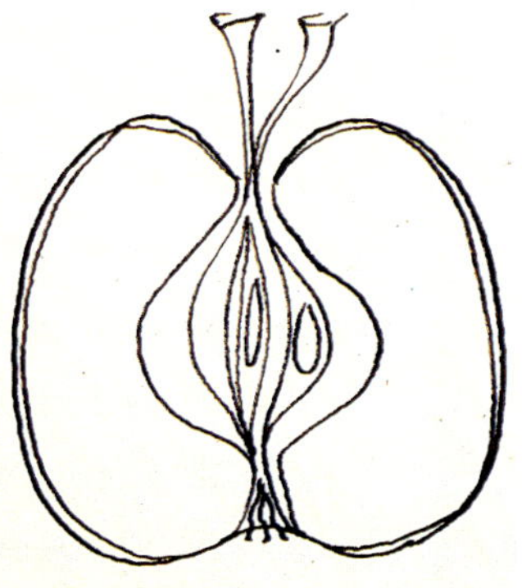

The illustrations above show a method of removing mistakes using chalk.

In the top picture, the apples show an ink blot and a wrongly positioned stalk. The lower picture shows the mistake rectified. The ink blot has been diluted with water, blotted and dried, and rubbed over with white chalk, while the unwanted stalk has simply been rubbed over with the white chalk. Both pictures have then had further drawing added, leaving the original mistakes only faintly discernible.

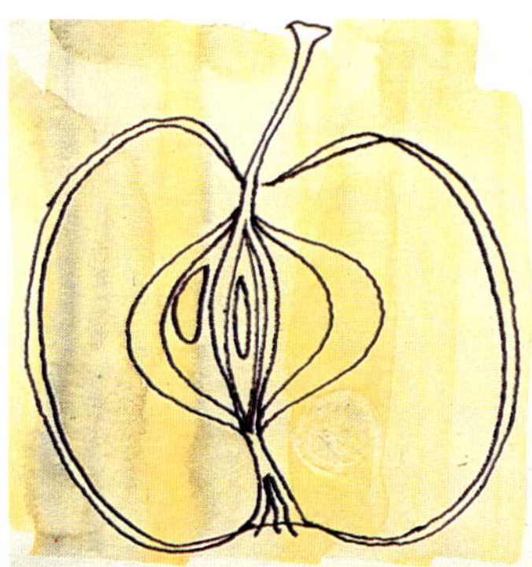

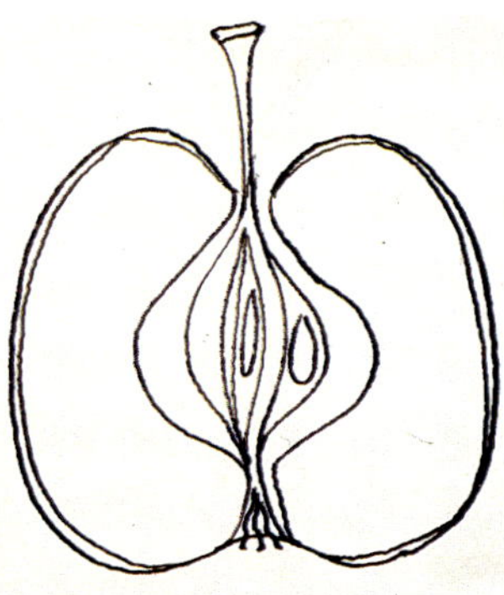

The illustrations on the left show the removal of unwanted marks using opaque white watercolour paint. This is usually the more successful method of the two, on account of the opacity of the paint and the fact that it can be applied in successive layers. Be careful, though, not to make a raised bump.

Once dry, the surface can be reworked.

Back-Up Exercise – Composition

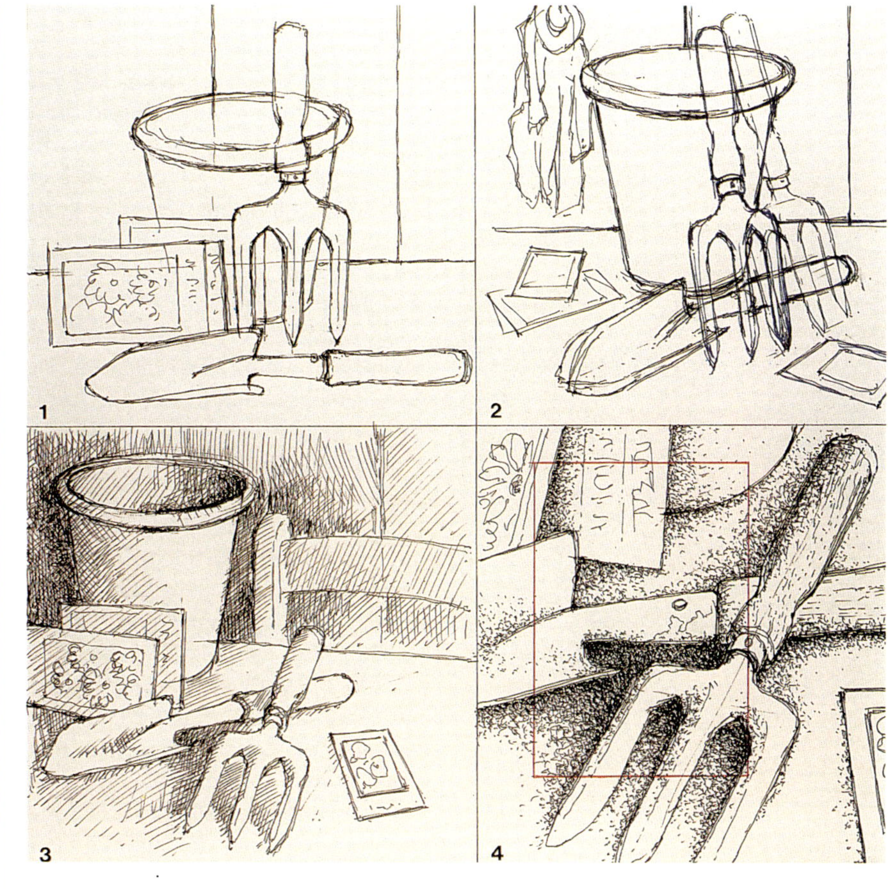

The purpose of these four sketches is to show how the composition of a picture can be roughed out in a series of small preliminary sketches until you find the most suitable arrangement. It is a way of exploring a subject before committing yourself to the final drawing. You will see how the same group of objects can be used in different ways to emphasise alternative aspects of picture-making.

Sketch 1 shows a simple composition based upon a vertical/horizontal concept. The group is placed in the foreground parallel to the spectator. There is no distracting detail in the background and little attempt to suggest depth. Most of the action takes place in the lower half of the picture.

In sketch 2, the objects have been rearranged to form opposing diagonal lines. This gives some sense of depth, even without the use of tone. The spectator's eye is now led into the picture and towards the focal point of the hat and coat in the background.

This sketch demonstrates how I worked out and arrived at the eventual composition. The original position of the fork was too far to the right which left an awkward gap in the middle. Re-drawing it further to the left overcame the problem and divided the flower pot in a more interesting way, thus improving the whole arrangement of the group.

In these first two drawings the objects are centrally placed on the paper in a conventional manner.

Sketch 3 gives a more off-beat arrangement, with the composition following a left-hand curve from the seed packet in the foreground to the flower pot at the back. This results in a picture with contrasted areas of activity and quietness. The shapes now dominate the left side of the drawing leaving the right side open. This emphasis is given more weight by the addition of broad areas of tone in hatched and cross-hatched strokes.

An asymmetrical composition can produce a certain tension in a picture, with interesting objectives to be resolved to ensure the final cohesion of the work.

With sketch 4, the concept has changed dramatically. The eye has moved in and focused upon an enlarged detail of sketch 3. The composition is becoming more concerned with shapes, and less with the identity of the objects. Negative shapes, the spaces between the objects, have become prominent, and these could be studied by tracing round them with a finger to realize their importance. This is highlighted by densely scribbled tone. Observe how uncompromisingly the group has been cut off at the edges.

Moving in closer still, to the area within the red lines, the objects lose identity, and distinctions between positive and negative are lost; all shapes have equal value and the composition points towards abstraction. Masking off the rest of the sketch will show this more clearly.

As a back-up exercise, arrange a simple group; approaching it in a similar way to mine. See how many variations you can produce, comparing the first sketch with the last to see how far it has developed.

PEN & WASH

MATERIALS & EQUIPMENT

- Paper
- Pen holder
- Nibs
- Brushes
- Inks
- Water
- Palette
- Drawing board
- Paper tissue

Wash is the name given to the technique of mixing and using ink with water. Combining this with pen drawing gives us one of the most varied and interesting of all pen and ink techniques, lending itself to many interpretations. Much depends on learning how to control the amount of water that is needed.

One method involves mixing up the ink beforehand into different dilutions, giving several tones, and applying it with brush or pen, or both, onto damp or dry paper. Use two brushes, one for mixing the washes, the other for applying them, and make sure you have plenty of clean water for rinsing afterwards. This will make it easier to manage what you do.

When the wash is dry, it can be worked on with pen and undiluted ink. Alternatively, the pen drawing can be done straight away, while the wash is still wet, giving rise to unexpected and interesting effects. Once waterproof ink has dried you will not be able to work it further with water. However, you can add more wash on top and draw again into this, building up your drawing in stages.

Another method is to use non-waterproof ink. Try drawing first, letting it dry, and then brushing the water over the ink. This will produce softened tones, giving a delicate touch to a drawing. Be careful, though, not to have your brush too wet or the tones may spread further than you intend! If this should happen, blot with paper tissue to remove excess water. Do this gently, without rubbing the paper and damaging the surface. The step-by-step guides in this section will show you these different approaches and how they develop through successive stages.

Other possibilities include combining waterproof with non-waterproof inks and the use of colour washes in addition to monochrome. These can be made with coloured inks or transparent watercolour paints. As I shall be dealing with these more fully in their own chapters later in the book, I shall do no more than mention them now.

Try using wash on different papers and see how it reacts according to the type of surface. A smooth and slippery surface will enable the ink to flow on easily, while a thick and absorbent one will cause the wash to soak in rapidly, with less spreading capacity. Tinted papers will affect the appearance of your work, especially when using colour washes, and can give attractive results.

The illustrations on these pages show combinations of brush and pen techniques and are just some of the effects that can be achieved. There are many options in pen and wash, so do experiment and be adventurous in your approach. You will discover more for yourself and find that the scope and quality of your drawing is increased.

A photograph of the equipment you will need for pen and wash: stretched paper, inks, pens, brushes, water, sponge, mixing palette, and paper tissue.

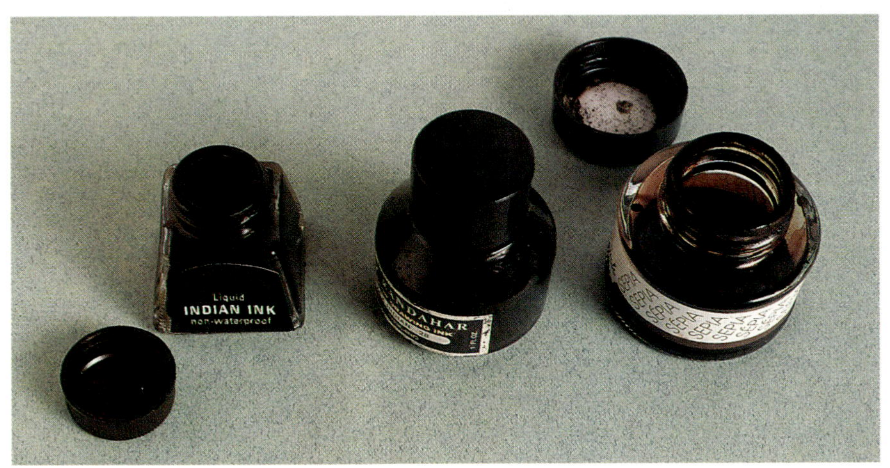

A close-up view of the inks that will be used in this section. From the left: liquid Indian ink (non-waterproof), black Indian ink (waterproof) and Sepia.

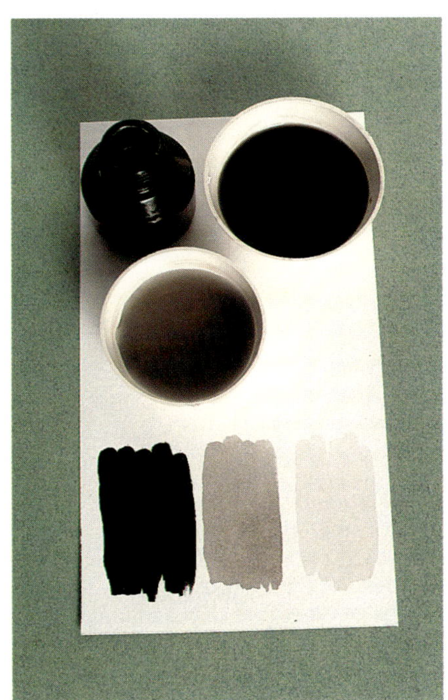

Mixing and Diluting Waterproof Ink *This illustration shows three tones: full black with no dilution; mid-tone with some dilution, and light tone with more dilution. The dishes contain the mixed dilutions, ready to be applied with brush and pen.*

Mixing up sufficient quantities beforehand will save time and avoid difficulties in remixing the exact tone again.

The top four examples were done with brush, using a sideways movement. The first two were obtained from a single loading of ink and a round brush. The two-toned effect was made by dipping one corner of a flat brush into ink.

The remaining examples were done with pen. Clockwise from the left: water brushed across pen line; water brushed lightly over paper texture, and ink applied; tip of pen placed on wet paper, causing ink to spread; water brushed from pen line; pen drawn down edge of water.

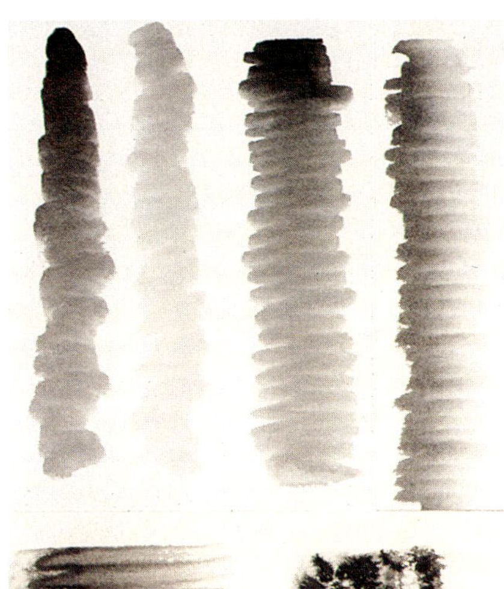

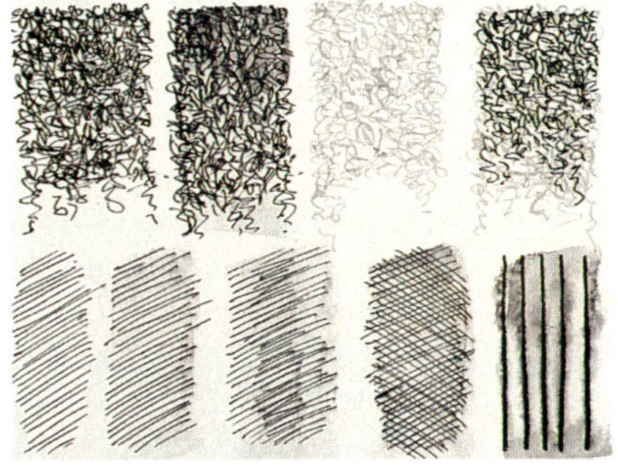

Mixing and Diluting Non-Waterproof Ink *The top row shows examples of ink, the first at full strength, the next two at different dilutions. The second row shows a wet brush dragged through dried ink.*

The third and fourth rows show samples of pen work, some using diluted ink which has dried and then had water brushed across them, causing the ink to run.

Pen & Wash

Waterproof Ink

Damping Paper *A pen and wash drawing can be done on wet or dry paper. Working on wet paper will give soft, blended areas, dry paper gives a sharper outline to the image.*

The easiest way to dampen the paper prior to drawing, is to use a sponge as shown here. The sponge will cover the area quickly and will enable you to make some progress with the drawing before the paper becomes dry again.

Take the sponge either down or across the paper in regular sweeps, so that the whole surface is covered. The sponge needs to be well moistened but not dripping with water. If you work swiftly apply the wash in broad strokes, one damping of the paper will be sufficient. If not, you will need to re-wet the dried parts.

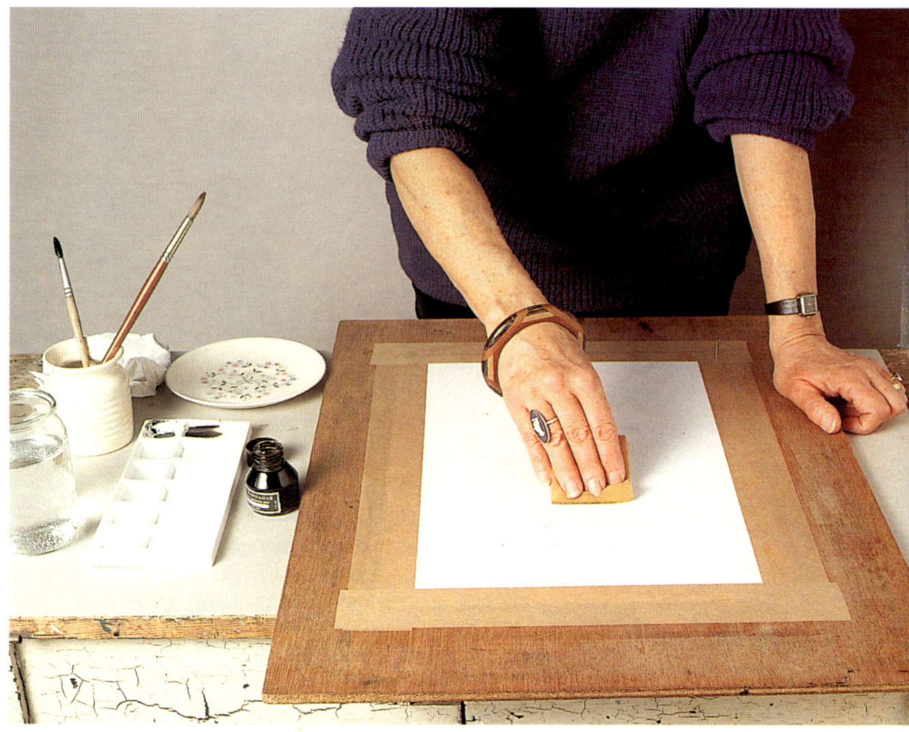

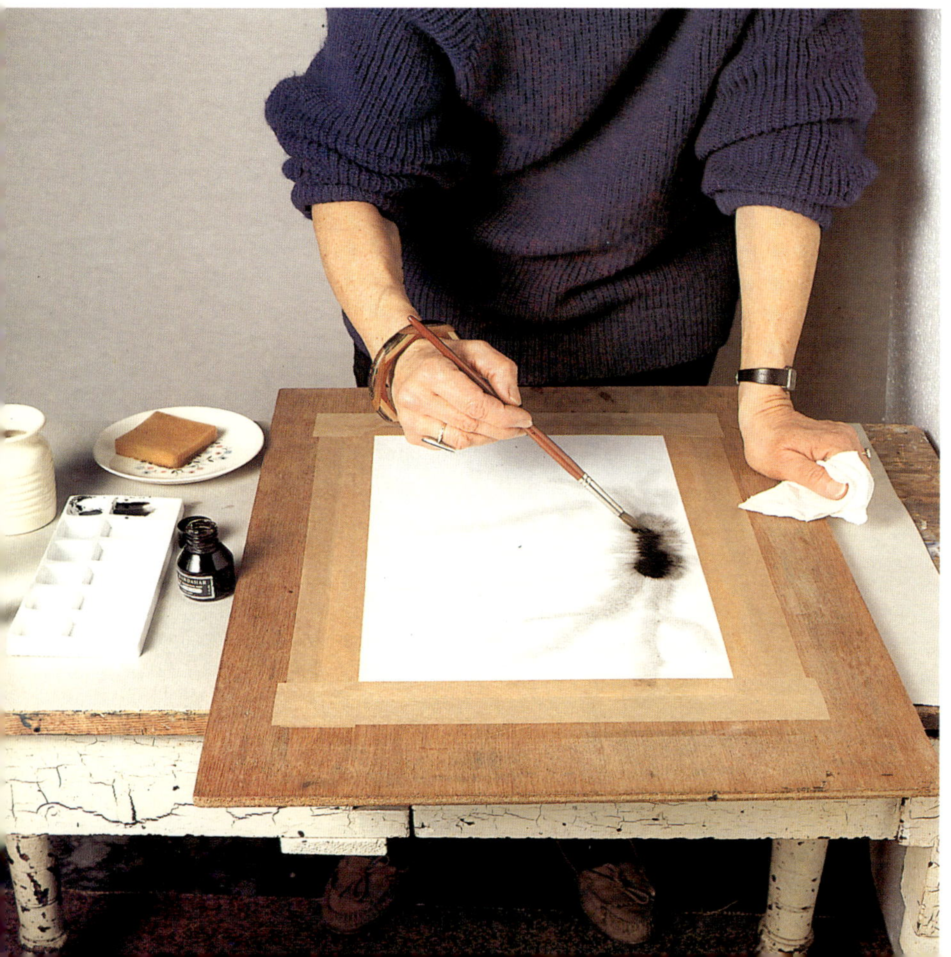

Applying Wash *The wash can be applied in a diluted or undiluted state. If you want several different tones of wash, then start with the lightest and work up to the darkest. The dark tones will look very black when you first put them on, but as they mix with the water on the damp paper, they will lighten and you may find it necessary to add more ink if you want a really rich, deep tone.*

In the illustration, a dark tone is being added to a much lighter tone, and you can see how it is spreading and blending near the edge of the paper.

An interesting combination can be produced by working first on damp paper, then letting it dry and adding more wash afterwards, mixing spontaneous with more controlled elements.

MATERIALS
Foliage – Pen on Wet Wash

- Stretched paper or Drawing block
- Pen and nibs
- Round brush No. 10
- Black Indian ink
- Water, preferably distilled
- Mixing palette
- Paper tissue

A light wash was applied freely by brush, suggesting the foliage growth. The paper should be damp, not saturated, so any excess moisture can be blotted with tissue.

As the foliage uppermost to the sky is lighter than that underneath, and the dominant light is coming from the right, a darker wash has been added to the left side and under the bushes.

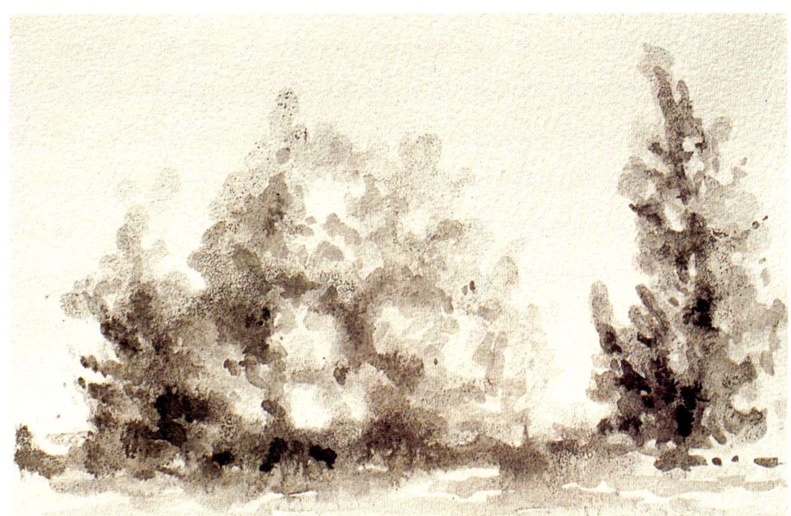

A stronger wash has now been added, increasing the three-dimensional effect, and establishing a sense of mass.

Here, we are concerned with the larger, general shapes of the bushes, although some indication of foliage texture shows in the smaller brush strokes. However, overdoing this would make the drawing too fiddly.

This middle stage establishes the main character of the foliage.

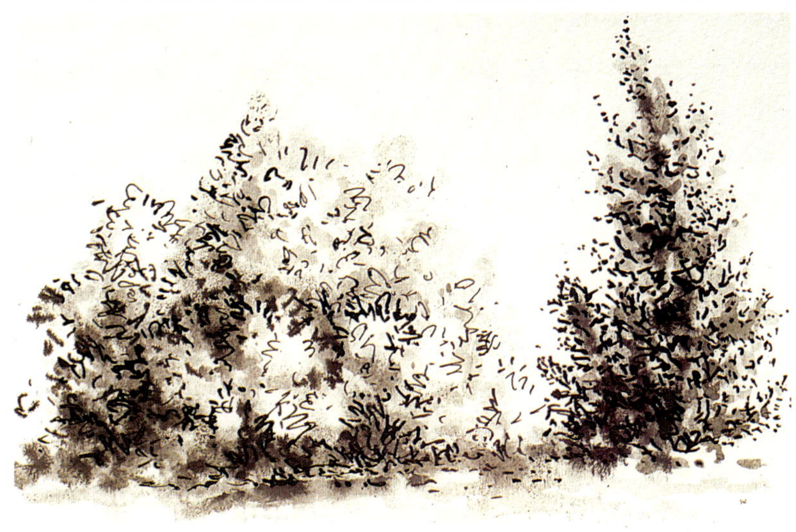

Finally, the detail was put in using thick and thin nibs to give variety. Initially, working on wet wash, the pen marks spread and produced an area of dark tone, seen in the lower parts of the bushes, but gradually, as the wash dried, the strokes became crisper and more easily controlled. This is shown on the upper foliage.

Clouds – Step-by-Step

MATERIALS
Clouds – Pen on Dry Wash

- Stretched paper or Drawing block
- Pen and nibs
- Round brush No. 10
- Black Indian ink
- Water, preferably distilled
- Mixing palette
- Paper tissue

A light wash was brushed on to dry paper in a swirling pattern indicative of cloud formations. This provides an opportunity for inventive use of the brush, rolling the handle in the fingers, while moving it across the paper, as well as dabbing and dragging it in the more usual manner.

After the wash had dried, the drawing was worked over in pen, using a medium nib. The strokes were small, involving both dots and lines, and were made in all directions. If the marks are too regular they will give the clouds a rigid appearance. The pen needs to move freely across the white and wash areas of the drawing.

The pen strokes continued to be built up as in the previous picture, with increased density in places to give tonal variety to the drawing.

Care needs to be taken here that the pen drawing is not overdone, otherwise the clouds will look too stiff. Using a finer nib can help to give a softer effect.

Clouds are very varied and it is a good idea to spend time observing the sky, noticing how the shapes are constantly changing.

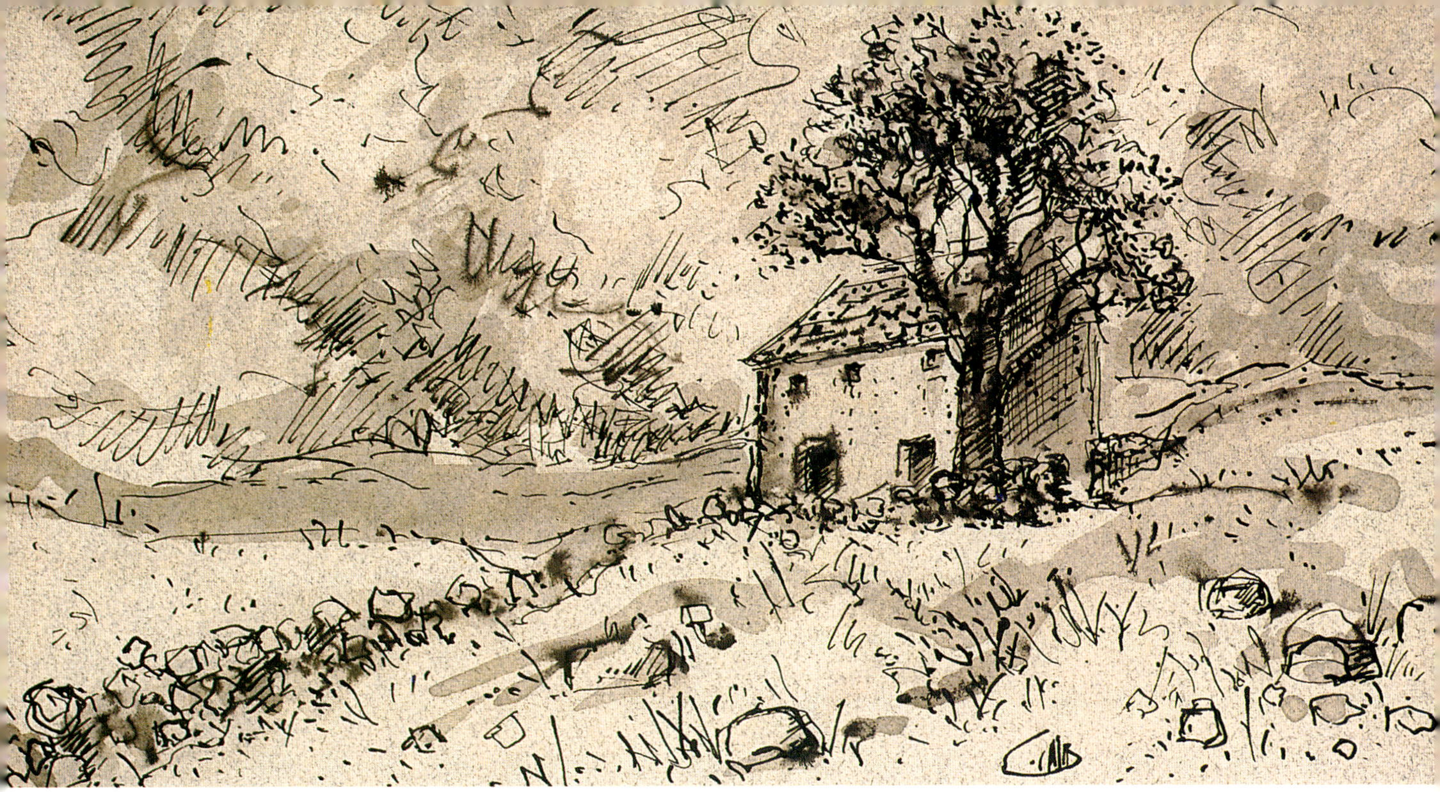

Landscape Above Brontë Bridge *A spontaneous drawing done with waterproof black Indian ink on tinted paper.*

The subject was brushed on to the paper in a light wash and drawn on with pen, using a medium nib, while the wash was still wet. This had to be done rapidly, leaving no time for unnecessary detail.

As the wash dried, more pen drawing was added, this time using a thick nib, maintaining the broad character of the approach. Finally, touches of a darker wash were put on to bring out tonal contrast and prevent the drawing looking too flat.

This is an enjoyable way to work and, as it is rapid, it is a good method if you are sketching out of doors, particularly if the weather is uncertain.

Barn Door – Heavy Technique *This picture, looking through a barn door, shows contrasted ways of using wash. Strong, to represent the interior of the barn, and light, for the building outside.*

Two inks were used, black Indian and Sepia, starting with pale washes and working up to the full intensity of the inks.

The technique involved working wet into wet with pen and brush, and also working on the dried surface, so that different effects were achieved; blending and spreading as well as sharp and clear cut. The pen work encompassed a wide range of strokes: stippled, tentative, scribbled and continuous.

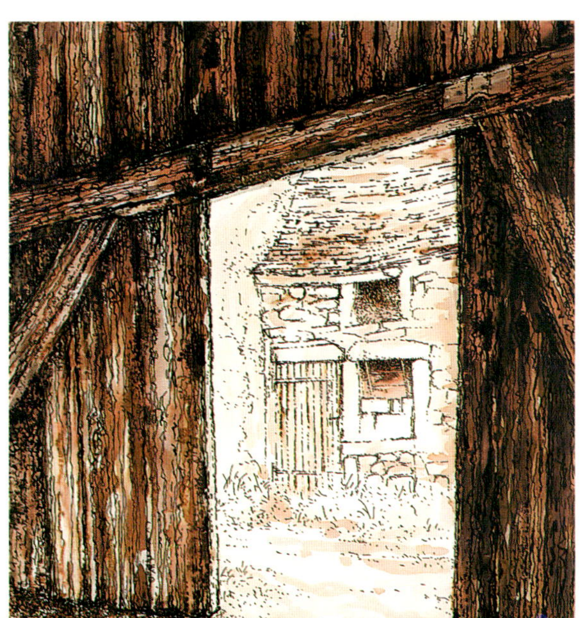

Using Sepia

Sepia was originally produced from the ink of cuttlefish but is now manufactured synthetically. It makes an attractive alternative to black ink if you want a change, and can also be used in conjunction with black to give an interesting two-colour effect, the brown introducing a note of warmth against the cooler black.

Sepia can be applied with pen or mixed with water to make washes. It is non-waterproof, so water can be brushed over it once it has dried to modulate the strokes or produce tonal effects. When it is used at full strength, Sepia is a rich, dark brown; diluted, it has a pinkish appearance.

Pen & Wash

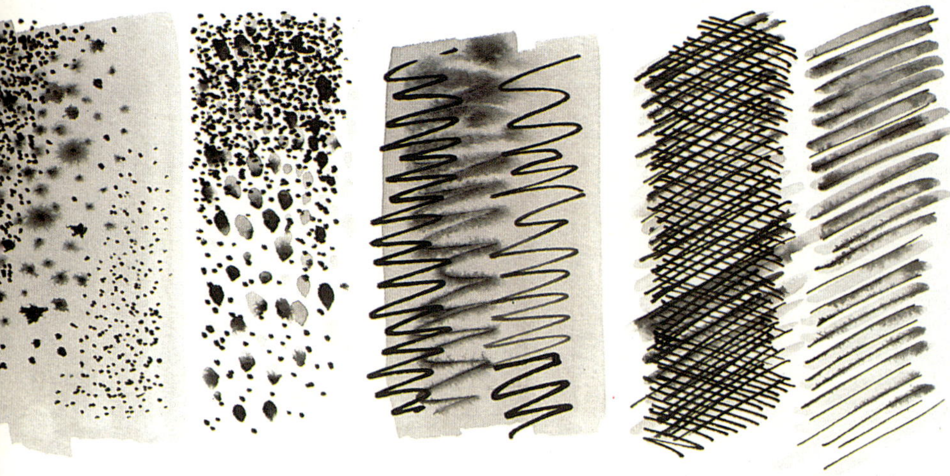

Non-Waterproof Ink

Wet and Dry – Try-Outs *Example showing stippling and an assortment of lines.*

First the pen is used directly on the damp wash or paper, which causes the marks to spread and dilute as they mix with the water. When the paper is dry it is worked over again with pen, but this time there is no spreading or dilution and the strokes remain clear and black.

This technique produces an interesting two-layered effect with a soft under-tone, and a strong over-tone.

Wet and Dry – Farm Gate *This illustrates a free way of working, showing how the wet and dry wash technique can produce unpredictable and accidental effects. A thick nib was used to give a chunky line.*

The composition was drawn in with brush and a pale wash and worked into with pen while still wet. The ink spreading into the wash gives texture.

The drawing progressed in this way, working on wet and dry areas with brush and pen, building up the textures and strokes until the picture was finished.

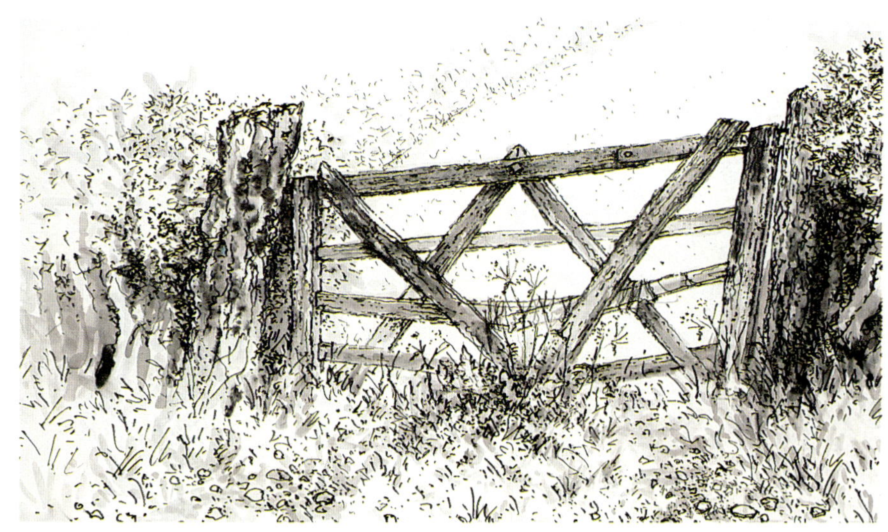

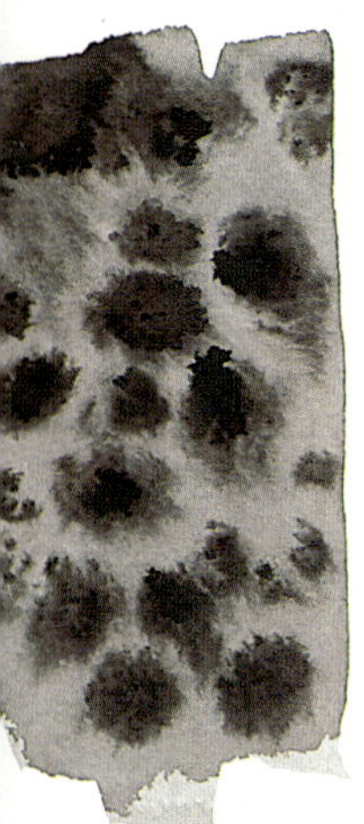

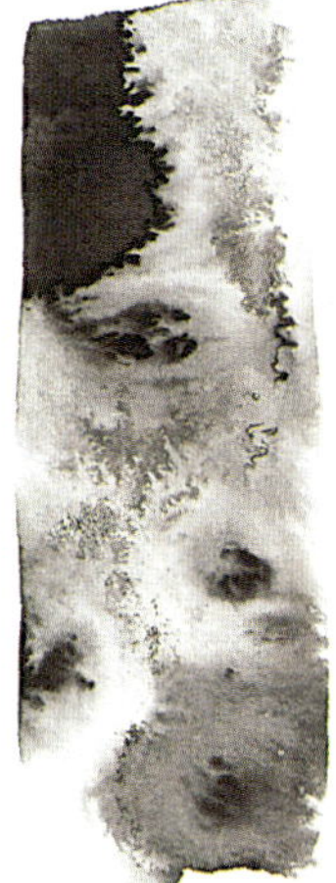

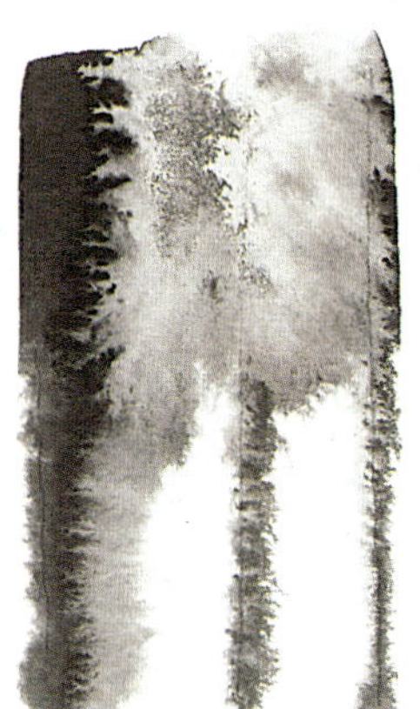

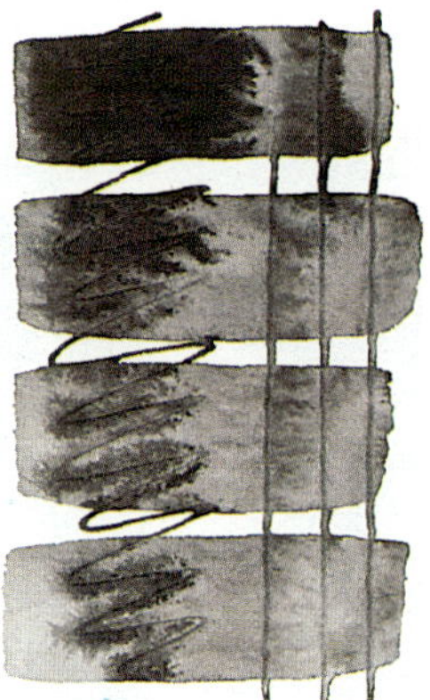

Running and Blending – Try-Outs *In these examples, the paper is made wetter, to make the ink flow and mix freely.*

Starting from the left: pen stippling on wet wash; pen stippling on wet paper; pen lines drawn vertically on wet paper; pen lines drawn on separated areas of wet wash.

In the wet wash samples, the wash was prepared before being brushed onto the paper. In the wet paper samples, only clear water was used. Note the tones produced according to whether the pen is used on a wash or clear water ground.

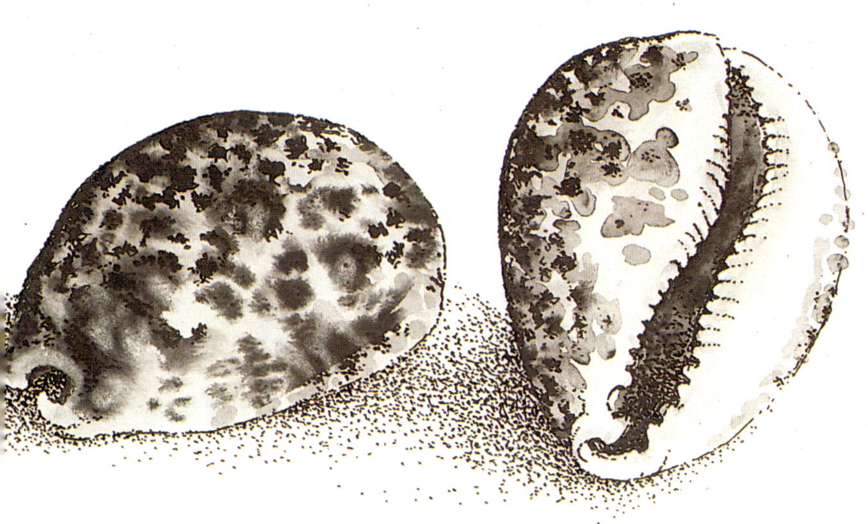

This illustration shows the running and blending technique used to suggest patterning on shells.

After the main shapes were drawn in with brush and wash, black ink was stippled on immediately with pen, which spread to give the soft-edged appearance of the spots. This was done heavily on the upper part, less heavily underneath. On the right-hand shell, there was also some brush stippling.

After the wash had dried, the outline and serrated edges along the opening were drawn in with pen. Some of the stippled spots were also darkened and emphasized to bring out the richness of the texture.

Smudging and Lifting *The first example shows an area of undiluted ink, to which dabs of water have been added by brush while the ink is wet. Blotting with paper tissue lifts the ink away. The lines were done in a similar way, except that pen was used instead of brush.*

The next example shows patches lifted from an area of wash with brush and water. Then the brush was squeezed out and used to blot with, instead of tissue.

The remaining examples show pen lines and stippled strokes smudged with a finger.

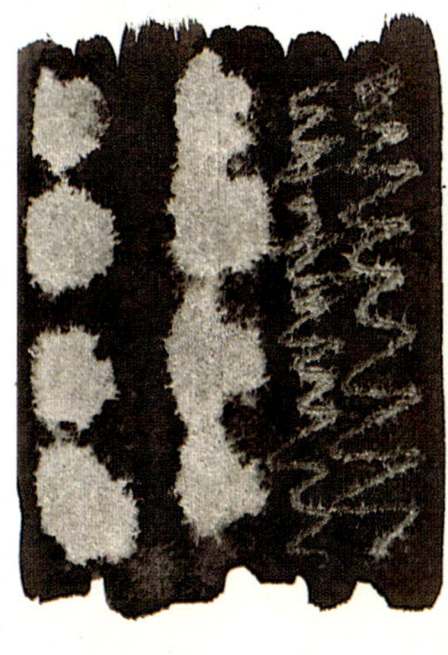

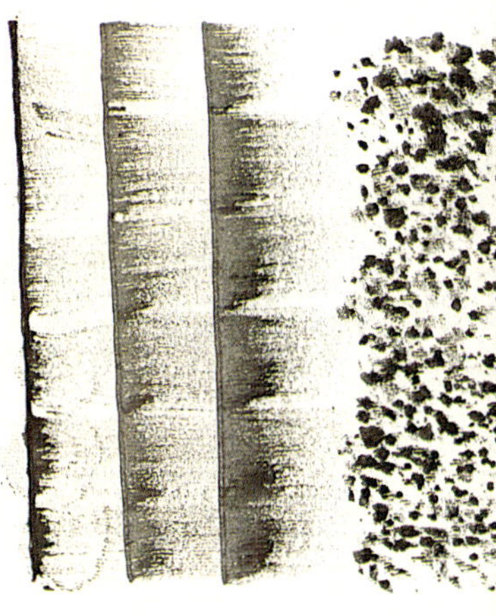

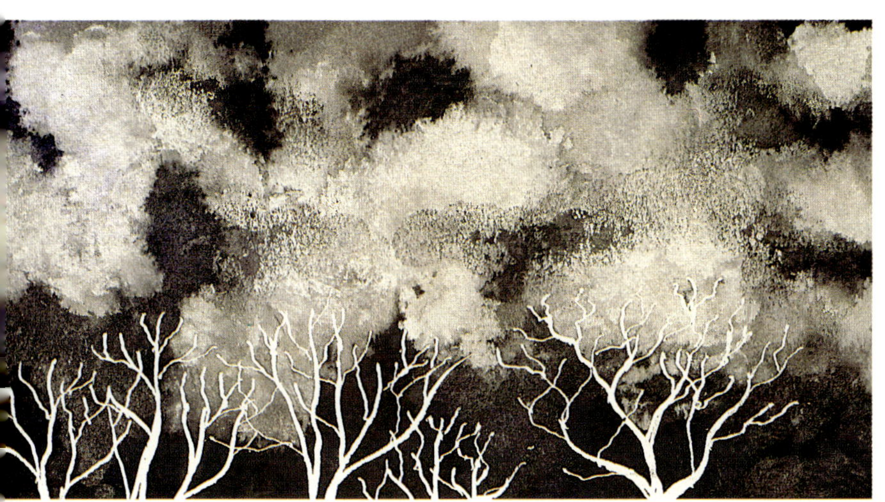

Smudging and Lifting – Clouds and Trees *This technique is useful for amorphous shapes like clouds, although since it relies more upon trick effect than technical skill, use it with discretion! As it is fun to do, it is worth a try.*

To get the white trees I used masking fluid (more about this in Experimental Work, see page 44) and then covered the whole picture with ink.

Clean water was blobbed on to the wet ink with brush and immediately blotted with tissue. Press hard to get the whitest areas, more lightly for the grey.

Group of Trees – Step-by-Step

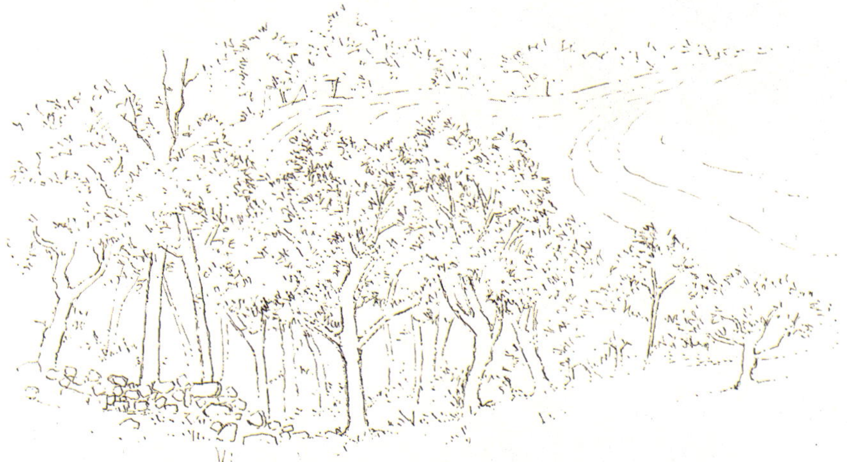

MATERIALS
Group of Trees – Non-Waterproof Ink

- Stretched paper or Drawing block
- Pen and nibs
- Brush
- Liquid Indian ink
- Water, preferably distilled

In this example, the main outline was drawn first, using a medium nib. The lines are light and understated. Later they can be thickened and strengthened to give a more positive appearance.

Some of the foreground trees have been subtly emphasized to distinguish them from those in the distance.

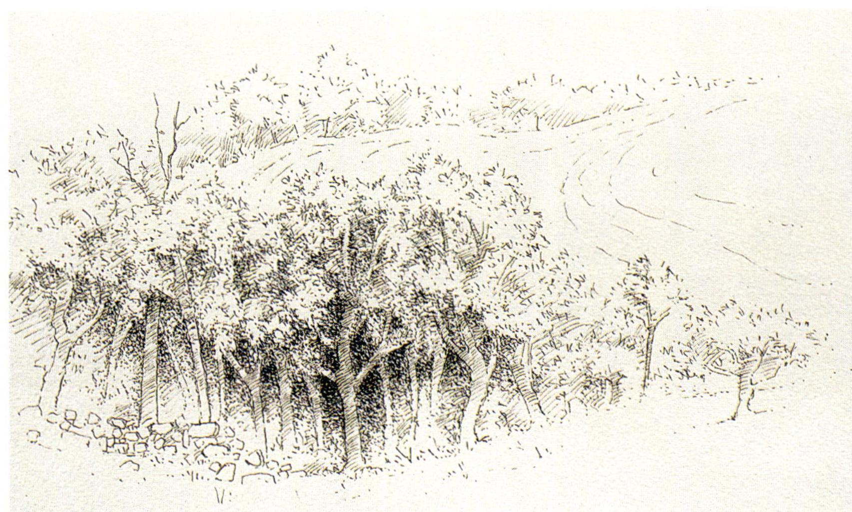

The tones have been added with pen, using hatched and dotted strokes. I made dotted strokes by lifting the pen sharply away from the paper, to give an irregular mark. This adds variety to the technique.

Notice the concentrated tones in the centre foreground and the diminishing of tone on each side. This focuses attention on the main part of the picture. In the background, lightly hatched strokes suggest distance.

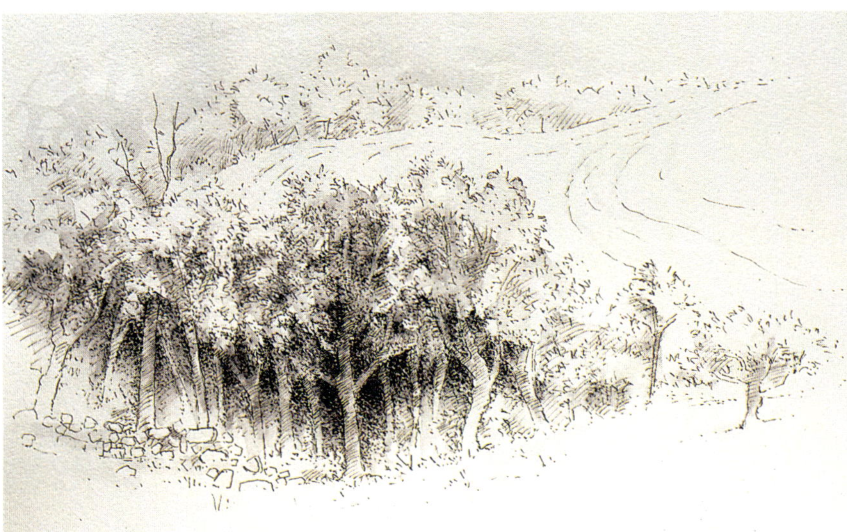

Dipping the brush in clean water and wiping off any excess, I dragged it lightly down the foreground tree trunks and the dark areas between. The lines blend, producing a wash and giving a more sensitive look. A dab here and there on the foliage, mixes and spreads the ink strokes.

Finally I brushed over and blended the distant trees. I was careful not to use too much water, to prevent the trees becoming uniformly grey. More pen work can always be added later to enrich dark areas.

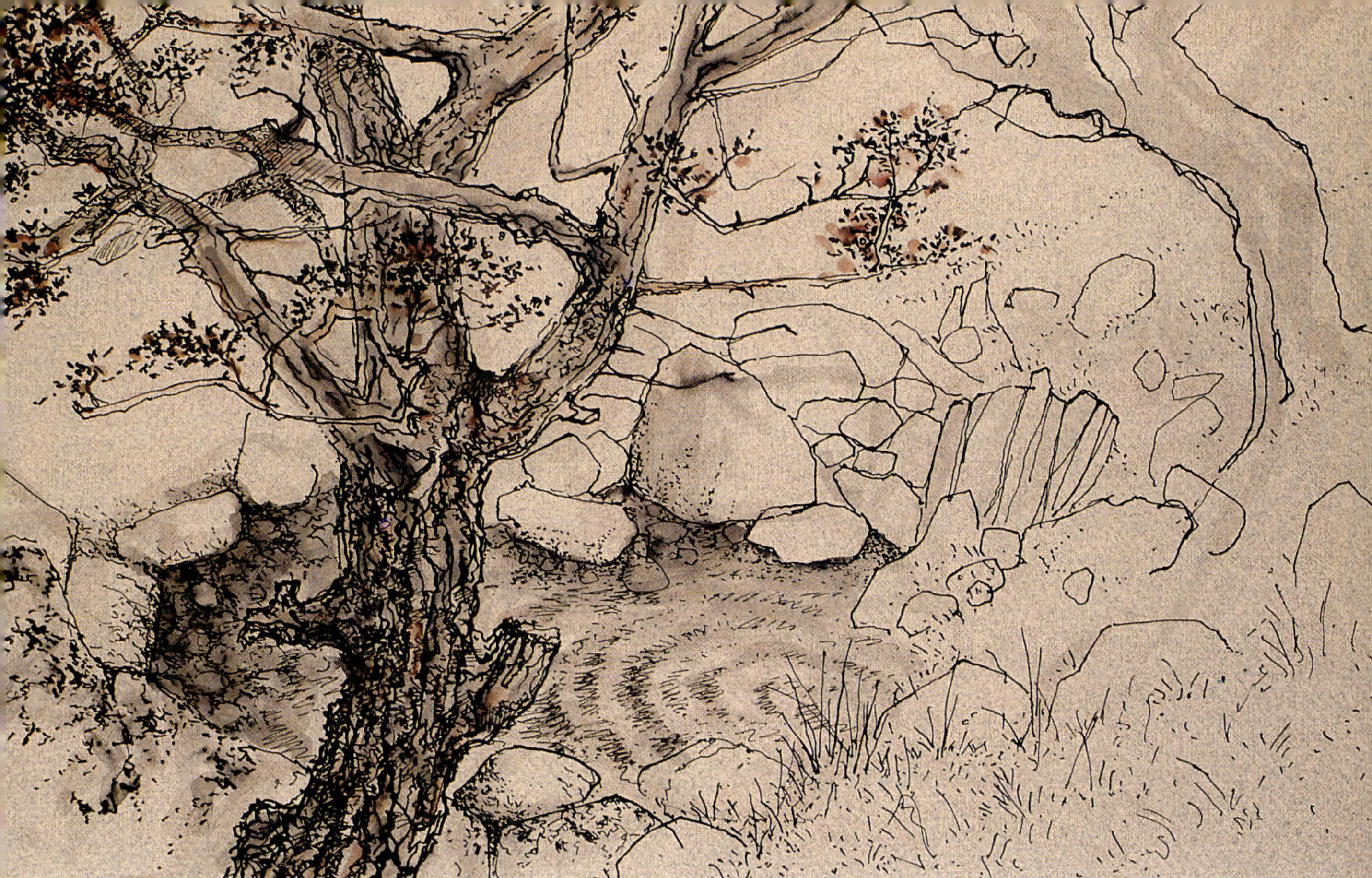

Hawthorns by a Pool *This illustration again takes trees as its theme, but whereas, in the step-by-step guide, the trees were seen as a distant united group, here two hawthorns are seen much closer and as individual trees.*

The picture encompasses all the stages of development so that you can see in one example how the drawing progresses from the wash and linear pen drawing on the right, to the finished and detailed work on the left.

Both waterproof and non-waterproof Indian ink was used, together with a little Sepia on the tree in the details of leaves and bark texture. The smudged effects were produced by lightly running a wet brush over the pen strokes.

This method gives more control over the spreading of the ink than working directly onto wet paper, as seen in the top illustration on page 25.

Back-Up Exercise – Using Wash

This chapter has introduced you to several ways of using pen and wash. You have studied, and possibly tried, the techniques shown in the step-by-step guides.

Almost all the illustrations show landscape-related subjects. As an exercise, do your own landscape, choosing a place that you know well, or have already sketched in another medium.

At this stage, while accustoming yourself to an unfamiliar technique, it is probably better to work indoors on a table with everything readily to hand. Later, with more experience, try working *in situ*.

Keep your picture simple in composition; a complicated format may cause muddles.

If you are unsure how to begin you could use the same method as the one shown in the example above. Start by mixing a pale wash to use for the initial planning of the picture. Because it is so light, it can easily be drawn over again.

Compare the two trees in my picture: the wash still shows through the drawing on the right. On the left, the initial wash has practically been obscured by subsequent working.

Once a shape has been found for your picture, draw into it with pen. Now introduce more wash or possibly some Sepia. Soon the drawing will start to flow, and you will become so absorbed you will hardly notice time passing.

PEN & WATERCOLOUR

Brushes

Watercolour brushes have shorter handles than oil painting brushes. The best and most expensive are sable, but others include ox hair, and a comprehensive range of synthetics, some of which contain sable mixtures, making a good substitute for pure sable. In addition, there are different shapes and many different sizes.

Choosing brushes can be difficult precisely because of this wide selection, and what suits one person will not necessarily suit another. Some people always go for flat brushes, and others round. My own preferences tend towards a flat 1 or 2cm (½ or ¾in), because I enjoy the broad sweep of colour these give, but I also use rounds, usually a 10 or 12.

In general I suggest you opt for larger sizes rather than smaller. Besides the expansive strokes created by a big brush, you can also make surprisingly small ones using the tip or the side, but try painting a large area with a small brush and you will have an uphill task!

So far, the techniques I have shown you have all related to using ink. However, in this section we shall be encroaching on the painter's territory.

Transparent watercolour paints are eminently suited to working with pen and ink, being used in a similar way to pen and wash and having the same consistency. Diluting the paint with more or less water will give the required strength of colour.

Watercolours can be purchased in either tubes or pans. Try one or two colours of each type and see which suits you best. In general, if you want to work on a large scale and require a lot of colour, tubes would probably be more convenient. On the other hand, if you are working out of doors, pans in a watercolour box might well be preferable.

There are two basic approaches to this technique: drawing added to colour; and colour added to drawing. In the step-by-step guides to illustrate each approach, I have chosen the same subject each time so that you can see how the alternative methods develop, and compare the similarities and differences.

Starting with brush and colour tends to produce a freer picture as you are less bothered about going over the edges.

Use the largest brush you can, a good-sized piece of paper, no smaller than A3 if possible, and try standing up to work for this first stage. Hold the brush near the end of the handle to give more freedom of movement and paint with your arm, not just your fingers! This bold approach should help you gain confidence. The combination of freely applied colour with the controlled drawing of the pen can produce work of great vigour.

Reversing the process – drawing with pen, and then adding colour – presents other opportunities. Pale washes brushed on to a completed ink drawing can have an attractive delicacy, the colour enhancing the pen work without subduing it. It is still predominantly a drawing.

A more full-blooded approach, where the colours are used with potency, may bring you right into the painter's domain, but this will depend upon the relative weight of colour, and the balance you want to achieve.

Do not be inhibited about keeping within the drawn lines. Let the brush

The equipment needed for working with pen and watercolour: stretched paper or sketchblock; pen holder with assorted nibs; black Indian ink; brushes, two round and one flat; watercolour paints and palette; water jar and paper tissue.

If you are going to work with your board upright, you will also want a table easel.

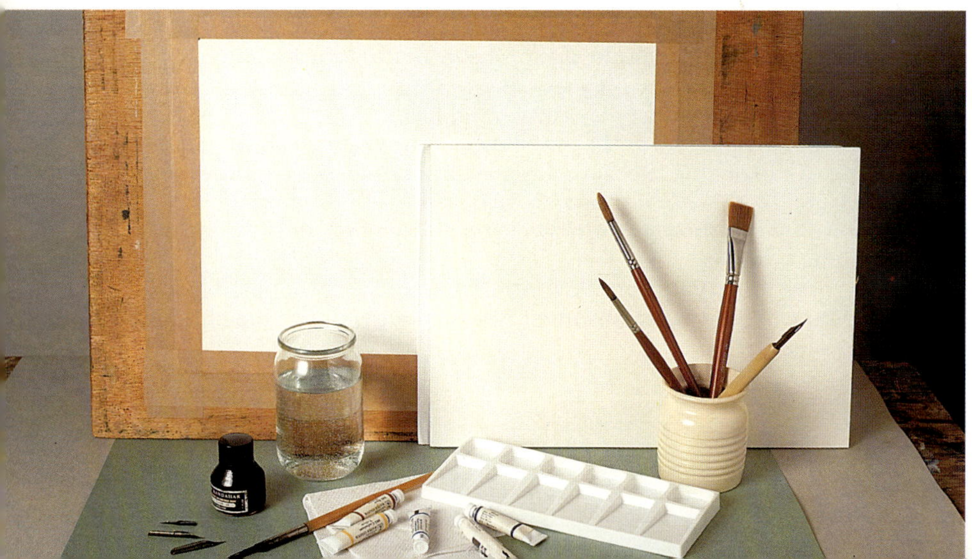

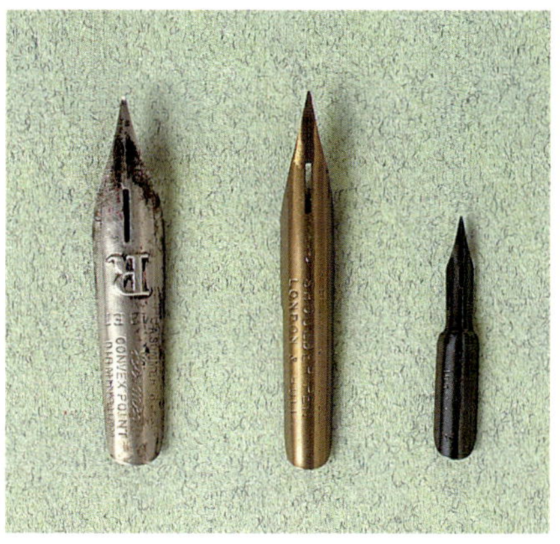

A close-up of the nibs shown in the previous picture, which will give strokes that are fine, medium and thick, adding variety to your drawing line.

have its head, allowing the colours to flow across the paper, even if they overshoot their mark.

Use watercolour expressively and delight in it. It should extend your pen work, and not merely provide a convenient means of filling in empty areas, reminiscent of painting by numbers.

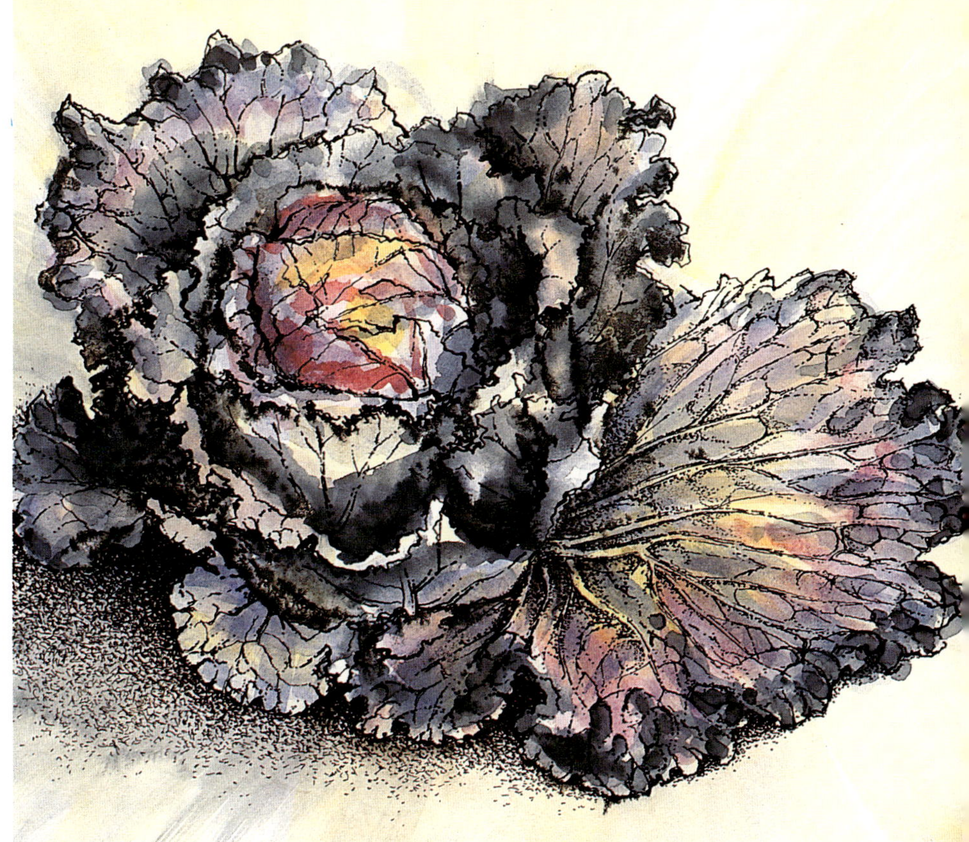

Drawing Added to Colour *This cabbage, glowing with dark purples and greens, seemed to be asking to be drawn!*

The colours were brushed on first and drawn into with pen and black ink while the paint was still wet, producing the crinkled effect seen on the central leaves. Final details of drawing were added when the paint was dry.

The purpose of starting a drawing with a brush is to keep the picture free and open, and to establish the essence of the subject before introducing the more controlled strokes of the pen. It is the dialogue between brush and pen that gives this technique its character and makes it so enjoyable to do.

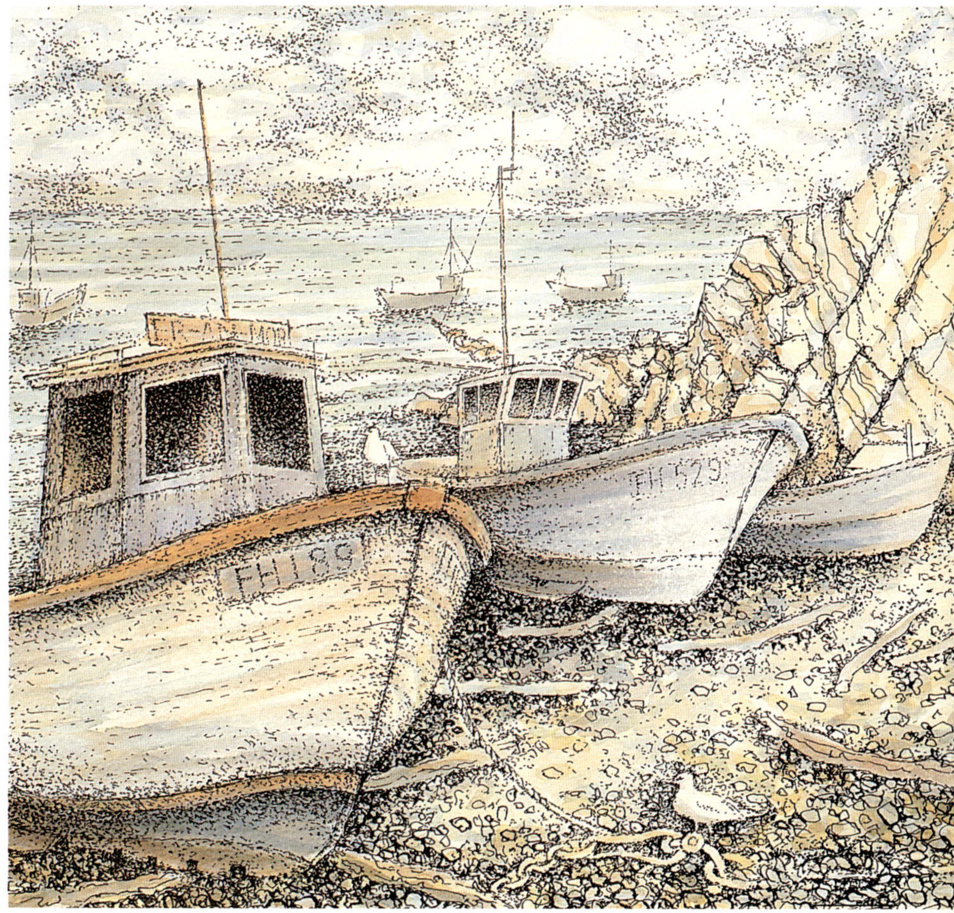

Colour Added to Drawing *Here, all the drawing was done and worked up in considerable detail before applying any colour. Then, very pale washes of watercolour were brushed on, keeping it fairly dry so that the white of the paper still showed through in places.*

Colour plays a much less dynamic part in this picture than in the one above, and the end result is a more careful and controlled piece of work – a tinted drawing.

These examples show two completely different approaches to using pen and watercolour.

Pen Added to Colour – Step-by-Step

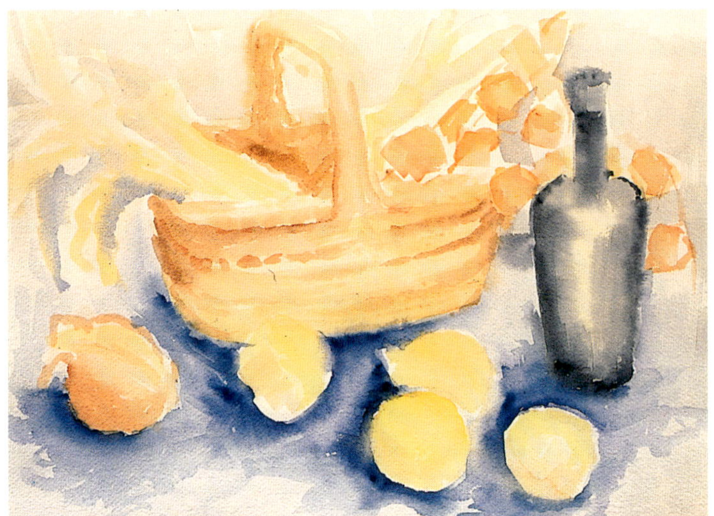

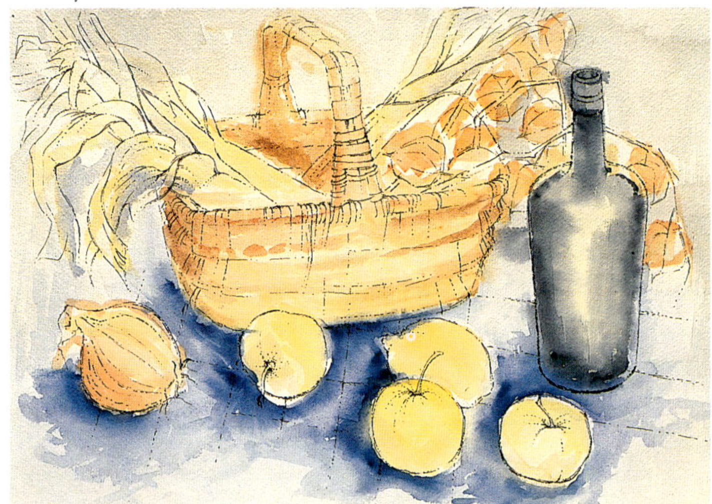

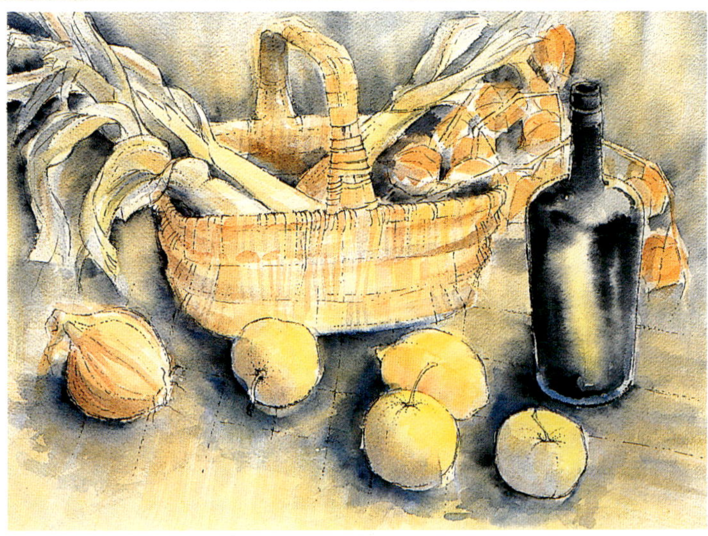

MATERIALS
Pen Added to Colour

- Stretched paper or Drawing block
- Pen and nibs
- Brushes
- Black Indian ink
- Watercolour paints
- Water
- Mixing palette

Before beginning, study the group to familiarize yourself with the objects.

I started by drawing in the shapes freely with a brush and Raw Sienna.

Having established the main composition, more colours were introduced, and the tonal range developed. Notice the darker blue around the fruit, and under the bottle and basket.

Using a medium nib, the first lines were drawn in tentatively. The initial, freely applied colour gives flexibility and the lines frequently overlap colour areas.

Some lines then needed emphasis to clarify complicated passages, (the leeks) and to strengthen the drawing generally.

Texture is shown on the basket, but the picture is still kept broad in character.

Now the paints are brushed on vigorously, with more colour and less water, to give glow and vibrancy. Notice how colour is used to unify the picture: for example, yellow is used not only on the lemon and apples which are yellow, but on other objects too.

Do not worry if colours run together; they will add vitality, and prevent the deadening effect that hard edges sometimes give.

As this is a bolder example than the following one, it is essential that the pen work should be in character, so the final drawing was done using a well-worn, thick nib, giving a broad, malleable line. The forms are reinforced, with a varied come-and-go line, while the tones are built up with a skittering action. Holding the pen half-way up the handle gives a loose, flexible movement and jumping, or skittering the pen over the paper scatters small, irregular marks in all directions.

Compare this picture with the last stage of the next step-by-step guide, especially noting the treatment of the basket.

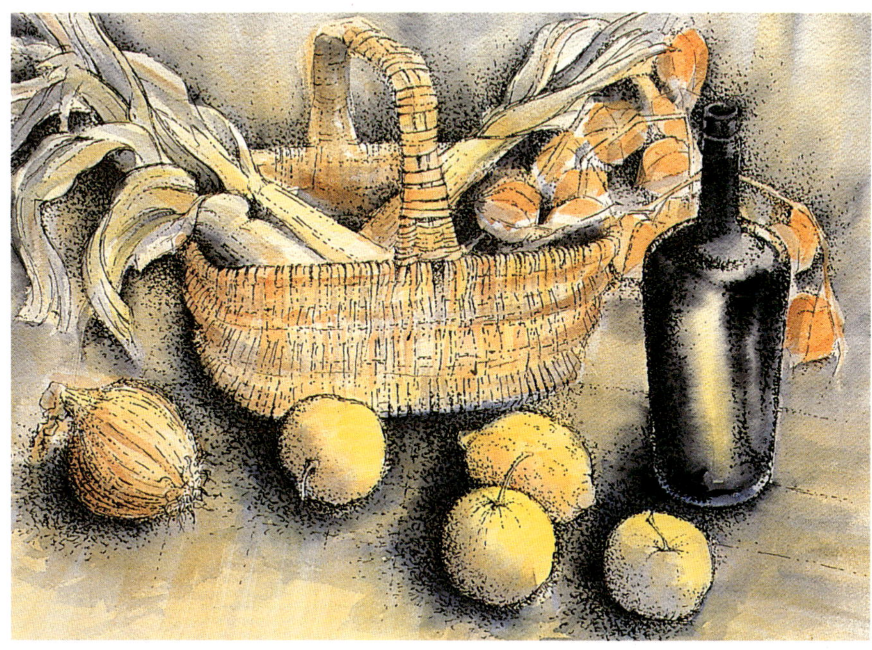

Russian Tomb *A watercolour and ink picture worked up from a drawing made in an overgrown St Petersburg cemetery.*

The original sketch was in black and white, with written colour notes. This approach allowed room for imaginative interpretation, which might have been restricted by a more finished colour sketch.

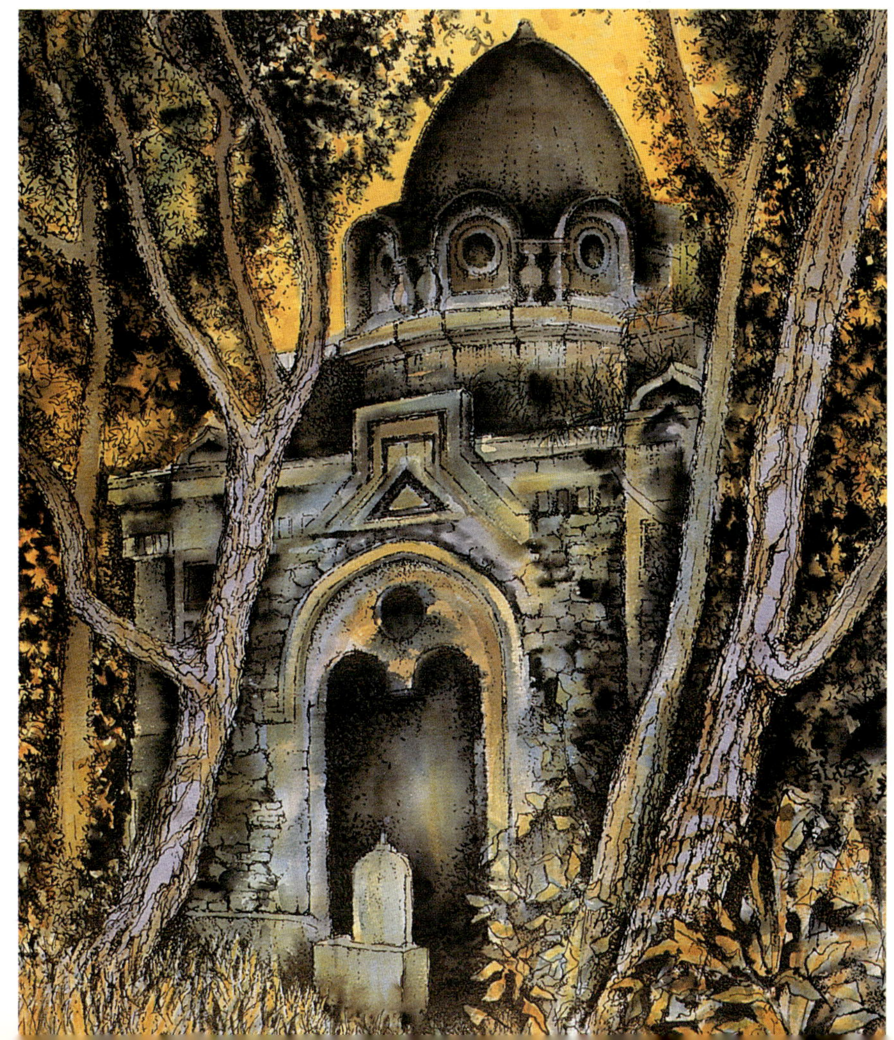

Using Colour

Colour can add an extra dimension to drawing, the broader technique of brush work contrasting with that of the pen.

Sometimes, lots of full-bodied colours are needed to give zip and intensity; sometimes, one or two will suffice. Even a hint of colour wash can give the desired atmosphere.

The study of colour is complex and books have been devoted to this subject alone, but a few basic facts might be helpful.

Colours fall roughly into two groups: warm and cool. Warm colours – the reds, oranges and yellows – advance in a picture, while cool colours – blues and greens – recede. Some colour groups, browns for example, can be warm or cool. Burnt Sienna is a glowing orangey brown, while Raw Umber is a cool green-brown.

This does not mean that warm colours should always be in the foreground and cool in the background. It simply gives an idea of the effects of colours and provides a lead for exploration in this region.

Colour Added to Pen – Step-by-Step

MATERIALS
Colour Added to Pen

- Stretched paper or Drawing block
- Pen and nibs
- Brushes
- Black Indian ink
- Watercolour paints
- Water
- Mixing palette

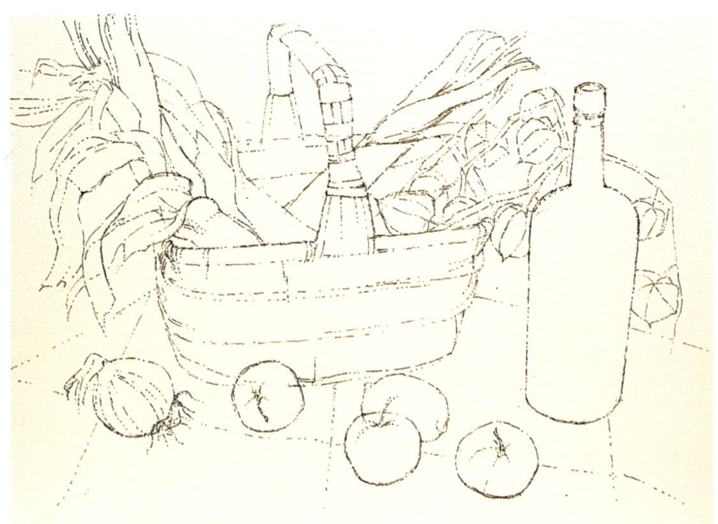

The approach here is more controlled than in the 'Pen Added to Colour' examples (see page 32).
The main shapes were drawn in using a medium nib. There is no indication of tone yet, although some emphasis of line suggests the space between two points, as shown in the basket handle.

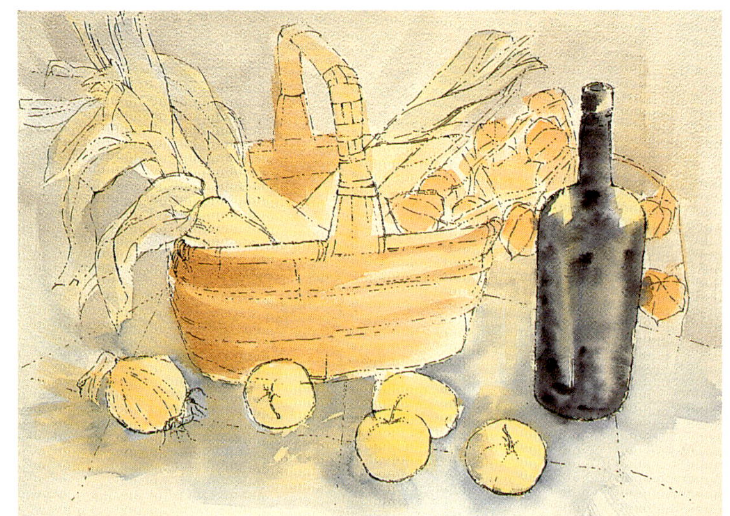

Using a flat 2cm (¾in) brush, a wash of Raw Sienna was worked over the whole drawing to give warmth and bring the composition together. Next, Winsor Yellow was added to the leeks, apples and the shoulders of the bottle; and then Cobalt Blue to provide colour and tone in these areas and the foreground. Indigo, orange and a grey background wash completed this stage.

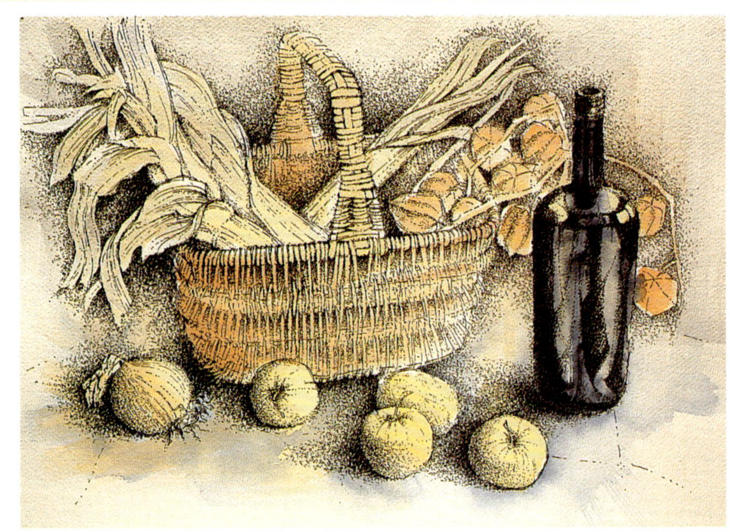

Now the character of the final picture will emerge.
The objects are drawn up in detail, paying attention to shape and texture. It is unnecessary to put in all the wickerwork of the basket. Notice how sketchily some of the outer lines have been drawn.
The background spaces are worked up with pen, pulling the picture together and pushing objects forward to give a feeling of depth.

With the drawing completed, all that remained to be done was to add the final touches of colour. As the picture looked rather pale, it needed to be livened up in appearance and given more zest. I felt that local colours ought to be intensified: for example, the orange on the Chinese lanterns and the yellow on the apples and lemon. At the same time, general unity had to be considered, so colours were subtly cross-referenced. Hence the cool blues, Cobalt and Indigo, and the warm brown, Burnt Umber, which are present in all the objects to a greater or lesser degree. This linking of colour was carried through into the foreground and background.

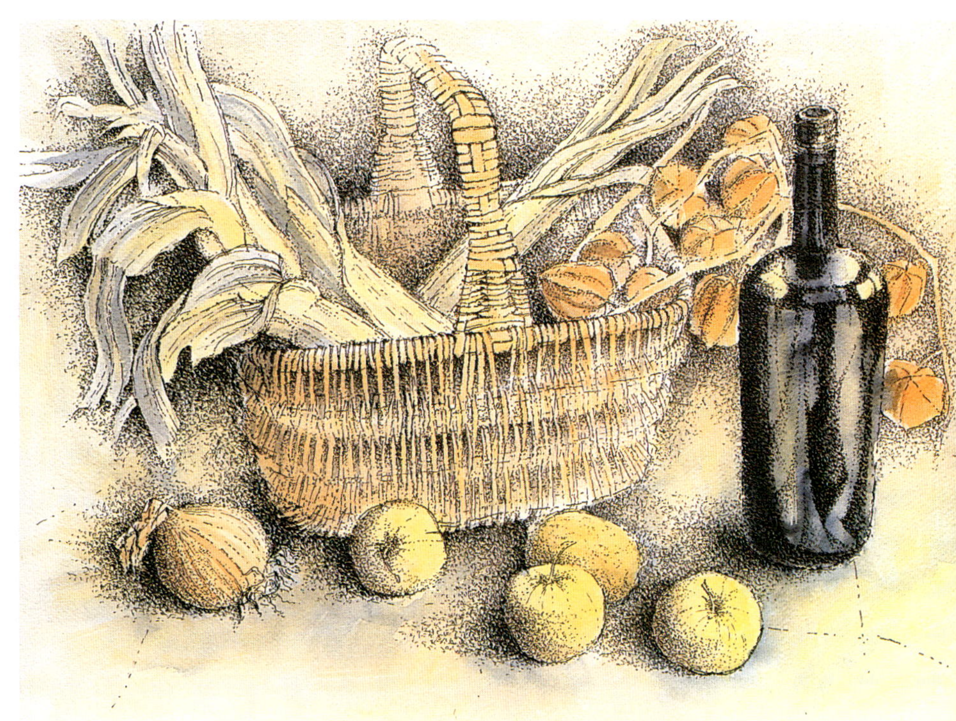

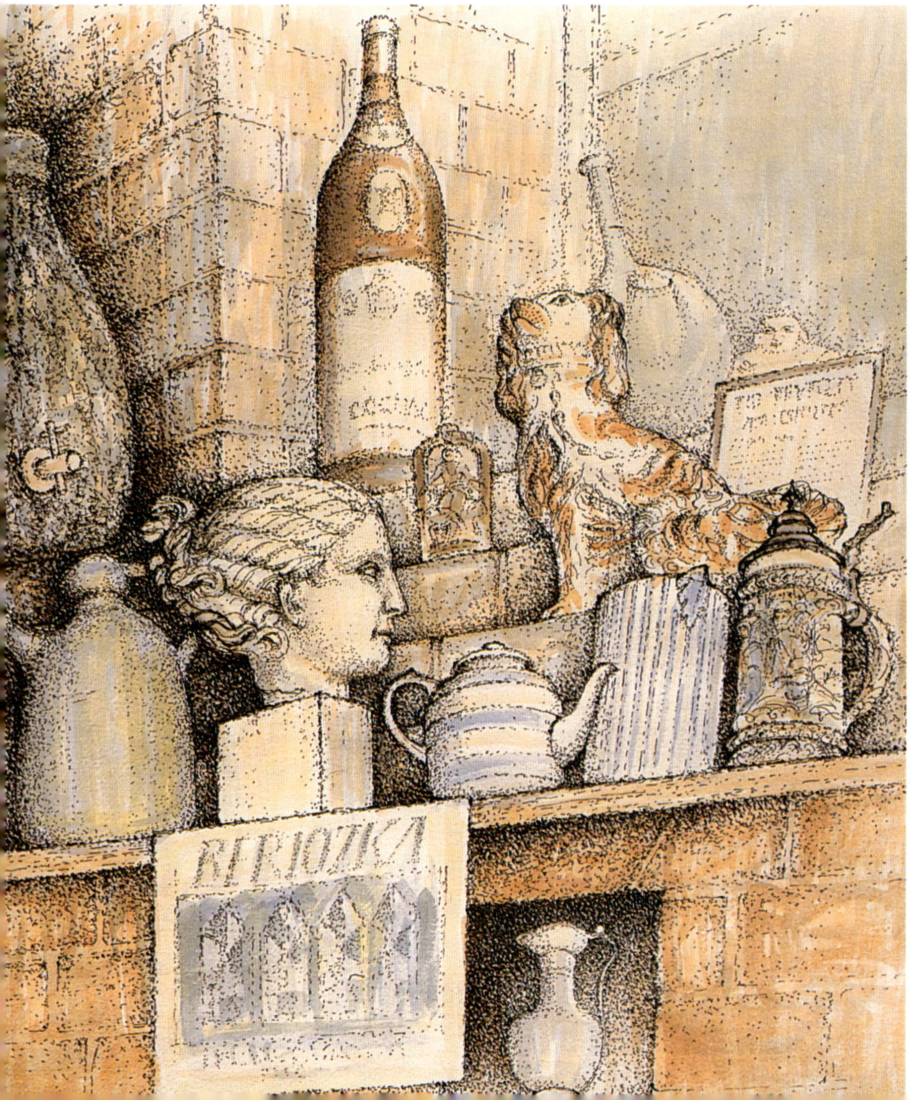

Studio Interior *Artists' studios offer many possibilities for drawing, with their incongruous assortment of objects.*

This was a chimney piece in one such studio, its accumulations making an unusual still life.

Since each object was interesting in its own right, (apart from its relationship to the whole group), and since the shapes dominated the fairly ordinary colours, I decided to emphasize the drawing side. This is the opposite approach to that in the 'Russian Tomb' on page 33, where colour and mood prevailed. The ability to play around with pictorial components is one of the delights of drawing.

I began the drawing with a medium nib and black Indian ink, keeping it light and open while I established the composition. Then I drew in more heavily, working up and accentuating the special character of the shapes. Tonal effects are noticeable on the brickwork; rather less so on the objects. Lastly, I added watercolour washes.

Variations

Amaryllis *The illustrated examples on these two pages show different ways in which pen and watercolour can be combined.*

In this first picture, it is the colour that predominates. Watercolour was used first, the red being put on at full strength to avoid too much overpainting, which could deaden the colour. Then the pen drawing was added and, lastly, Indigo and the textured pen strokes were brought in to heighten the contrast against the red.

Flowers are some of the most intensely coloured subjects you will draw. It is impossible to match exactly this brilliance, but by placing Indigo in the flower's centre, the red seems to explode against it giving a sense of vibrancy. Leaving the paper white would have had less impact.

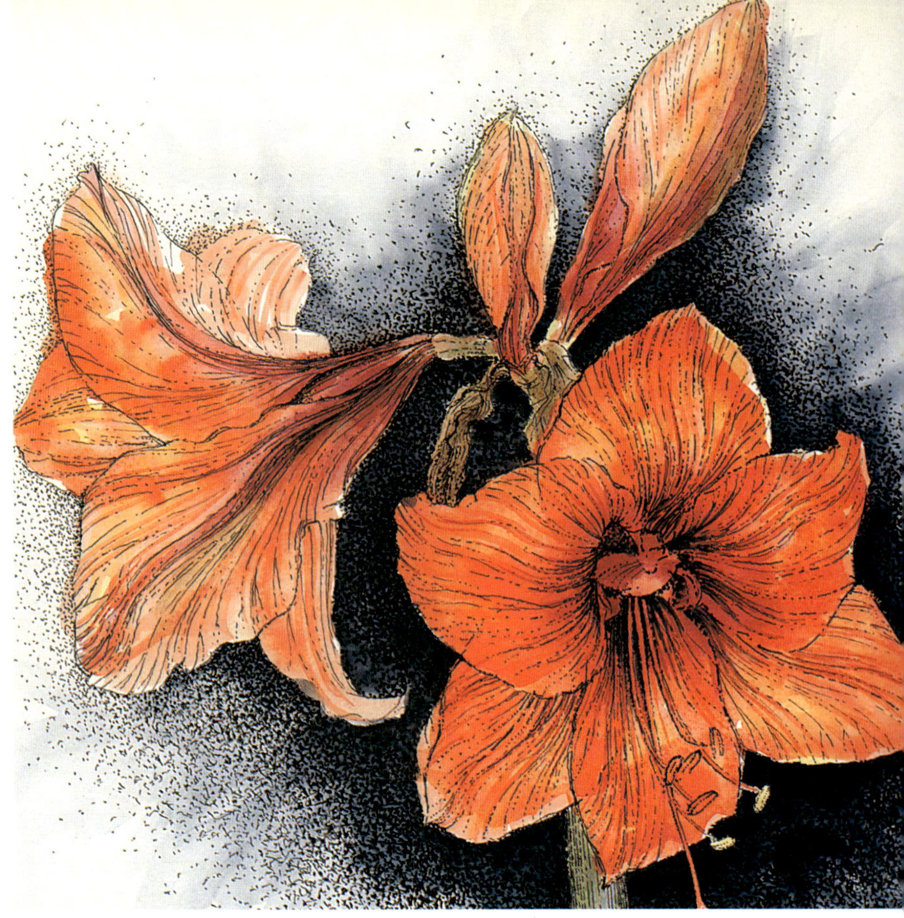

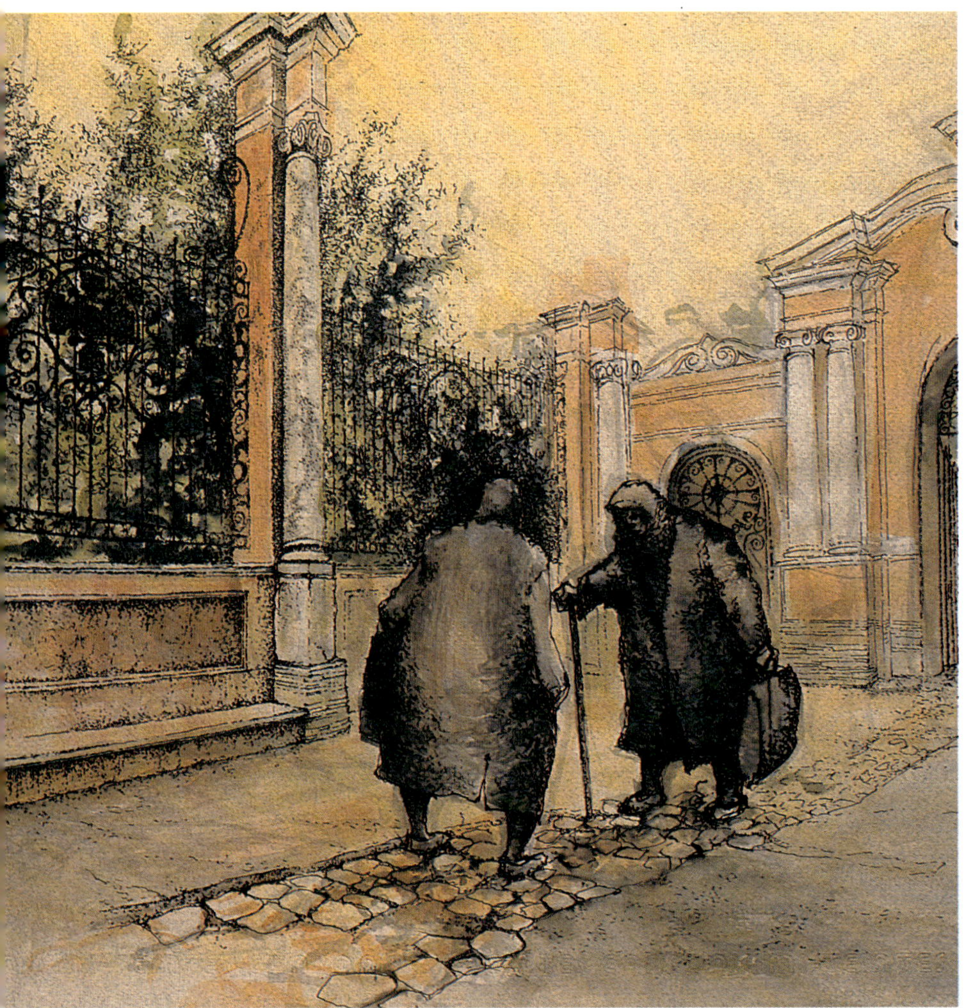

Babushkas *Two babushkas gossiping in a once opulent St Petersburg street. This subject offered some interesting contrasts to be translated into ink and colour. Unlike the amaryllis above, which required colour to sing out, this picture needed a faded look, a sense of something past. I chose the grey-tinted paper to work on, to mute the colours in the way that was wanted.*

Washes of colour were brushed on first, the grey paper not only reducing the colour brightness, but harmonizing and pulling the picture together. These same washes on white paper would look more colourful.

The ink drawing done on top consisted of several techniques: linear, stippled and scribbled strokes. In the drawing of the wrought-iron railings, notice how the nearest railings are darker and more emphasized than those farther away, to suggest the distance and space beyond the women.

Rabbit *In this illustration, the pen drawing was carried to a high degree of finish before any colour was added. This was applied in pale washes to enhance, but not dominate, the pen work. It echoes the hand-coloured engravings that were popular in the last century.*

Notice the different drawing techniques on the rabbit and the surrounding plants.

Bird Boxes *I was immediately struck by the resemblance of these wooden bird boxes to a row of little faces. It was an amusing and original subject which I felt called for an immediate and direct approach, a complete contrast to the rabbit above.*

Earth colours, Raw and Burnt Sienna, Raw and Burnt Umber, were brushed on with a flat 2cm (¾in) brush, the drawing being done straight away with a thick nib, causing some of the lines to run. Indigo was finally added to give depth.

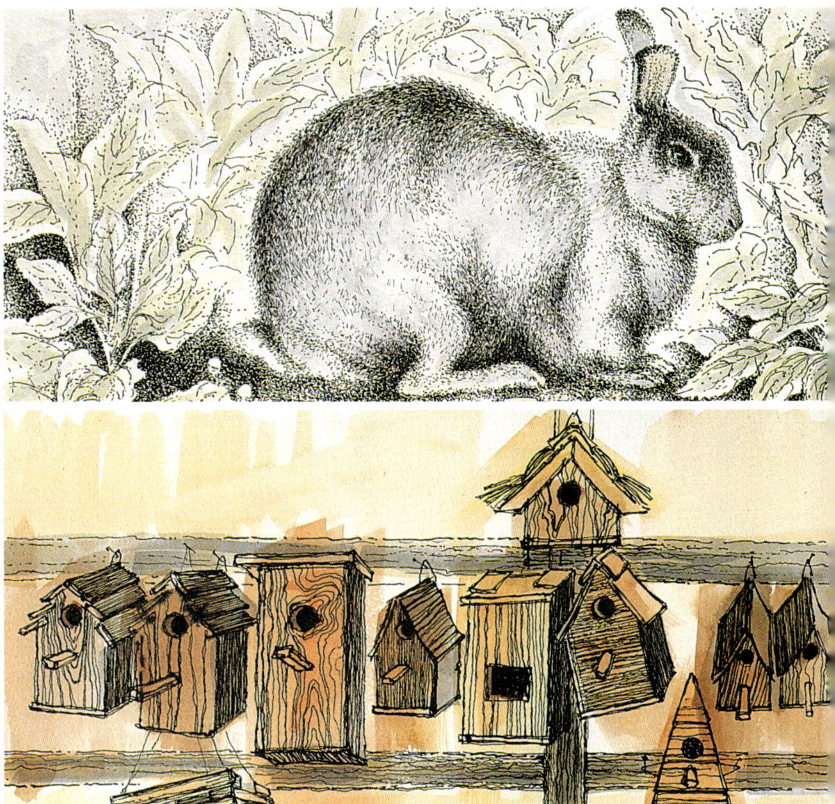

Back-Up Exercise – Using Watercolour

For an exercise, set up a similar group to the one shown below.

The illustration shows how the picture progressed from the initial brush drawing on the left to the final stage shown in the teapot.

Having completed the initial drawing in yellow wash, the larger areas of colour were blocked in with a 2cm (¾in) flat brush, shown in the leaves above the cup. Deeper colour and tone were added to give substance. The ink drawing was done with a thick nib, holding the pen high up for flexibility, which produced the coarse strokes, in keeping with the broad treatment of this subject.

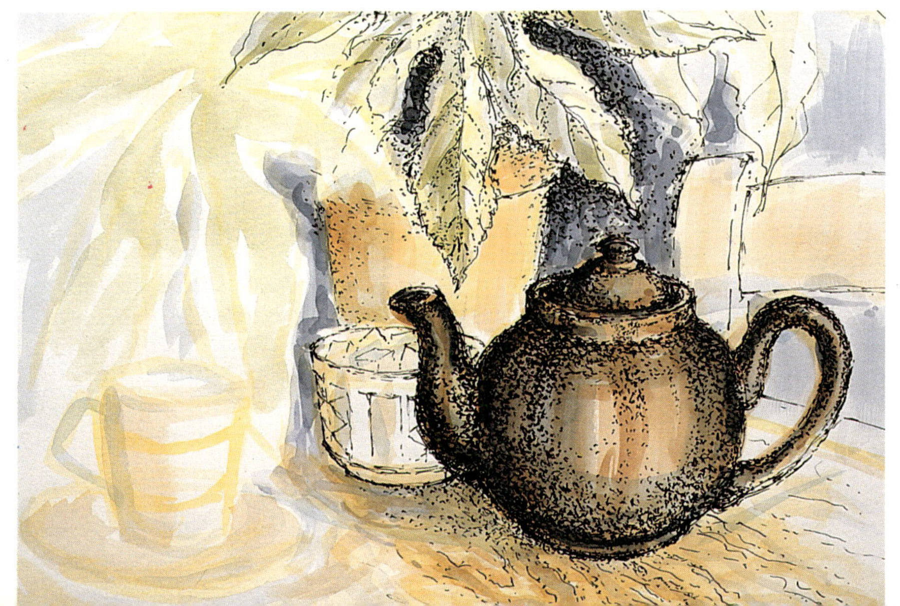

Summary

The illustrations in this section give an indication of the varied techniques and ways in which pen and watercolour paints can be used together.

There are examples where colour dominates the pen, and others where colour is subsidiary to pen.

Some pictures have been built up in layers: first colour then pen, repeating this until the picture is completed. This method produces a work of some substance, although a layer too many will cause the colour vibrancy to be lost – a question of knowing when to stop!

Work on tinted papers opens up other possibilities, with their subtle colour changes and harmonies.

Pen and watercolour is a lovely medium for producing images that are full of vitality, or quietly sensitive.

COLOURED INKS

MATERIALS & EQUIPMENT

- Paper
- Pen holder
- Nibs
- Brushes
- Coloured inks
- Watercolour pens
- Water
- Palette
- Drawing board
- Paper tissue

For many people, pen and ink conjures up the idea of a drawing done solely in black ink. We have already seen how watercolour washes can add colour to a pen drawing, but another way in which colour can be introduced is by using coloured inks.

These, too, can be put on in the form of washes, either diluted with water (preferably distilled) or used at full strength. They can also be used with pen and drawn with directly.

Their use opens up the opportunities for coloured drawings in a number of exciting ways, and there are some examples of these in the illustrations on the opposite page.

The colours of inks are generally more potent than those of watercolours, and for this reason can sometimes look garish when used at full strength. However, there are occasions when brilliance of colour is called for, particularly when doing decorative or design work, and coloured inks are ideal for this purpose. If more subtle colours are called for, they are easily diluted into softer tints.

One advantage is their mixing capability. They will readily intermix to give good, clear hues, either in the form of pre-mixed colours before you commence work, or as overlapping layers on the work itself. Because they are transparent, the first colour will show through the second, and this can be seen in the illustration of colour mixtures at the foot of this page. As with all colours, it is not a good idea to mix too many together at once as they can soon look muddy. Experimenting with colour will teach you just how far you can go.

There are many different kinds of ink available on the market; some are waterproof when dry, others are not. Be sure you know which sort you are purchasing or using. Some are specially prepared to be used with a particular type of pen, so make your selection carefully. Not all inks are lightfast, which may also be a point for consideration.

Besides liquid ink in pots, there are also watercolour, felt-tip, and fibre-tip pens. These are good for quick drawing and sketches, as they cover the paper rapidly and can be used boldly. They are also convenient to use.

The illustrations in this section show several techniques for using coloured inks and pens; some are very free and others more controlled, but each has its own special character, conveying something of the diversity to be found in drawing.

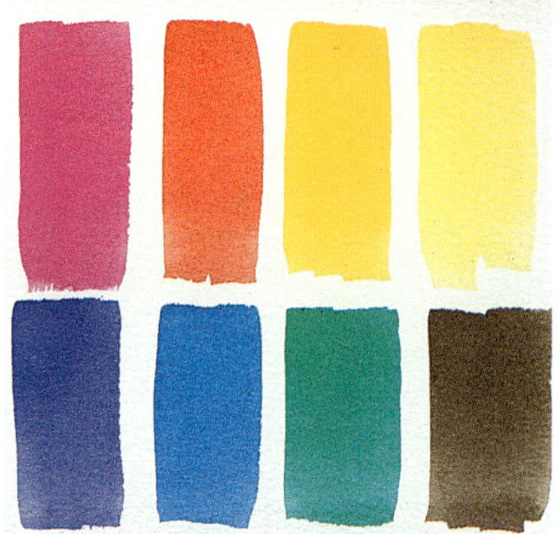

Selecting Colours *A selection of inks. Warm colours on the top: Crimson, Vermilion, Bright Yellow, Pale Yellow. Cool colours below: Ultramarine, Cobalt, Viridian, Brown. All samples were made with a single brushstroke.*

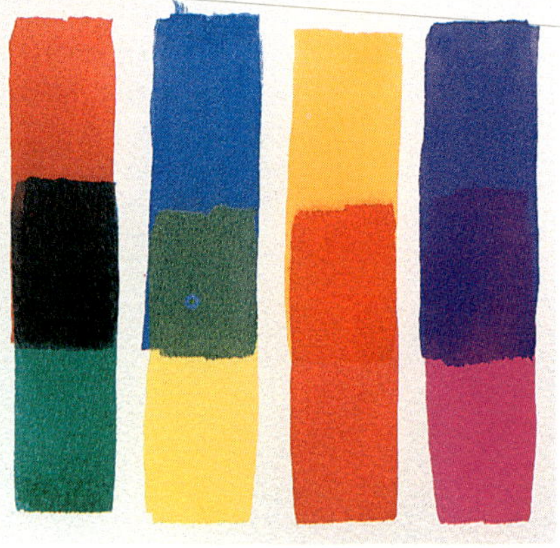

Colour Mixtures *Combinations of colours shown in the previous picture, demonstrating the mixtures that result. Again, all samples were made with a single brushstroke. Additional strokes would deepen the colours.*

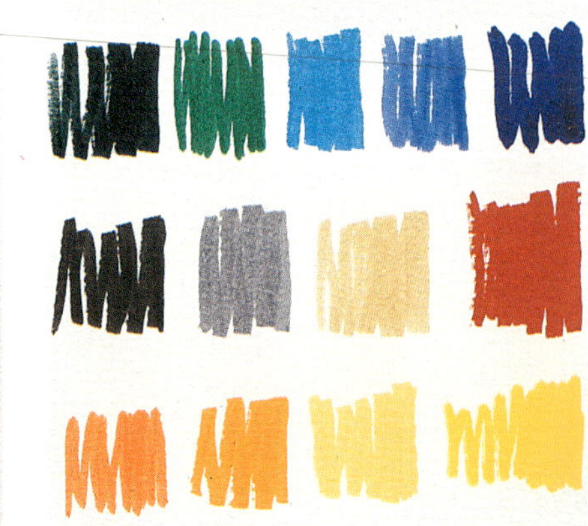

Watercolour Pens *Watercolour pens come in many colours. A selection is shown here. They can be used for line drawing and blocking in large areas. They are transparent and can be overlaid to give colour mixtures.*

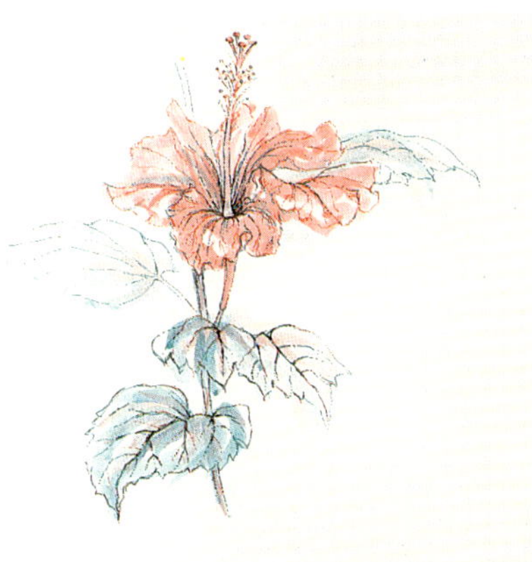

Hibiscus Flower (1) *A pen and wash drawing of a hibiscus flower using two colours, Vermilion and Viridian.*

The wash was put on first with a No. 10 round brush. Notice the third colour produced by overlapping. The pen drawing done with a medium nib appears more intense in colour because the ink was used undiluted, in contrast to the wash.

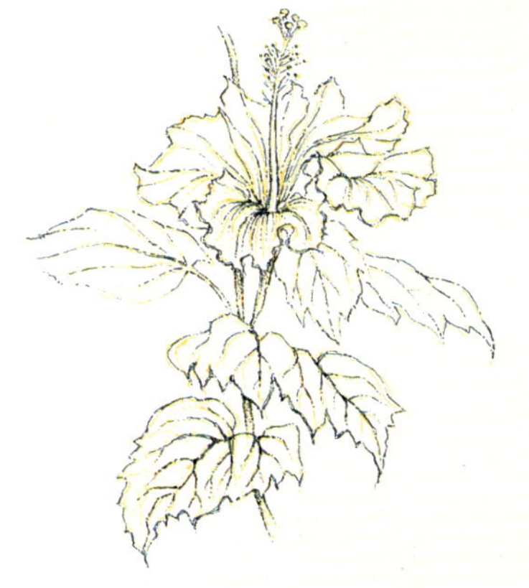

Hibiscus Flower (2) *Another study of the same flower using Cobalt and yellow.*

This predominantly linear drawing uses just a little stippled tone on the stem to push the leaves and petals forward. A thicker nib reinforces the line in places to give movement to the drawing and prevent it from becoming monotonous.

The quality of this type of work depends upon the variation of line that can be produced.

Selecting and Buying Colours

One of the difficulties confronting a beginner purchasing equipment for the first time is knowing which colours to select.

It is unnecessary to buy a large number, but instead choose those colours that, when mixed together, will produce secondary colours. Crimson, Vermilion, Ultramarine, Cobalt Blue, and yellow will also make violet, orange, green and brown (as shown in the illustration of colour mixtures on the opposite page). Add black to these and they should be enough to get you started.

Some manufacturers produce packs of inks, made up in groups of six or twelve. They come in convenient plastic cases, which you might prefer, but you have to accept their choice of colours.

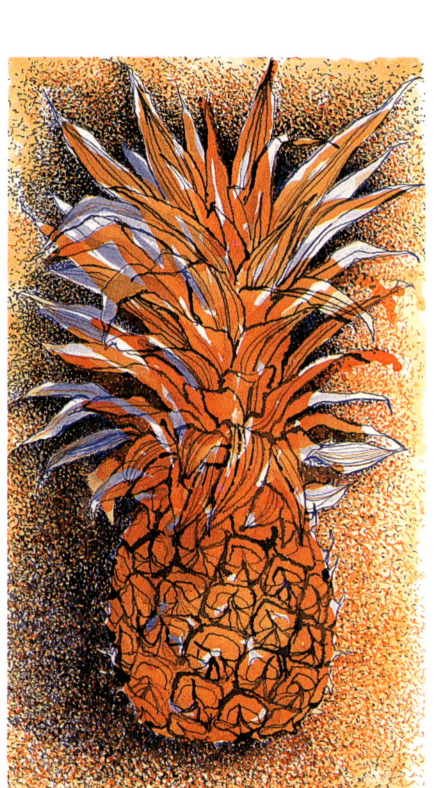

Pineapple (1) *Ultramarine and orange were used in this more dramatic pen and wash treatment of an exotic subject.*

The colours were brushed on freely, then worked on with pen while they were still wet, which produced the spread line effect. Later more pen drawing was added to the dried surface. Both thick and thin nibs were used.

Pineapple (2) *This decorative drawing relies entirely upon line for its effect. Crimson and violet were used with medium and fine nibs.*

It is a lovely way to draw but needs some practice first and a less complicated subject to start with. The secret is to make sure there is sufficient ink to complete each shape in one continuous movement.

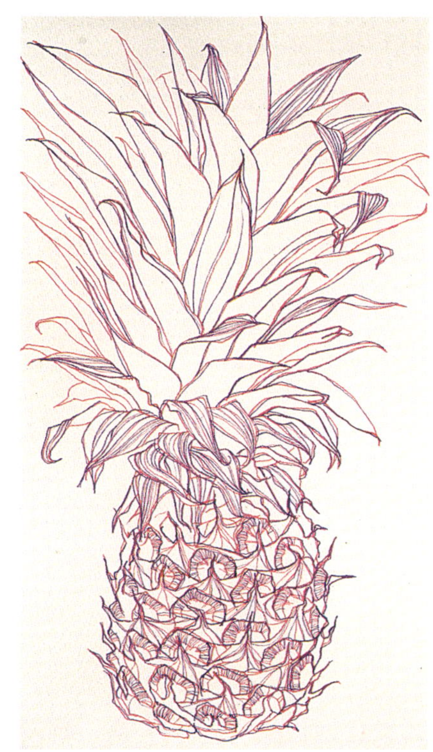

Peppers and Aubergines – Step-by-Step

I started this picture by drawing in the pepper and aubergines with a No. 10 brush and a diluted wash of yellow ink. Having established the composition, I strengthened the shapes with a wash of Ultramarine.

Compare the washes with the undiluted colours in the corner. As the picture progresses, notice how the colours intensify and become closer to these undiluted ones.

Using a flat 2cm (¾in) brush, I added a blue wash to the background, linking the shapes together and breaking up the white areas. To complete this stage, all the lines were reinforced with a stronger yellow.

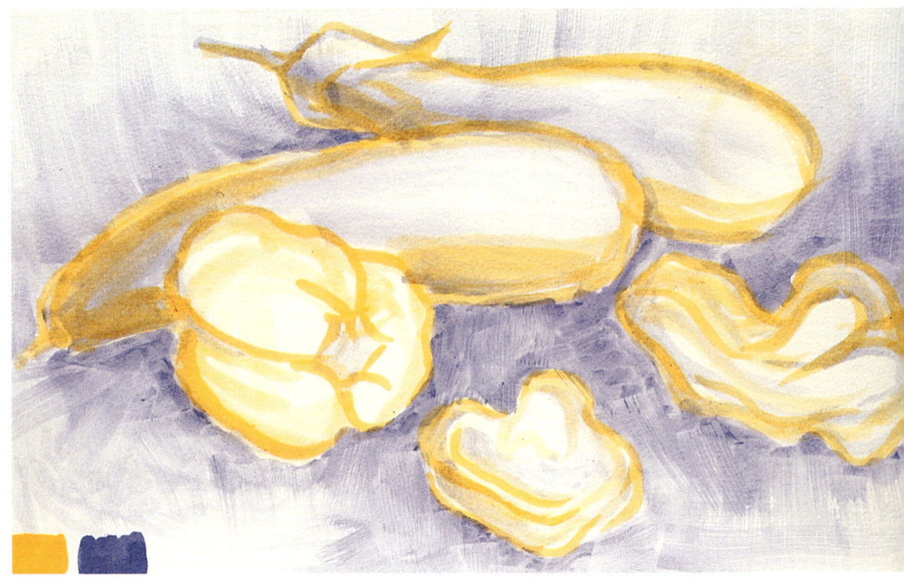

MATERIALS
Peppers and Aubergines

- Drawing paper
- Pen and nibs
- Brushes
- Coloured inks
- Water, preferably distilled
- Mixing palette
- Drawing board
- Drawing pins or clips

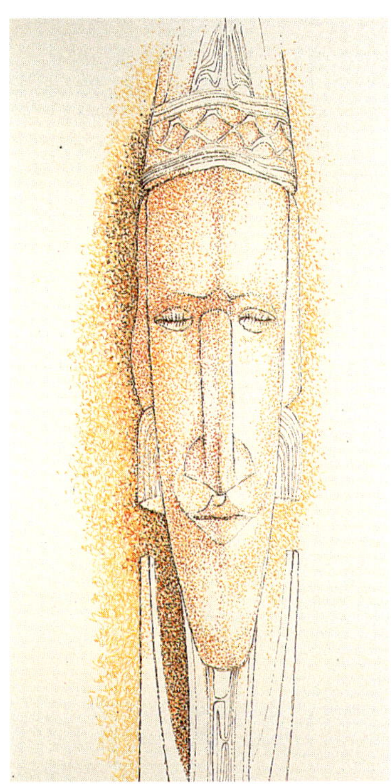

Papua New Guinea Carving
This drawing of a carving from Papua New Guinea illustrates how tones may be built up from tiny dots of colour.

Brown, Burnt Sienna, and yellow inks were used in this first stage.

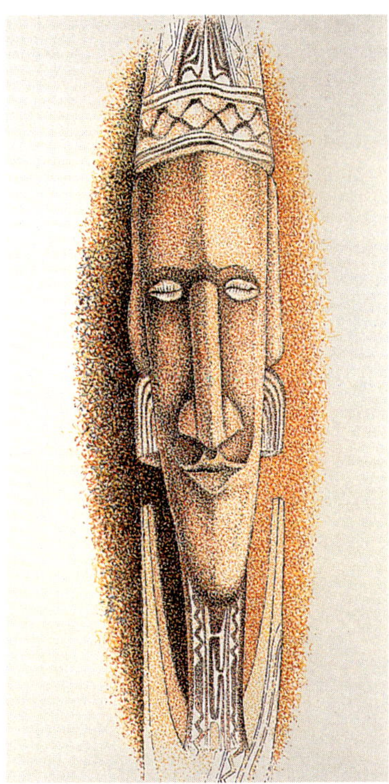

Ultramarine has been added to the drawing to deepen the darker tones. The lightest tone uses only yellow; the mid-tones use yellow with Burnt Sienna; and the darkest tones consist of all four colours.

Continuing with the same two colours, I drew over the whole picture with pen, using a thick nib.

The main drawing technique is made up of scribbled and dotted strokes, worked around the objects and, to a lesser extent, on them. This produces a vigorous effect and maintains the breadth of approach that I want to keep throughout this drawing. The pen work adds substance to the forms and helps to pull the image together.

More linear drawing has been used on the vegetables to bring out the rhythm of their distinctive shapes.

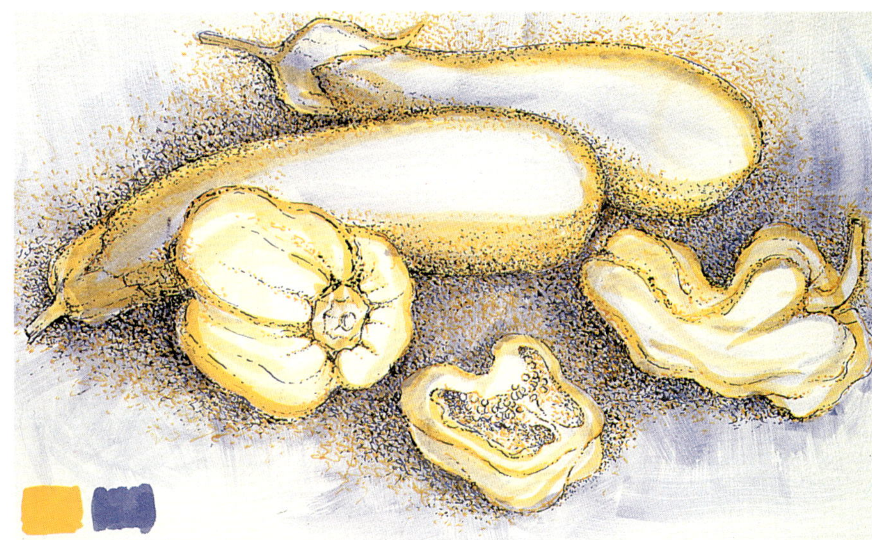

I brought in the third colour, Crimson, first as a wash and then as pen drawing, again using broken, stippled strokes. This is used lavishly on the aubergines, acknowledging their local colour, and with more restraint on the peppers. Introducing it to the background and linking spaces between the vegetables, prevents the overall unity becoming submerged in the delight of drawing individual objects.

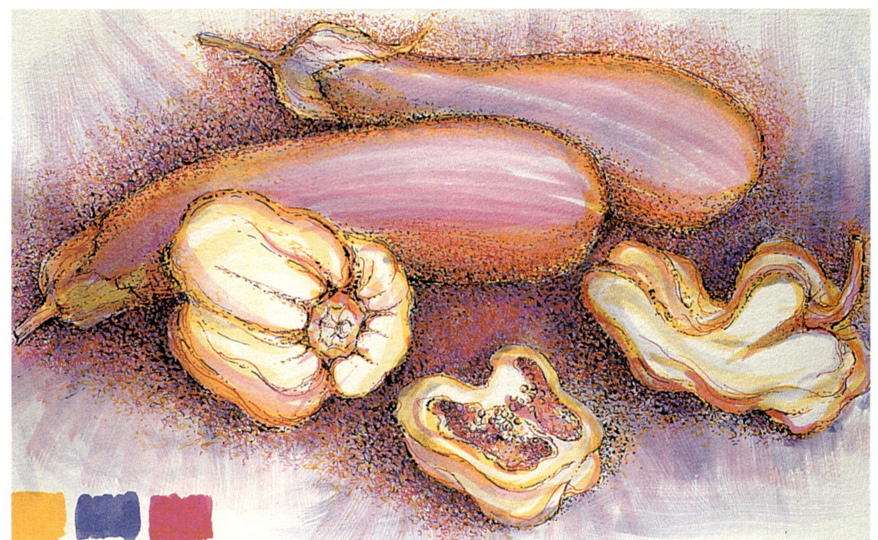

The final colour, brown, I used first as a wash, to subdue the harshness of the colour, particularly on the aubergines, and then to increase the depth of tone in the pen drawing.

Now it was time to stand back and assess the picture as a whole, making any adjustments where necessary. I felt more blue was needed to enrich the dark tones and make them sparkle, so this was added and, as a final touch, I brushed more yellow on the peppers, which looked too light against the heavier aubergines.

This is an exuberant illustration which seemed to suit the medium. It is quite different in mood to the previous still-life drawings.

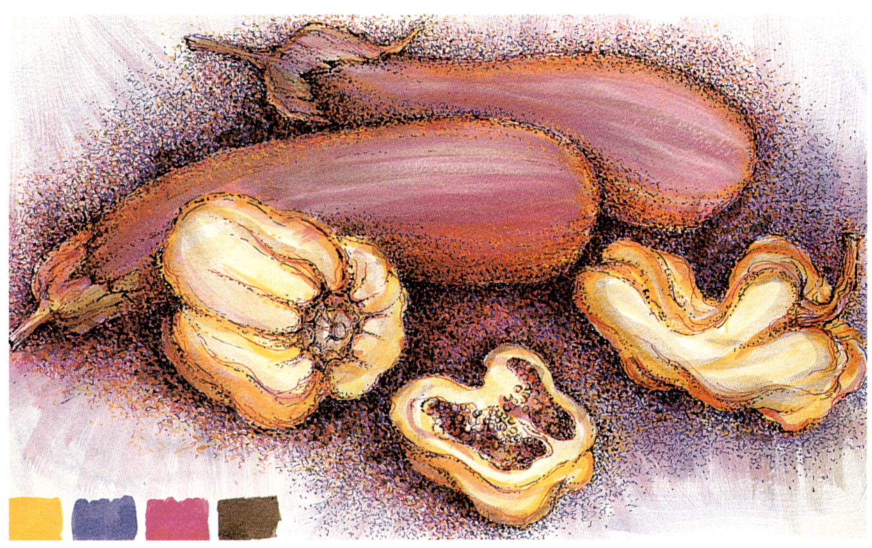

Coloured Inks

Watercolour Pens

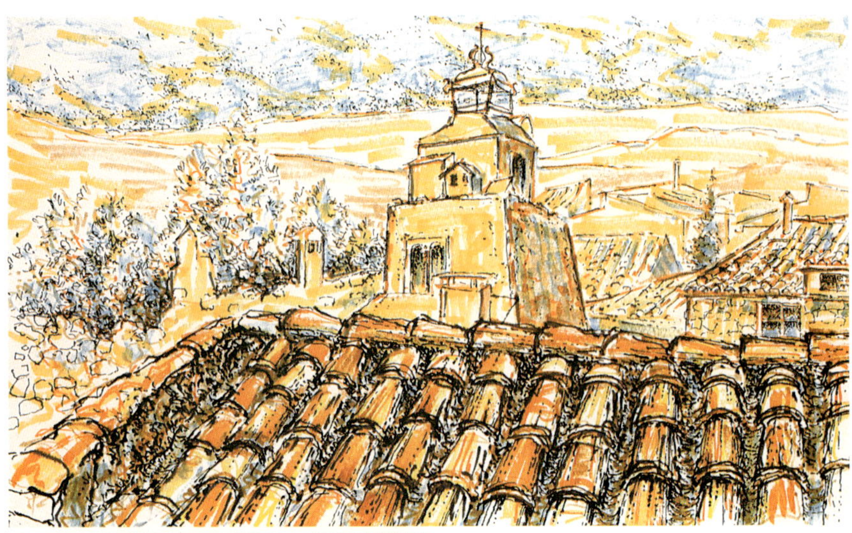

Watercolour Pens with Pen and Ink – Le Barroux *Watercolour pens produce a thick line suitable for broad, spontaneous drawing such as sketching and quick colour notes.*

This drawing was done with watercolour pens first, allowing the white paper to 'sparkle' through, reinforcing the sunny atmosphere. The colours are predominantly warm, with blue used in the cooler sky, foliage and shadows.

The final drawing in pen and ink brings out the shapes and textures of roofs and walls.

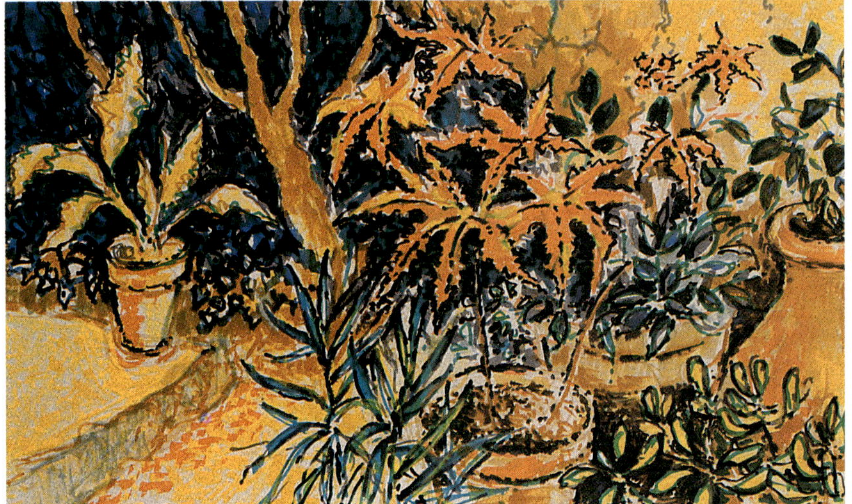

Watercolour Pens – Barbara's Garden *A subject with strong contrasts of sun and shadow.*

Only watercolour pens were used, worked on grey/green-tinted paper to reduce any brashness of colour. Compare this with the picture above, drawn on white paper.

Colours were applied densely, with several layers superimposed in the darkest parts. Since they are transparent, underlying colours affect those on top.

Colour is used interpretatively, not realistically, to emphasize the strong lighting.

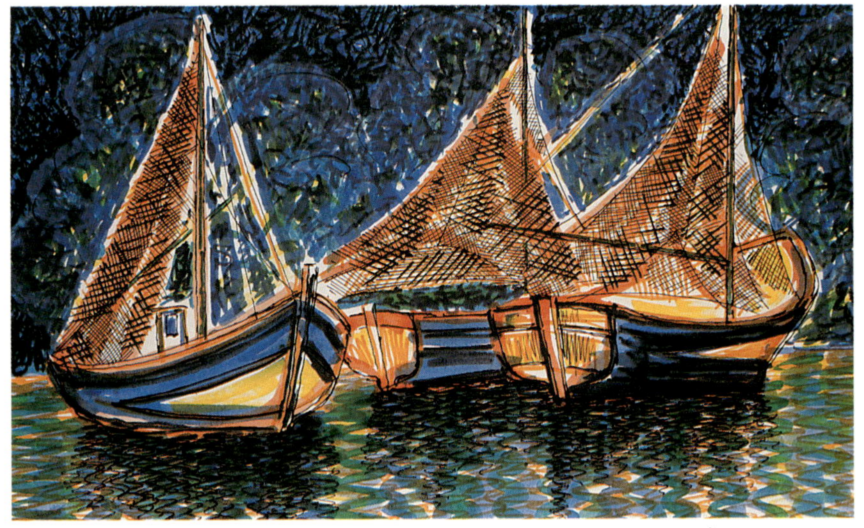

Watercolour Pens with Colour and Black Inks *The intention here was to capture the colour and essence of fishing boats without recourse to much detail (in contrast to the boats on page 31).*

Watercolour pens were used with Indian and coloured inks. The coloured inks were used first and put on with a brush; then the watercolour pens, to bring out the textures of sky, nets and water; and lastly some pen and black Indian ink was added.

The broad treatment suits the character of these chunky pens.

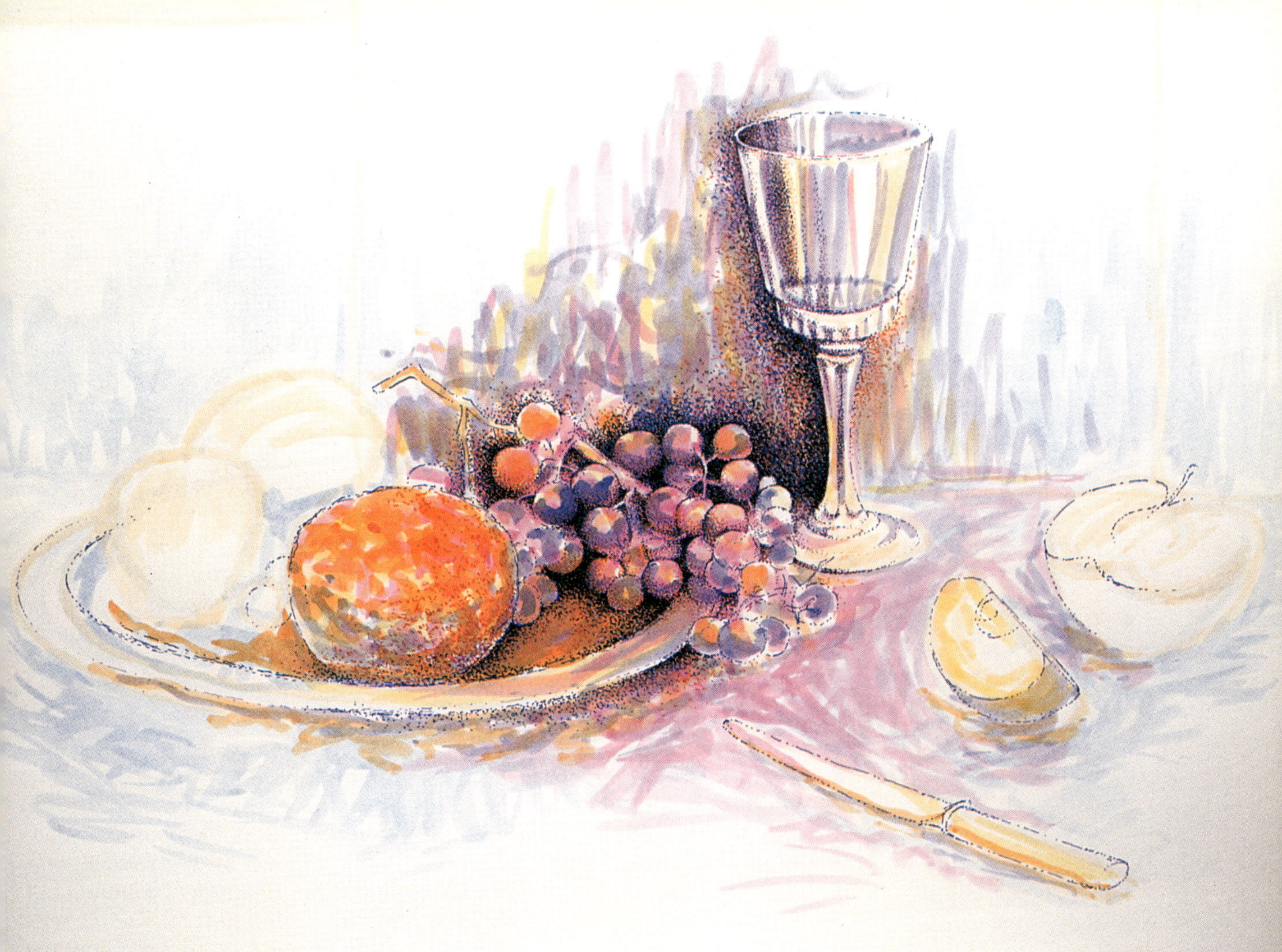

Fruit on a Plate *This picture has only been partially finished so that you can see how it evolved, from the first pale washes of Cobalt blue and orange, through the building up and intensifying of the colour, to the final pen-drawn details. The colours used were Cobalt blue, orange, Ultramarine, yellow, and Crimson. The techniques included freely applied brushwork, linear pen drawing, and finely stippled pen work to bring out the tonal contrasts. By stippling the colours on top of each other, it is possible to get a depth of tone that is very dark, and yet still retain its vitality. Mixing all the colours together beforehand and then applying them would have a deadening effect.*

Back-Up Exercise – Using Coloured Inks

As a back-up exercise, I suggest that you set up a group of your own, similar to the one in the picture above, and approach the working of it in the same way. Start with the brush, and keep the washes very pale indeed until you are sure about the composition, and then proceed along the lines I have just indicated.

The advantage of this method, rather than a straight copy of my picture, is that you are working directly from three-dimensional objects, which you can examine closely, and even pick up, to understand fully their shape and form. This will give you a much better sense of what you are drawing and provide a first-hand experience rather than a second-hand one. It also means that *you* are doing the creative work in transposing the group from three dimensions into two dimensions on your paper. It will be your own interpretation, and not a copy of someone else's.

In this way you will be able to follow and learn from the example that is shown, and yet produce a picture that is unique and personal.

EXPERIMENTAL WORK

MATERIALS & EQUIPMENT

- Paper
- Coloured papers
- Pen holder
- Nibs
- Brushes
- Inks
- Resists
- Spray diffuser
- Toothbrush
- Stick
- Quill
- Sponge
- Salt
- Water
- Palette
- Craft knife
- Paper tissue
- Drawing board
- Cutting board

This is a long list of materials and equipment and is intended to give you some idea of the diversity and range of experimental requirements. Make sure that everything is in good condition beforehand, as it will be so much nicer and easier to work with.

Until now the chapters in this book have dealt with traditional and orthodox methods of using pen and ink, and the step-by-step guides and illustrated examples are mainly representational or figurative. This is because I believe it is essential to learn to draw things as they appear naturally in everyday life. The demands and disciplines this imposes on a developing ability provides an excellent training of mind, hand, and eye, which you will need to become an accomplished artist. It will also teach you to understand and appreciate the structure of forms and encourage awareness and greater enjoyment of the world you see about you. Anything that can be seen or imagined is grist to the artist's mill.

This leads us to imagination, a most vital ingredient that must not be ignored. Imagination gives rise to creativeness and unique personal vision. All the artists mentioned in this book have had these qualities in common: superb technical skill allied with imaginative vision, but it is important to remember that the technique has always been subservient to the vision. Although few of us will ever attain the heights of these masters, we can learn from them and try to put this into practice in our own drawings.

This section aims to open up the field beyond conventional pen and ink techniques and give you the opportunity to discover and develop your own creativity, and have some fun at the same time.

All the methods shown involve the use of inks and some will involve the pen as well. It is always feasible to combine unconventional with traditional techniques, and this can be seen in some of the illustrated examples.

There are many ways in which inks can be applied to paper, besides the obvious ones of pen and brush. Sharpened sticks, toothbrushes, spray diffusers, paper tissues, sponges and fingers can all transfer ink from a pot to the working surface. The pictures on this page and the next show the sort of marks and effects you can

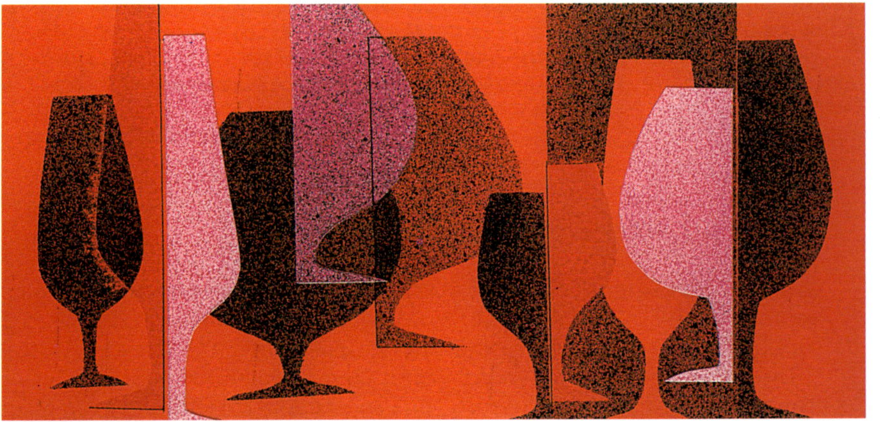

Collage: Wine Glasses *Collage is made by sticking pieces of extra material to the background surface.*

For this collage design I worked on red paper. The black shapes were sprayed directly on to the background, but the pink shapes were made on separate paper, then cut out and glued on. The black lines were drawn in afterwards.

I wanted the overall effect to be bright and jazzy.

expect to get from these implements. Some will not only apply the ink but also remove it as you can see with the sponge, paper tissues and salt grains.

Many of these techniques can be used to achieve background effects. Spraying with a diffuser, for example, gives a textured surface simulating the roughness of stone or brick; dabbing with a crumpled tissue suggests foliage; reversing the process and using the tissue to lift the ink will produce cloud or smoke images; salt grains leave an impression of a starry sky or snowflakes.

The sharpened stick comes closest to the pen in that it makes a drawn line, but the line differs in quality, being crumbly and irregular compared to the firmer, regular pen stroke, which is the difference between the tool that holds the ink and the one that must be replenished constantly.

The relevance of experimental work to the developing artist is in providing the chance to try out new techniques, or familiar techniques in new guises, without feeling encumbered by a set subject. It is a sort of artistic freewheeling, and involves shape, colour, texture, or various combinations of these.

If, however, you find it difficult to work away from a subject, try to approach it in a different way and see it afresh. Use methods that you have not tried before and enjoy the experience of doing something new. It will help to get you out of the 'habit' drawing, which can occur once you have mastered a technique and become adept at executing it, particularly if it elicits the admiration of family and friends!

Ideally, each drawing that you make

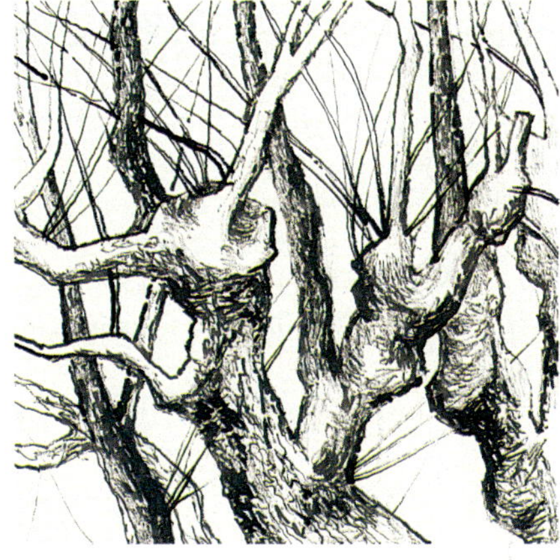

Drawing with Stick and Quill *A sharpened stick used with Indian ink gives a line that starts black and quickly becomes grey and charcoal-like. Because the ink dries quickly, this technique is suitable for quick sketches and other drawings requiring little detail. It makes an unusual method of drawing that has a distinctive grainy quality.*

The quill is closer to the pen, retaining the ink in a similar way and allowing greater control and a longer stroke. The twigs were drawn with a quill.

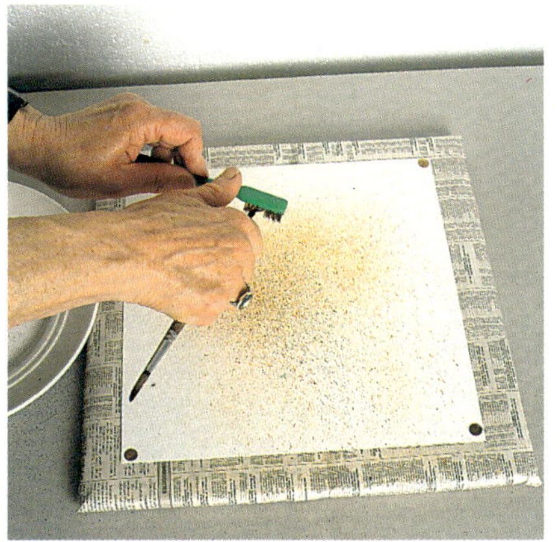

Toothbrush *Splattering with a toothbrush can be messy, so make sure there is newspaper to protect the surrounding area. It is easier to control the splattering if your paper is horizontal rather than upright.*

Put some ink on a plate and dip the toothbrush in. It should not be saturated, otherwise it will make large drips. Use the handle of an old paintbrush, dragging it across the bristles of the toothbrush, and as they spring back into place they will splatter ink across the paper.

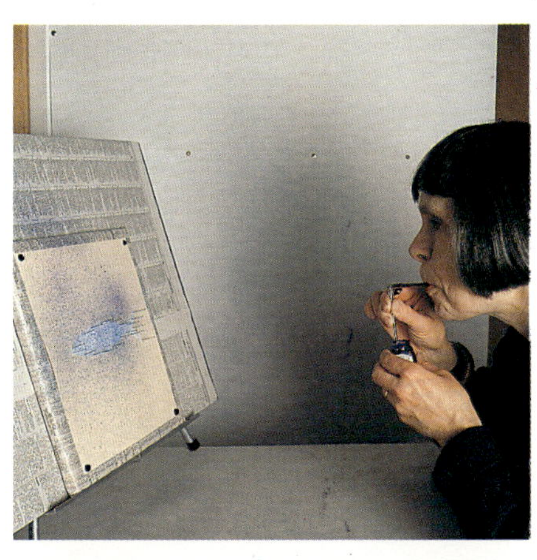

Spraying with Diffuser *Spraying should be done upright, again using newspaper as a protection.*

Hold the diffuser as shown in the illustration and blow. The ink will be sprayed on to the paper. Work swiftly, placing the paper flat once the desired level of colour has been reached, to prevent ink dribbles. Allow each colour to dry before adding another.

Spraying gives a more even texture than splattering.

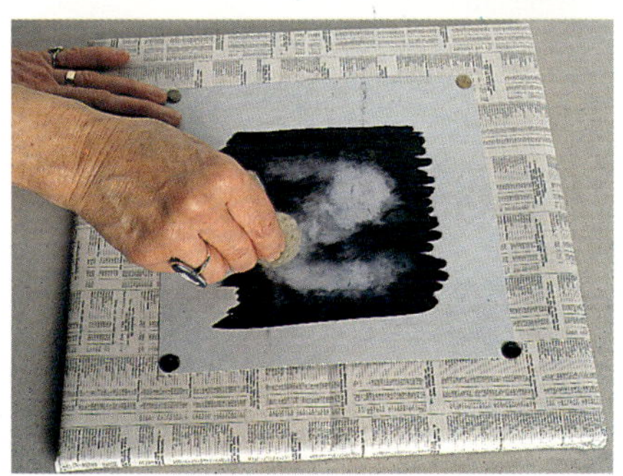

Lifting with Sponge *Brush non-waterproof ink onto the paper and let it dry. Dampen the sponge and press it down on the ink. Lift it and the ink comes away. The longer and harder you press, the lighter the image will be.*

Rinse the sponge to prevent it clogging with ink.

Experimental Work

Ideas

Almost anything can provide the raw material for ideas; these are the vital sparks that set off the imagination.

Natural forms, with their infinite variety of pattern, texture, and colour, provide inexhaustible material for many artists, and most artists are collectors. Pebbles, drift wood, seed pods, plants, feathers, shells, tiny skeletons, an animal's jaw bone, perhaps even a discarded snake's skin: these are all objects to be found, looked at, drawn and used for inspiration; so start to make your own collection and you may be amazed and delighted by the many fascinating things you will find. Your searchings should also help you to use your eyes more perceptively.

Other sources may lie within ourselves, waiting to be stimulated by music, a poem, or a half-remembered scene from the past. Even doodling and letting the pen idle at random on the paper may produce a promising starting point.

At times you may want to make careful studies, for use at a later stage. On other occasions, plunging straight in is appropriate: dispense with preliminaries and let the work evolve as you go along, one idea generating another – this often leads to the best results.

Train yourself to notice what is around you, to look with a 'seeing eye' and a sense of wonder. Build a 'vocabulary' of images, which in turn will feed the imagination and increase your range of ideas for drawings and designs.

should be an excursion into unknown territory, with fresh challenges for your skills. It should not be a collection of well-tried recipes which you turn to when you want to do a landscape, a still life, or an interior. If you should choose to work in this way, you may well become skilful, but your pictures will lack vitality and purpose.

The illustrations in this chapter are different from those in the rest of the book, having a distinctly design-based bias. Much of the work is two-dimensional and decorative, with scope for the imaginative use of pattern and colour.

Attempt some of these ideas yourself. You will discover a lot about using shapes, becoming more aware of their intrinsic values as forms in their own right, not always representing something else. When you return again to more orthodox means of drawing, this increased comprehension should help to give greater breadth to your work. A teapot will not just be a teapot, but a beautiful, rhythmic abstract shape: you will have found something of the poetry of picture-making.

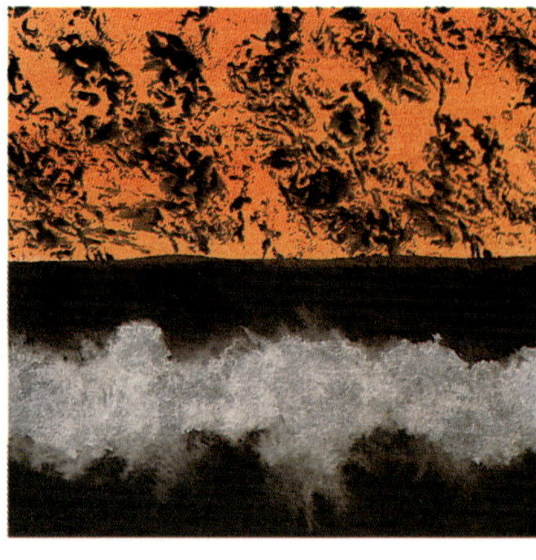

Paper Tissue *Top example: black ink dabbed over orange ink with a crumpled tissue. Lower example: damp, crumpled tissue pressed hard on to wet, non-waterproof black ink.*

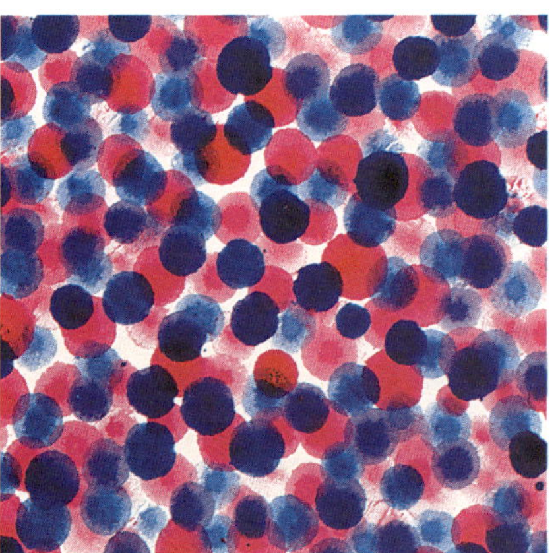

Finger-Marks *Blobs made with the finger using three coloured inks: Crimson, Cobalt Blue, and Ultramarine. The lighter marks give the impression of a fingerprint.*

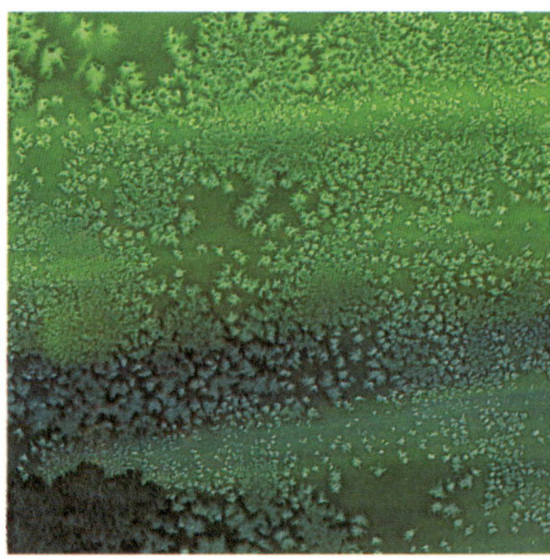

Salt Grains *Salt grains sprinkled on wet, non-waterproof green and blue inks, and brushed off when the inks are dry.*

Using Resists – Step-by-Step

The function of resists is to prevent the ink from coming into contact with the surface you are working on, to mask out certain portions of the picture.

The most commonly used resists are masking film, masking fluid, paper or card, and wax. There are step-by-step guides on the following pages demonstrating how these can be used.

Of all the resists, wax is the one most usually associated with drawing. It is used in conjunction with washes, and there is an element of the unknown about it which makes it fun to use, because being colourless, its effect will not be seen until the wash has been added. Using the stub of an old candle draw with it in the way you would use a thick crayon and see the exciting textured quality it gives to a drawing.

Masking film, fluid, and paper are more generally connected with design work, although fluid is useful in drawings or pictures where very fine white lines are required against a darker background. It can be applied with pen or brush, but remember to clean these thoroughly in water after use to prevent clogging.

Masking film and paper will be used for larger areas, cut to shape with scissors or a craft knife. Paper can also be torn, giving a less rigidly controlled shape, which again introduces an element of chance.

Alternatives

As alternatives to the more conventional resists that have been discussed, try using leaves, flat pebbles, pieces of wood, wire mesh, plastic netting, and anything else you can find that would make a resist. You should find it entertaining, and although not all your choices may work, you will be surprised by some of the results and unusual effects you achieve. The value of this exploration is that you are exploiting different materials and extending your creative experience, storing up new images and ideas in your mind that may, eventually, be used to liven up a more orthodox drawing.

Museum Poster *A poster design that is an amalgamation of free, spontaneous elements with others that are more tightly controlled and detailed. The colour, too, heightens the sense of contrast: the glowing orange of the fearsome dinosaur skull stands out against the cool blues of the background. The lettering, although standing aside from the main thrust of the design in order to be easily read, echoes the warm colour of the skull.*

Several methods were involved: wax resist; splattering; using masking film; brushed-on colour washes; pen and ink drawing; and collage. After it had been drawn on orange paper, the skull was cut out and superimposed on the background.

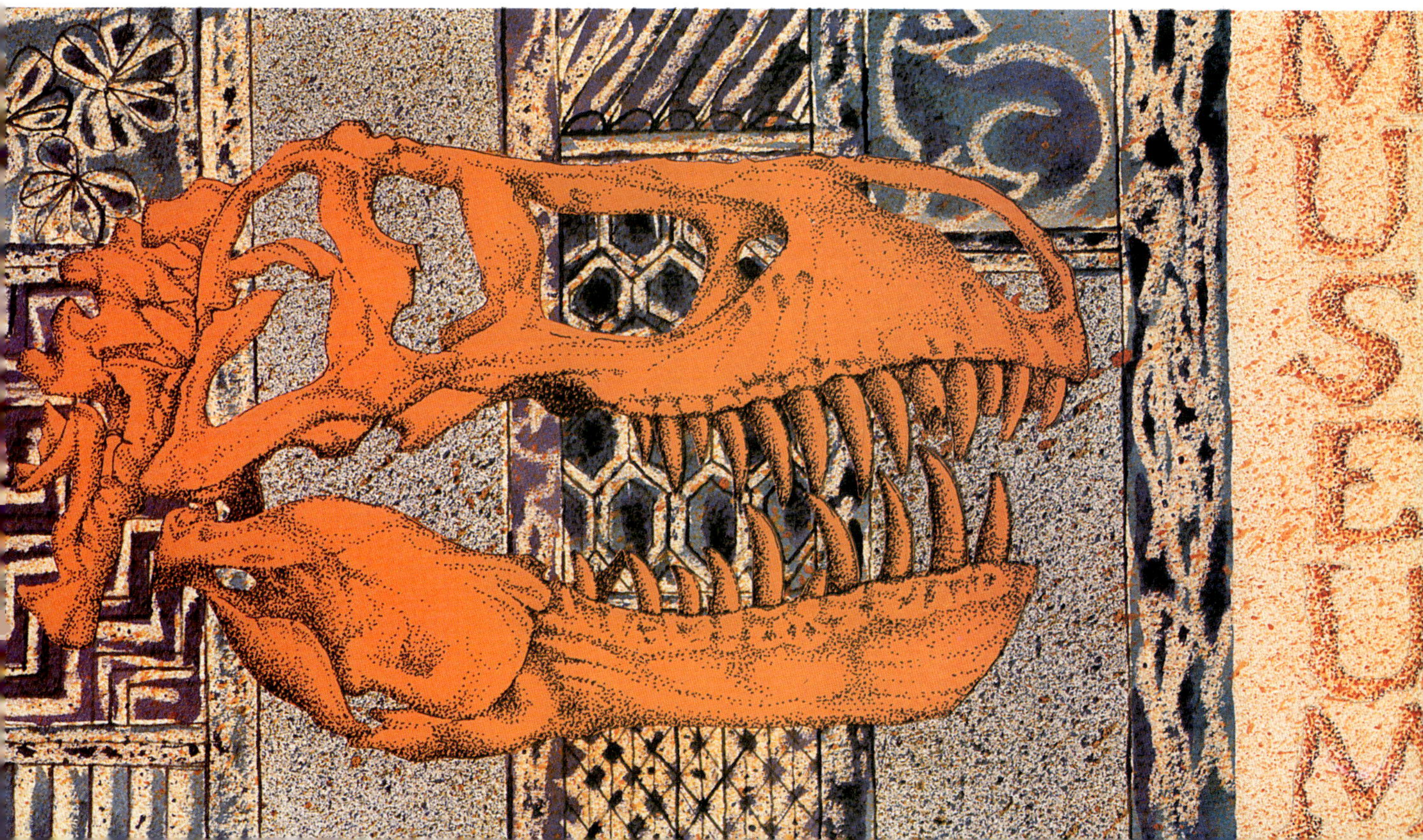

Masking Fluid and Film – Step-by-Step

MATERIALS
Using Resists

- Drawing paper
- Pen and nibs
- Brushes
- Stencil brush
- Coloured inks
- Black Indian ink
- Craft knife or scissors
- Water
- Masking fluid
- Masking film
- White candle

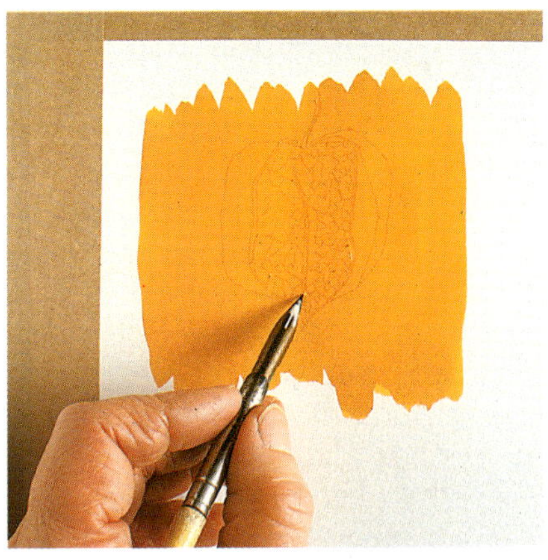

Masking Fluid *Yellow ink was brushed on to the paper and left to dry. Using a medium nib and masking fluid, I drew a Chinese lantern on the yellow background and allowed it to dry.*

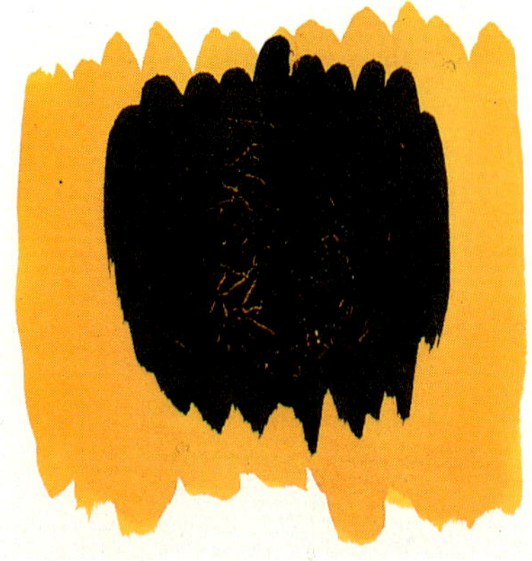

Black Indian ink was brushed over the drawn design and left to dry thoroughly.

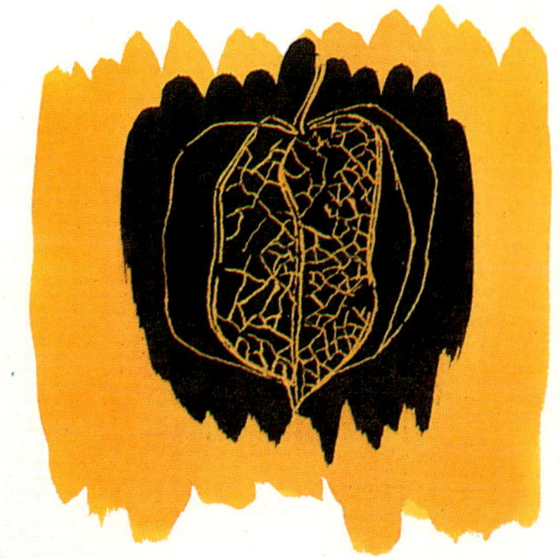

Making sure that the black ink was absolutely dry first (it can be left to the following day), I rubbed away the masking fluid with my finger. This needs to be done carefully.

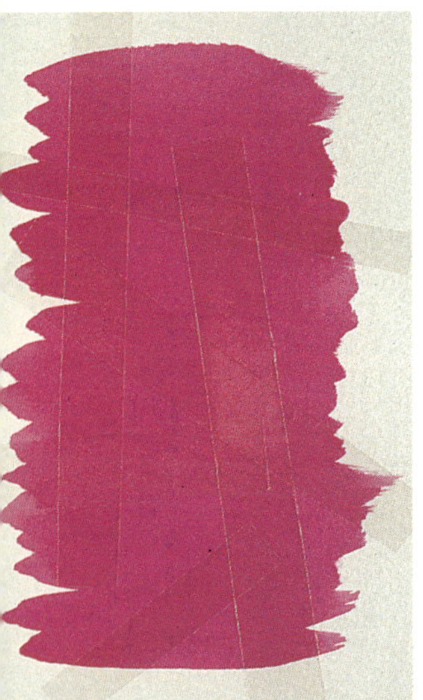

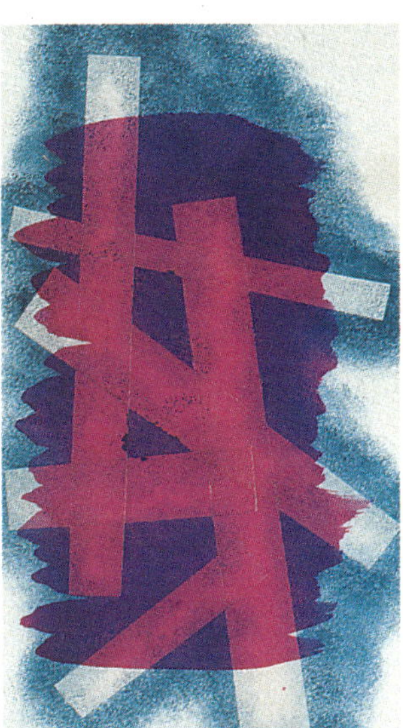

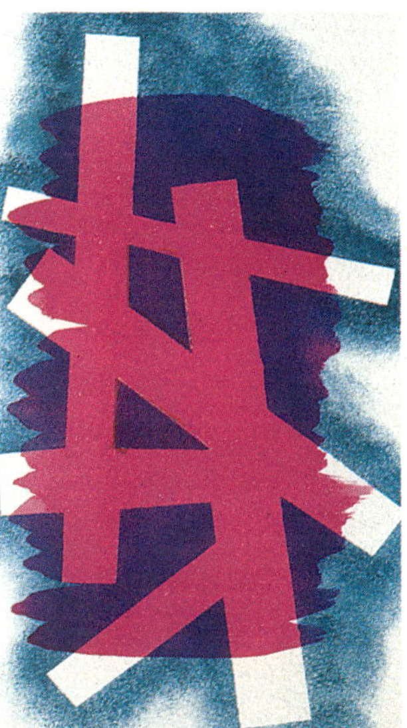

Masking Film *First I brushed a background of Crimson ink on to the paper and let it dry. Then I cut strips of masking film and pressed these down firmly on the background.*

Using a stencil brush, I dabbed blue ink over the design. It is important not to miss out any edges of the masking film or you will not get a crisp shape.

When the ink was dry I peeled away the masking film. This demonstration shows the method at its most basic. It can be greatly expanded with many more areas of film and colour being applied.

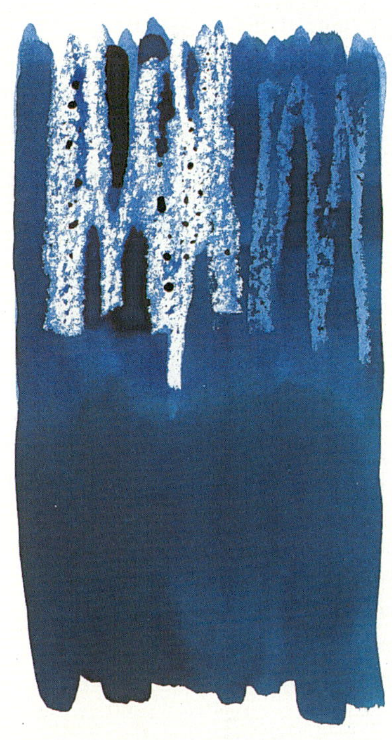

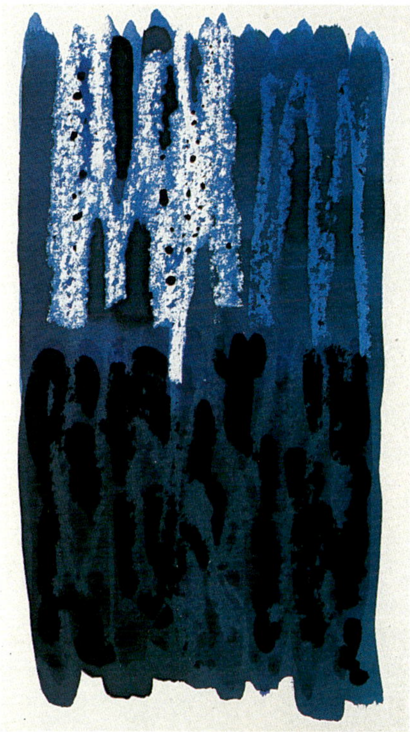

Wax *Wax produces an attractive texture when used with inks or watercolours, and adds liveliness to graphic work.*

Here I rubbed a candle on paper and then brushed Cobalt ink on top, extending it towards the right. The greasiness of the wax has repelled the ink and produced the characteristic effect.

More wax has been applied, this time on top of the Cobalt ink. Now I have brushed a darker blue over the whole area, and you can see the result in the contrasted wax textures, one showing the white paper and the other Cobalt Blue.

In the final stage I rubbed wax on the lower part of the example, and then brushed it over with a mixture of Ultramarine and black Indian ink. The top part was left untouched.

A simple illustration to show how a rich combination of texture and colour can be produced.

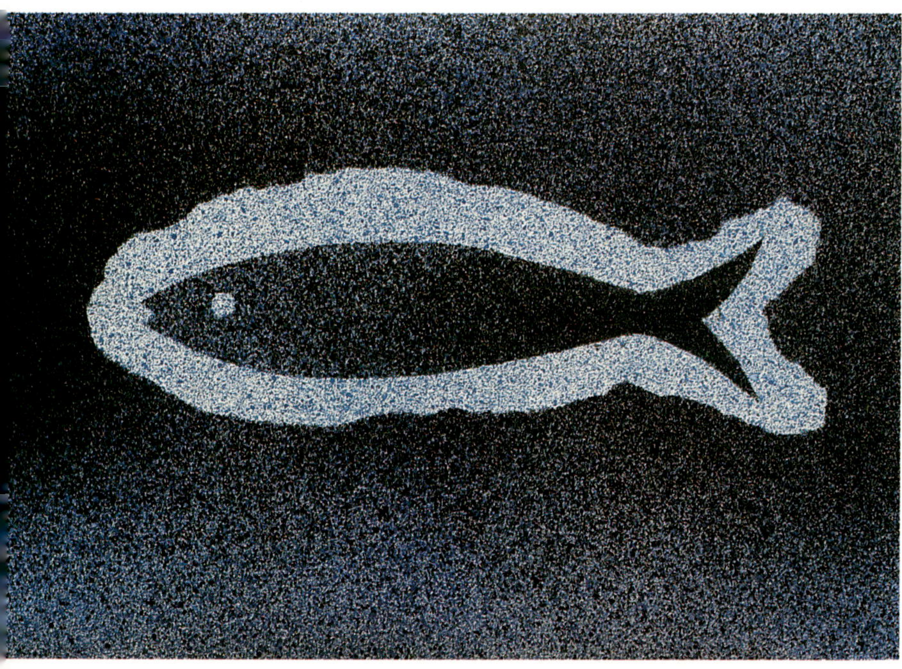

Paper Resist – Fish *Paper makes an efficient, economical resist, particularly when masking out big areas.*

I find the best way of fixing it is to use dressmaker's pins and a cork or polystyrene tile as a backing. Pins are easily pushed into the flexible surface, without making your fingers too sore.

Apart from economy, the advantage of paper is that it can be torn as well as cut. Both these methods are illustrated here, demonstrating the different quality of shape that results.

Coloured inks were sprayed on to produce the textured effect.

SPLATTERING & SPRAYING

Splattering and spraying inks onto paper makes an attractive mottled texture, particularly effective in design and illustrative work. It can also liven up a drawing provided it is not overdone.

One of the finest exponents of this method was Toulouse-Lautrec, who made bold use of it in his large lithographic posters for the cabarets and dance halls of Paris during the 1890s. He developed his own technique by splattering the inks onto the lithographic stone through a sieve. These posters are a striking example of the telling effects ink spraying can have when balanced against broad, flat areas of colour.

The final results of the two techniques are similar although produced in different ways. Splattering is done with a stiff-bristled brush (a toothbrush is ideal). It is easier to control than spraying, but it takes longer to build up an equivalent accumulation of colour.

Spraying with a diffuser requires more effort as the ink is blown on to the surface, and if there is a large area to cover you might get a bit breathless towards the end. The size of the mottles that are produced will depend upon the diffuser. Those with the narrowest tubes make the finest spray but some of them are hard to blow. It can take a little practice to acquire the knack of blowing; some people find it much easier than others. If you have difficulty, try altering the angle formed by the two tubes.

Both methods are illustrated below. Applying successive layers of ink, using either technique, will give a rich density of colour.

Unless you want an all-over textured background, these techniques are normally carried out in conjunction with a resist, as demonstrated in the step-by-step guides opposite. This should be a simple procedure, but problems do arise sometimes, which I have described in the caption to the illustration 'Machines' (*see* page 52). It is important to make sure that resists adhere closely to the area to be sprayed or splattered, otherwise you will not get the clean edge that is a feature of this technique. To prevent ink runs after spraying, put the work flat immediately.

MATERIALS
Pebble and Capital Letter

- Drawing paper
- Pen and nibs
- Fine brush
- Black Indian ink
- Coloured inks
- Spray diffuser
- Toothbrush
- Craft knife
- Masking fluid
- Masking film

These step-by-step guides demonstrate only a few ways in which these techniques can be combined.

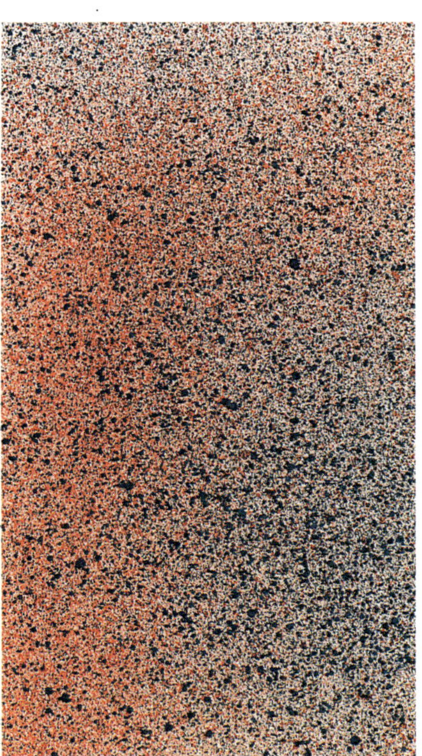

Spraying *The example on the right shows the result of blowing ink on to paper through a spray diffuser. It makes an attractive texture and colours can be built up to produce a rich effect.*

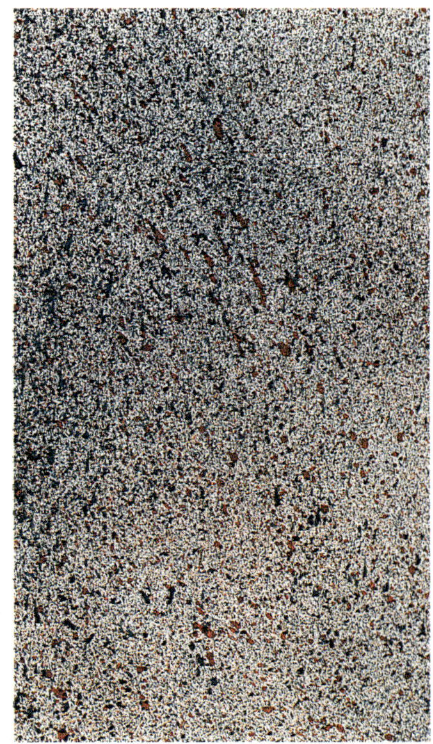

Splattering *The example on the far right illustrates the effect of splattering ink on to paper. It is similar to that achieved with spraying, but it is a slower method.*

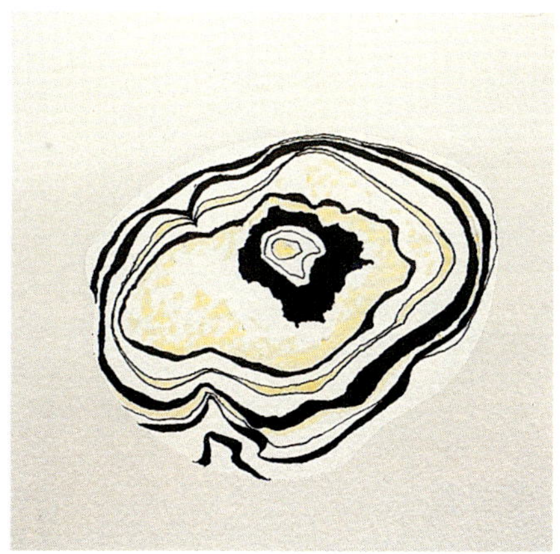

Pebble *The patterned pebble design shown here combines several of the methods you have met in this section, involving resists, pen drawing and splattering.*

I cut out a pebble shape from masking film. I then discarded the shape and stuck the background that was left to a piece of paper. I drew in the black lines with pen and Indian ink, and areas I wanted to remain white, with masking fluid.

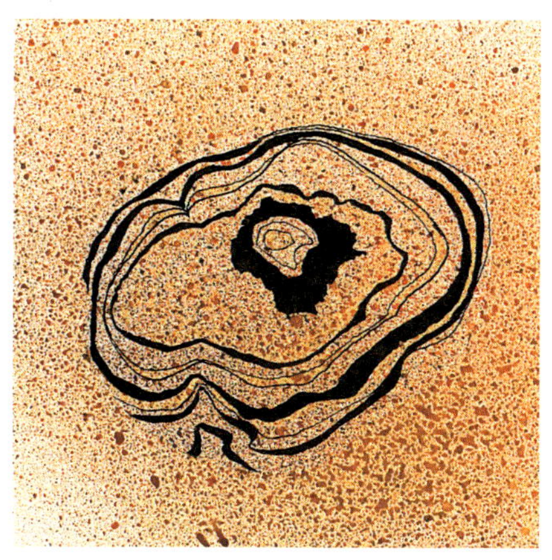

When the ink and masking fluid were dry (and making sure the film was firmly attached, particularly along the edges), I splattered yellow ink over it. After this had dried, more ink was splattered on, this time Burnt Sienna. Finally, brown ink was added in places, to give movement to the surface. I wanted to avoid a static, all-over look, which would have been monotonous.

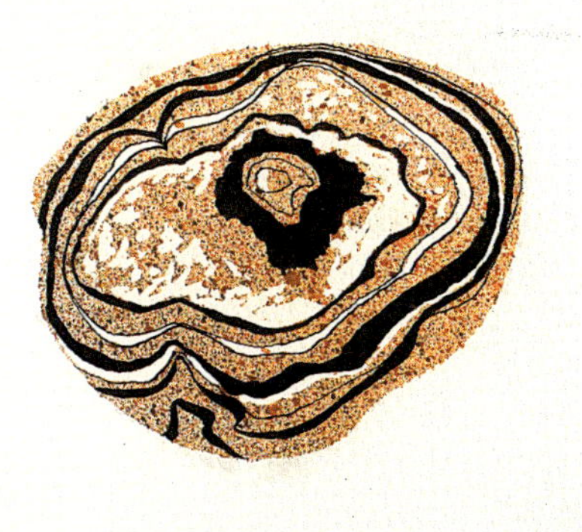

When everything was dry I removed the background masking film, leaving the positive pebble shape. The masking fluid was rubbed off with a finger. Usually this comes off easily, but at times it may need more persuasion. If so, try scratching very gently with your finger nail.

It is important with this type of work that each stage is allowed to dry before moving on to the next.

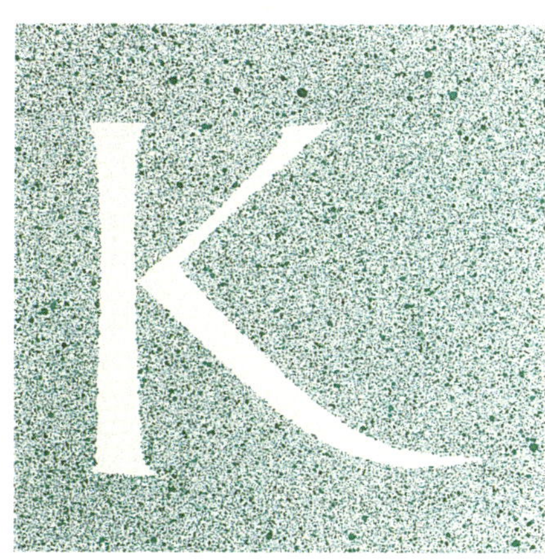

Capital Letter *The alphabet makes a good source of varied shapes for design work.*

The letter shown here is uncomplicated, but as the method is more tricky I wanted to keep the shape simple.

The letter was cut out of masking film with a craft knife and stuck down on the paper. Then I sprayed it with green ink and left it to dry.

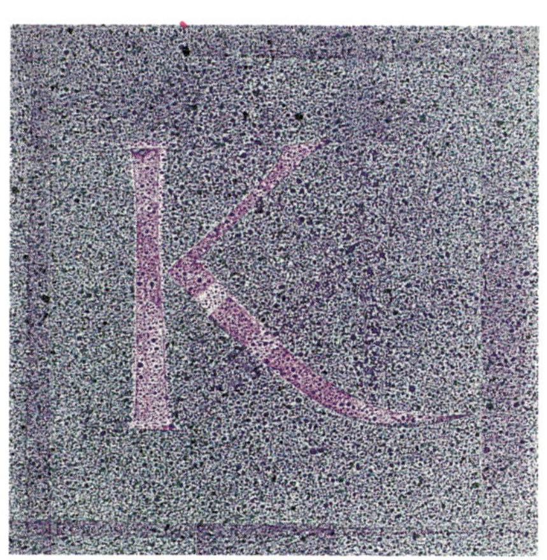

Having kept the background shape from the first letter, I used this as a template to draw the second (purple) letter on masking film, but this time in reverse.

For this second stage, the negative background shape is used, the letter discarded. After fixing it in position, I sprayed it with violet ink and again left it to dry.

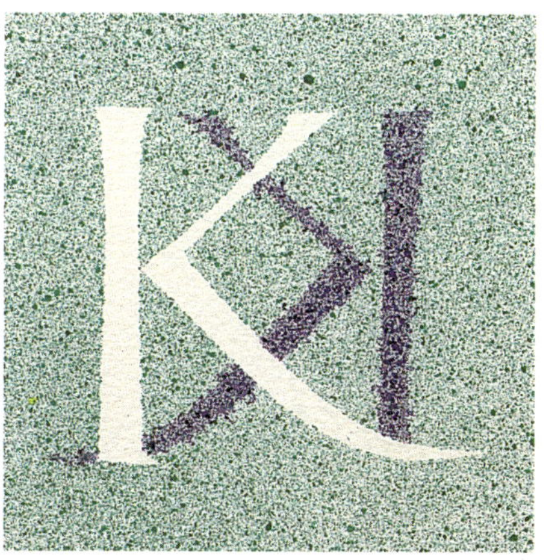

I removed the masking film only when the ink was absolutely dry. If the film is removed too soon it can cause smudging.

Spending a lot of time waiting for things to dry can be irksome and it might be an idea to have several projects on the go at once.

Variations

Machines *A design which nearly became a disaster!*

Shapes cut from masking film were fixed to a background, previously sprayed with yellow and orange inks. After further spraying and removing the masking film, the ink was found to have seeped under the edges.

There is always a slight risk of this happening with masking film, particularly when using it on textured paper. In this case, the initial spraying had caused minute bumps of ink to form, preventing a close enough contact between the film and the background paper, and this allowed the ink to creep underneath.

The remedy was simple: I cut out the design and remounted it, thus restoring the crisp outlines. Learn to be resourceful!

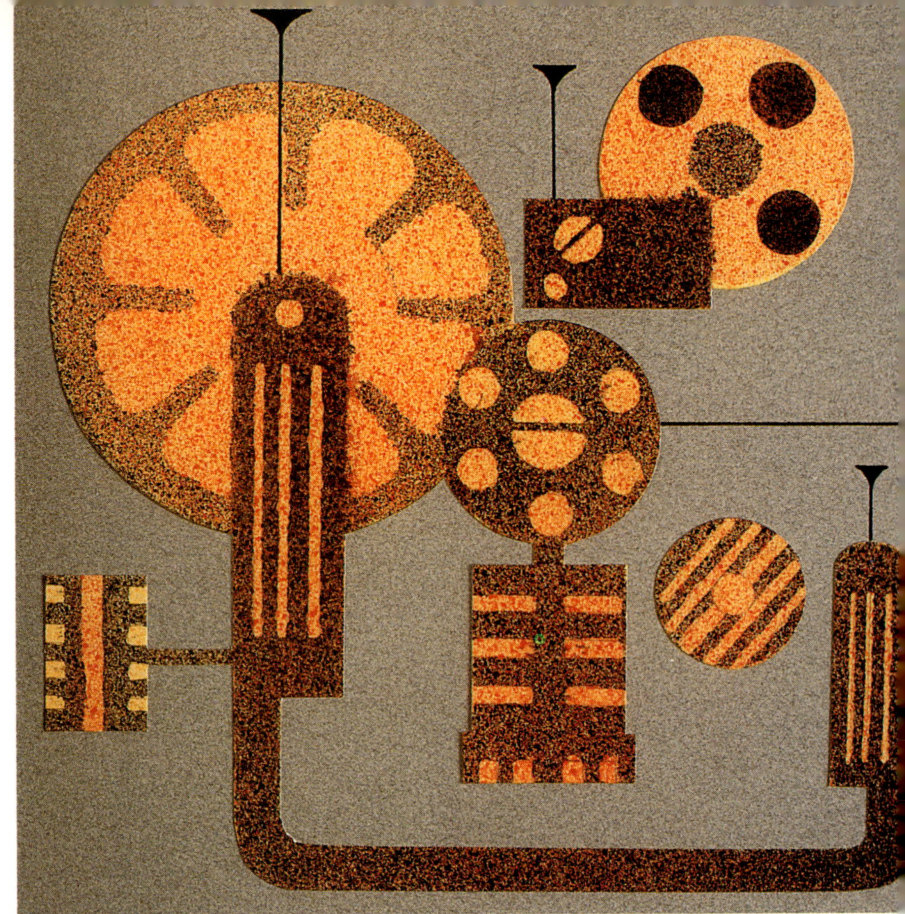

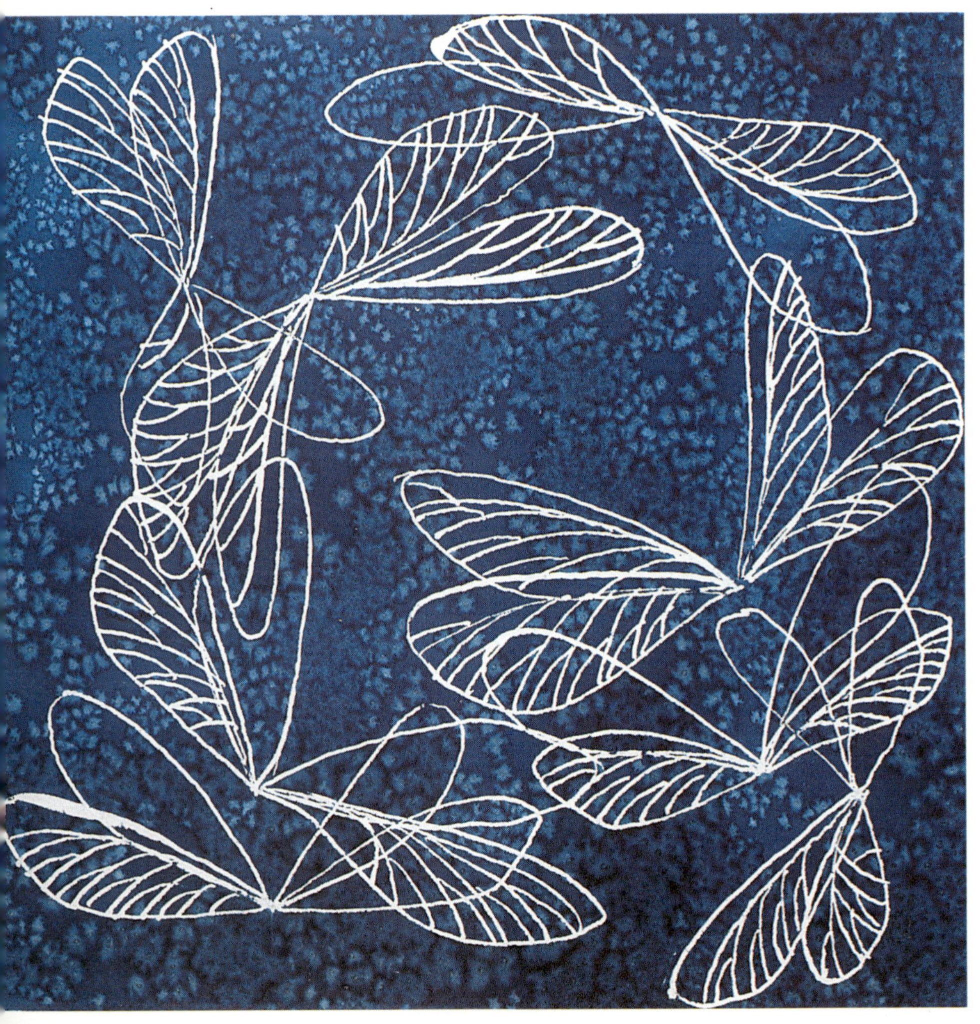

Insects *Flying insects were the inspiration behind this illustration, demonstrating how a motif can evolve from natural sources. Because I wanted to capture the essence of delicate gossamer creatures, I decided to use only their wings, dispensing with the rest of their bodies as being superfluous to the design.*

Since the drawing was to be detailed, the technique had to be simple. The wings were drawn in with pen and masking fluid. Then non-waterproof colour was brushed on and salt grains sprinkled over while it was still wet. When it was thoroughly dry, the salt and masking fluid were removed.

The background texture suggests a shimmering atmosphere, in keeping with the subject.

One of the delights of this kind of work is choosing and adapting forms to suit your own purposes. There are no hard and fast rules about this. Mobility of ideas and imagination is what matters.

Stencils

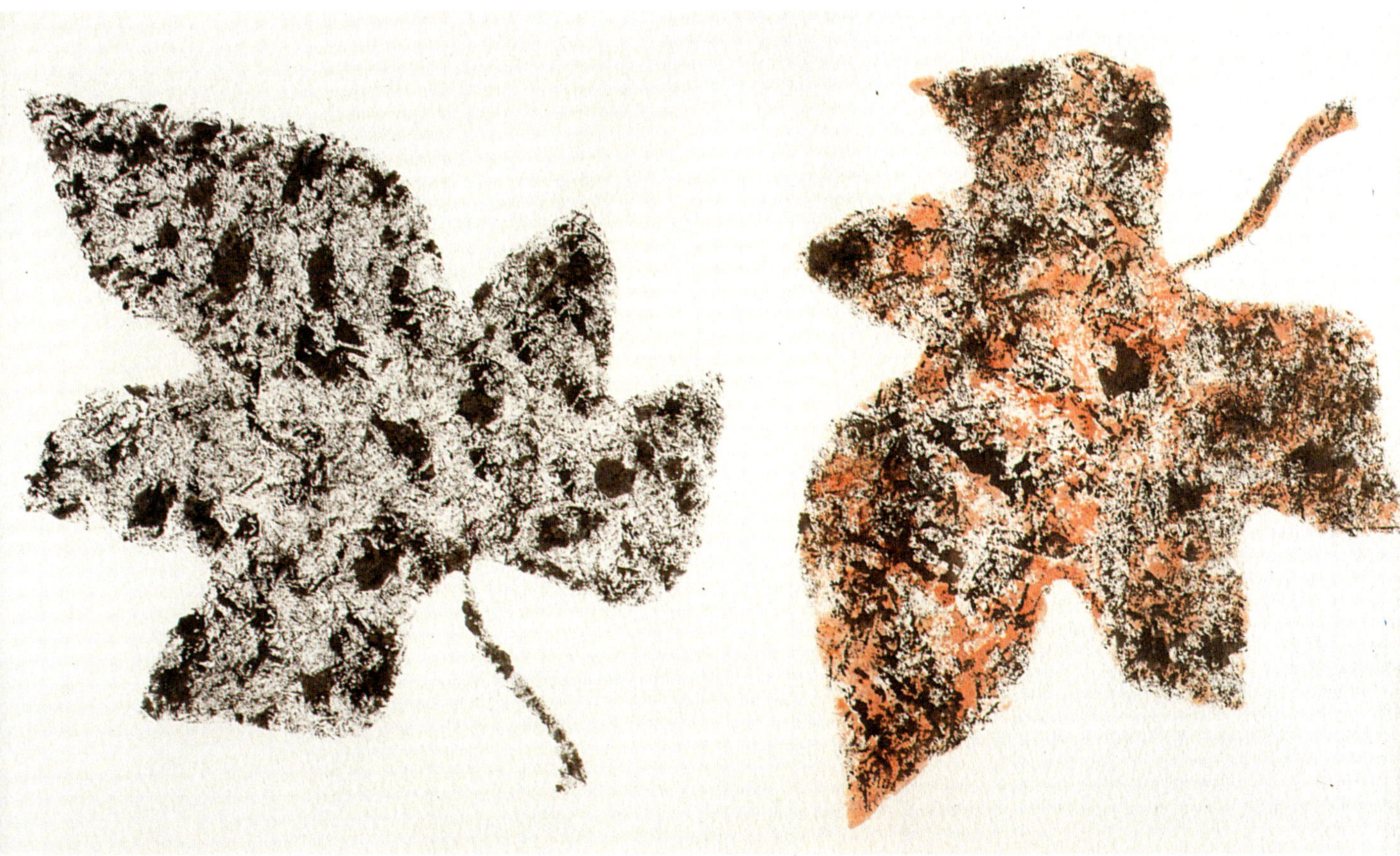

Leaves *Using one of the simplest and easiest techniques of all, these two leaves were made by cutting a stencil and dabbing on the ink with a crumpled paper tissue. The ink makes contact only through the cut-away portions of the stencil.*

When crumpling the tissue, screw it up several times to get plenty of creases, as it is these that give the interesting marks in the texture. A plate makes a good receptacle for the ink, as it gives plenty of room for dipping the tissue, and mixing the colours.

In the illustration, black Indian ink was used for the first leaf; for the second, black with Burnt Sienna. The mottled effect is reminiscent of the splodges found on leaves when they have fallen from the trees in autumn. This is a naturalistic interpretation, but you can be as fanciful as you wish, with colours unrelated to the shape's source.

For those of you who need to make posters, or like to do your own greetings cards, this is a quick and attractive method of producing them. Once the stencil has been cut, you can turn them out like a production line but, being handmade, each will be slightly different.

Cutting a Stencil

To make a stencil, use thick paper or card, cutting out the shapes with a craft knife or scissors. I always use a knife as I find it cuts more precisely, but it takes practice to handle it efficiently. If you have not used a craft knife in this way before, start with very simple shapes moving on to complicated ones only when you have proper control over the cutting.

Always cut either away from, or parallel to, your hand; never towards it, in case the knife slips and you cut yourself. Craft knives must be very sharp in order to do their job properly!

Doorway – Step-by-Step

MATERIALS
Doorway

- Drawing paper
- Black Indian ink
- Coloured inks
- Watercolour paints
- Pen and nibs
- Brushes
- Spray diffuser
- Toothbrush
- Stick
- Masking film
- Masking fluid
- Wax

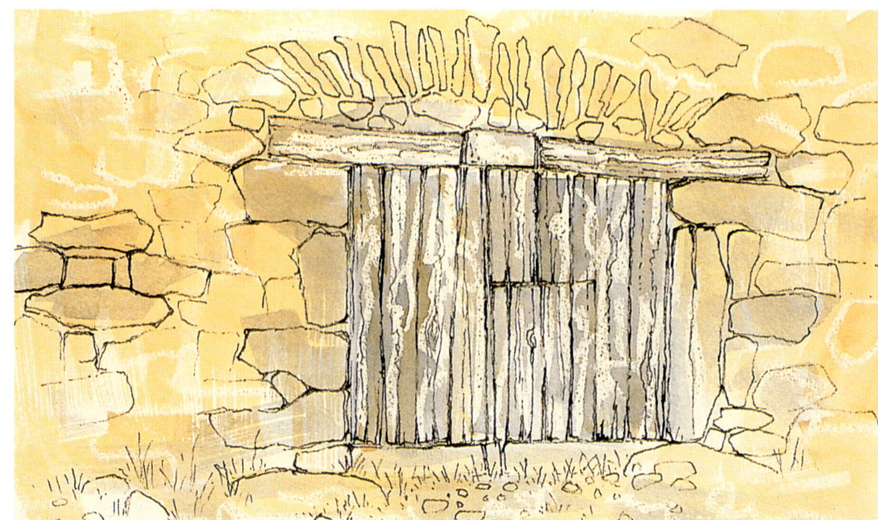

This sequence demonstrates a more pictorial approach to experimental work. I drew the outlines with a stick and rubbed wax on the door and some stones, washing over the whole area with Raw Sienna. Touches of Indigo were also added.

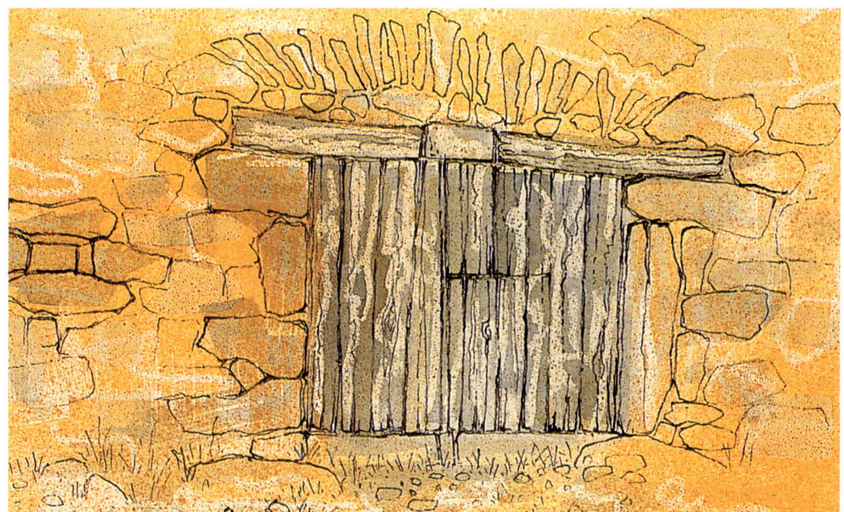

I traced the doorway on to masking film, cut it out and stuck it on. Film was also added to some stones, and wax to the walls. The picture was sprayed with yellow ink and left to dry.

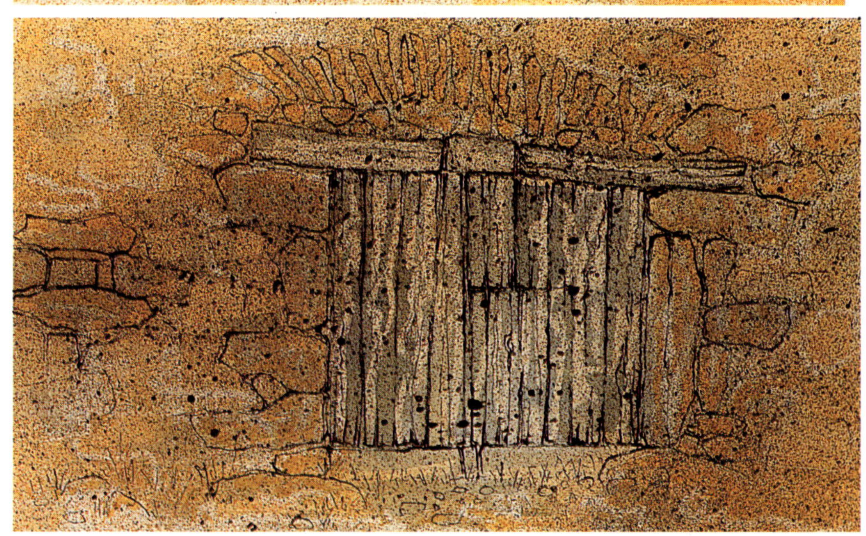

Now the rest of the textures have been included. Masking fluid has been drawn in on the stones around the door, window and the foreground grasses, using both pen and a fine brush.

Brown ink has been splattered on with a toothbrush. The effect I am after is one of rough and weathered surfaces.

To some extent I am working blind as I have to imagine how the picture will look without the film.

It is time to remove the resists and see what else needs to be done. The masking film is peeled away, revealing the lighter stones and the door. This gives greater tonal contrast. During the last stage, the tones had become too uniform. Next, the masking fluid is rubbed away.

When all the resists have been taken off the final pen drawing must be put in, and any other adjustments made. In this case I decided to add only a few details of drawing around the stones and on the wooden door planks, for which I used black, brown and yellow inks.

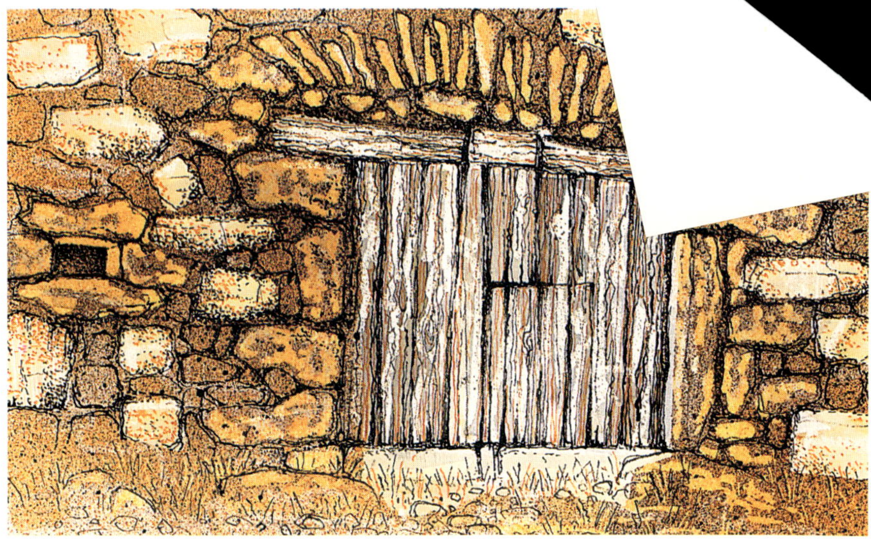

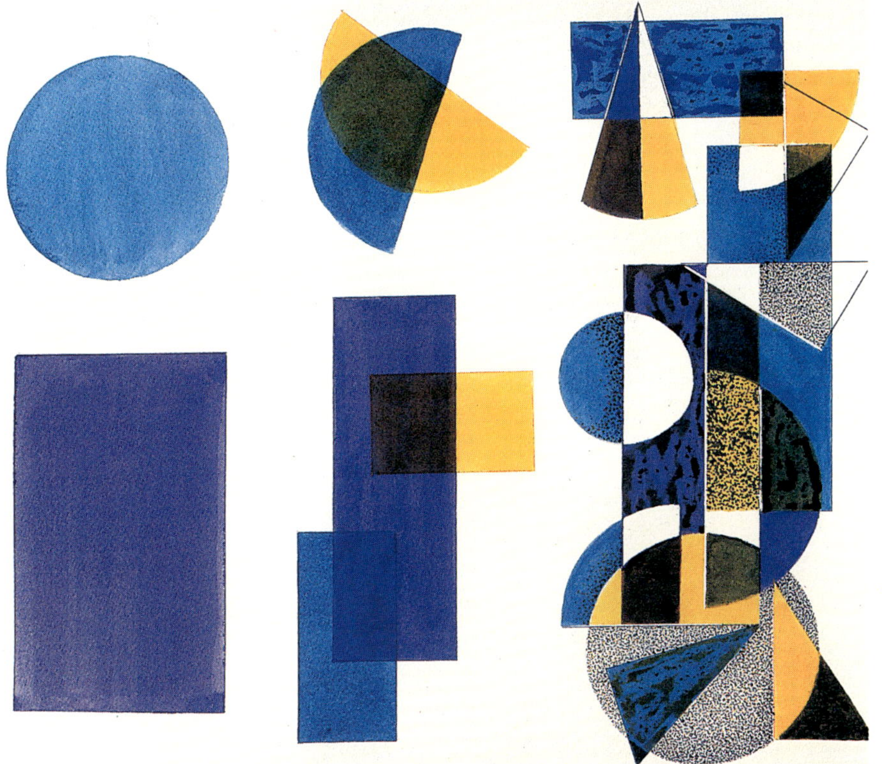

Summary

The intention behind this section has been to provide the opportunity for working in a more innovative way than perhaps you would do normally, to give you the chance of using a wider range of materials than is usually associated with pen and ink; to explore colour, shape and texture; to take a few risks and test the possibilities of fresh themes.

Some of the techniques are 'tricky' but they are fun to do and produce quick, attractive results, which can make a refreshing break from longer-term efforts. I would stress that they should not be thought of as a substitute for traditional drawing, but as a complement. The outcome of these experiments should invigorate your approach generally and set you off on new tracks.

Allow yourself plenty of time for experimental work. Projects sometimes need to be readjusted and tried again before reaching a successful outcome. It can be annoying if exciting ideas have to be curtailed before being properly worked through.

Back-Up Exercise – Geometric Shapes

Cutting and overlapping basic shapes can produce complex arrangements, as illustrated in the abstract above.

Try this exercise with your own choice of shapes and colours, moving and rearranging them until you make a design you like. They can be further embellished with texture and colour.

TEXTURES

MATERIALS & EQUIPMENT

- Paper
- Pen holder
- Nibs
- Brushes
- Inks
- Watercolour paints
- Water
- Palette
- Drawing board
- Paper tissue

By now, you will have become familiar with the main pen and ink techniques. You will have worked in black and white and also in colour, and you will have done some experimental work. Your prowess will be developing with pen and brush and you are ready to use these accomplishments to further advantage.

The use of textures will enliven the appearance of your drawings and also offer a challenge to your greater ability.

Textures fall into two main groups: surface pattern, and surface feel. The first group is concerned with visual appearance: the variegation on a leaf, the spots on a leopard's fur, the markings on feathers. These are all patterns that are *seen*, but in the second group we are concerned with the way things *feel*, their tactile sense: hard, soft; rough, smooth; shiny, dull. These are the textures that are so fascinating to the artist, and so demanding of technical skills.

Develop an awareness and sensitivity to the surface you are portraying, first by looking and also, if possible, by feeling. Get to know the form not only through your eyes but through your fingertips as well. Then choose the technique that will suit the image, deciding what type of nib and pen strokes are needed and whether a wash of tone or colour is required.

Sometimes less conventional methods can help, using wax to give a woody effect; dabbing with a tissue to soften the edges of clouds; or you may prefer a mixture of approaches, incorporating the unorthodox with the more traditional. Exploit all the variety of techniques you know, to give added interest to your drawing.

A word of warning. It is easy to be beguiled by mere skill. It can become over-important, to the general detriment of your work, which may then become nothing more than a clever collection of technical tricks.

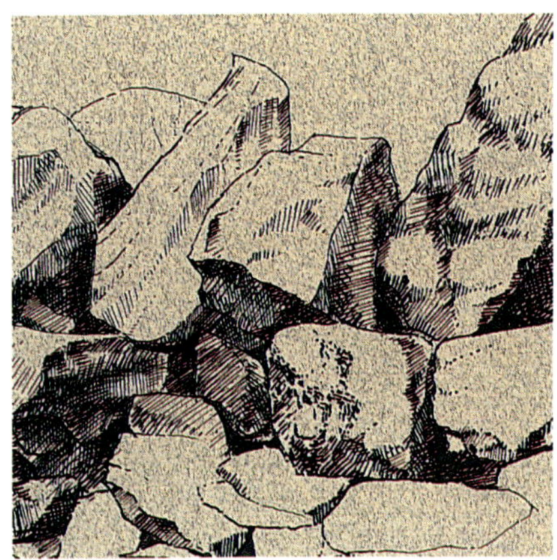

Stone Wall *A detailed study to explore the varied shapes found in a Cumbrian wall. Note the different pen strokes: linear, hatched, cross-hatched and broken strokes, noting also the tonal range.*

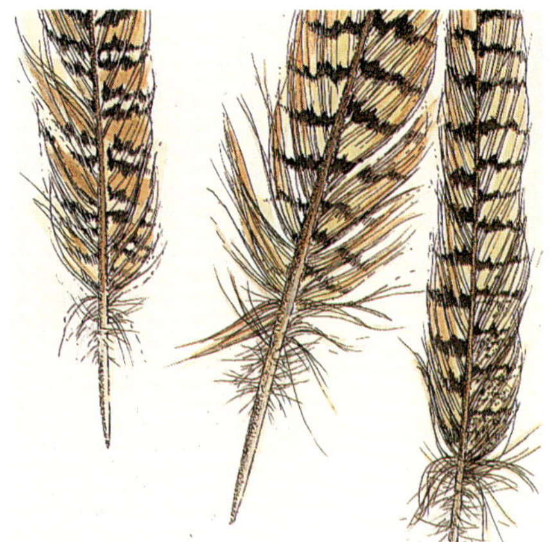

Feathers *A drawing to show the pattern on the feathers as well as their physical characteristics. A fine nib and brush are needed to give the desired effect of lightness and delicacy.*

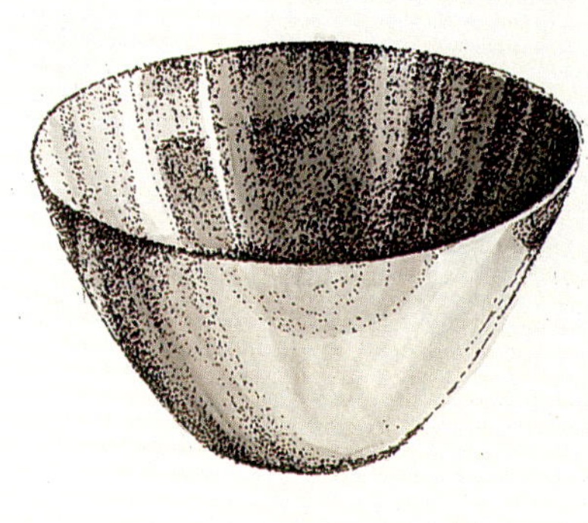

Metal Bowl *The objective here was to suggest a metallic and reflective surface. Wash was used first and then pen. Observe the counterplay of light and dark tones, and how they follow the curve of the bowl.*

Young Cats Asleep *Animals make special demands on the artist's skill. In addition to representing the texture and patterning of the coat, you need to be aware that under the fur lies a skeletal structure.*

One problem is deciding how much to include without drawing every hair. It is important to show enough information about the way the fur grows and how it follows the body contours, but not necessary to work over all areas equally. Notice how the curled position pushes up the shoulder hairs.

Non-waterproof ink was used with a medium nib, and a damp brush softened some strokes.

Drawing into the background helps to define shape and anchor the subject. See how the dark tone blends into the fur. Too distinct an edge would flatten the form.

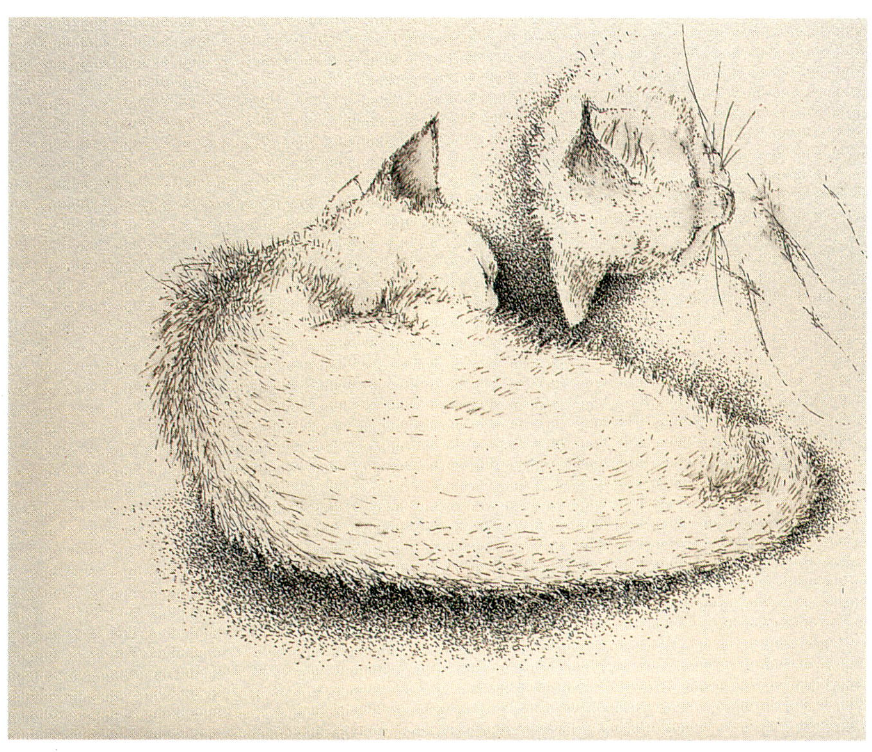

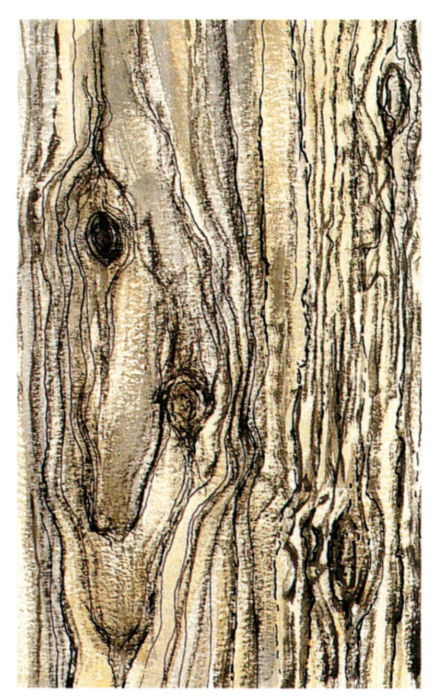

Wood *A combination of dry brush – a brush wiped almost dry on a tissue – and a light top drawing in pen was used for this effect.*

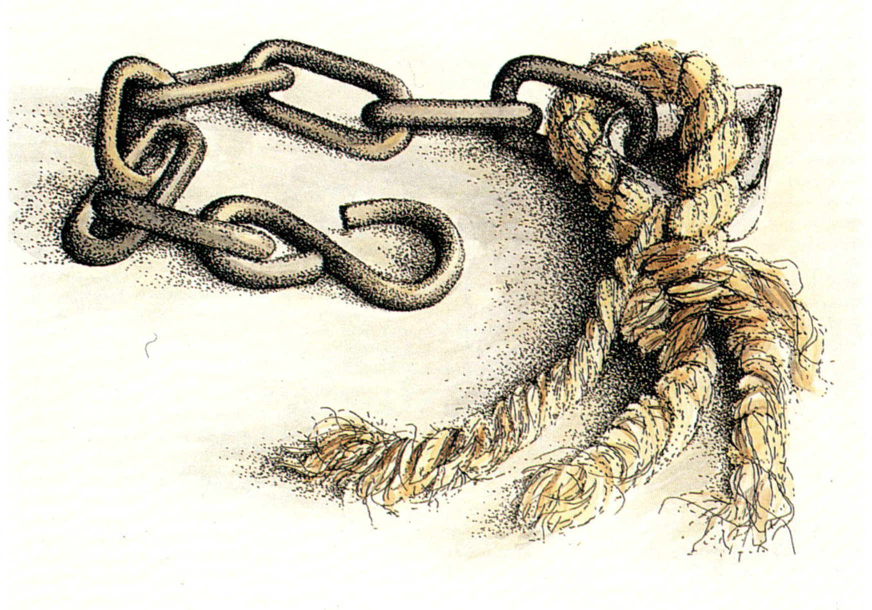

Rope and Chain *In this illustration, pen, brush, wash, and colour were all used to show a hard, inflexible material, the chain, against the softer, flexible frayed rope. The technique used on the chain is regular and dotted with a hard, smooth outline; the technique used on the rope is fluid and wispy, with a less defined outline. Two nibs were used: fine and medium.*

Bridge – Step-by-Step

MATERIALS
Bridge

- Stretched paper or Drawing block
- Pen and nibs
- Brushes
- Liquid Indian ink
- Watercolour paints
- Water
- Mixing palette

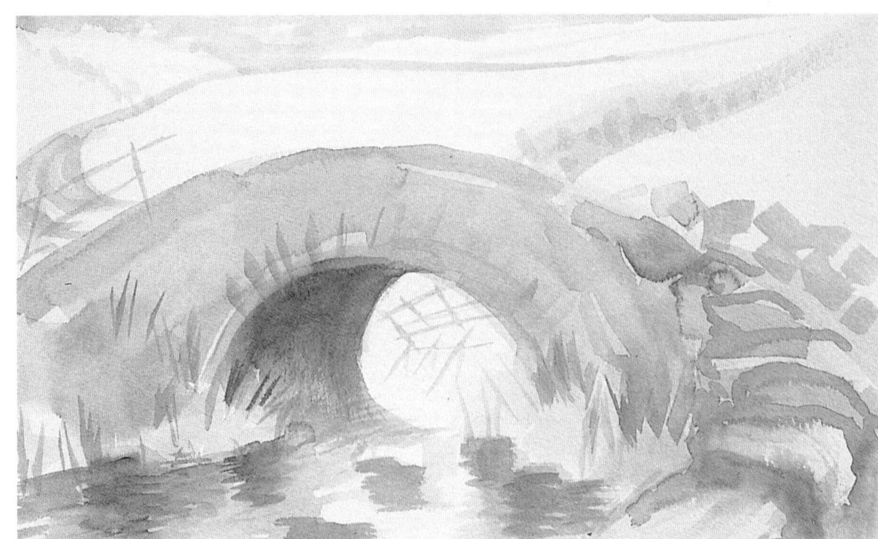

Mixing up a light wash of non-waterproof black ink, I blocked in the main shapes, using a flat 13mm (½in) brush. A darker wash was used for the tones under the bridge and in the water. A side-to-side movement of the brush produced the broken reflections.

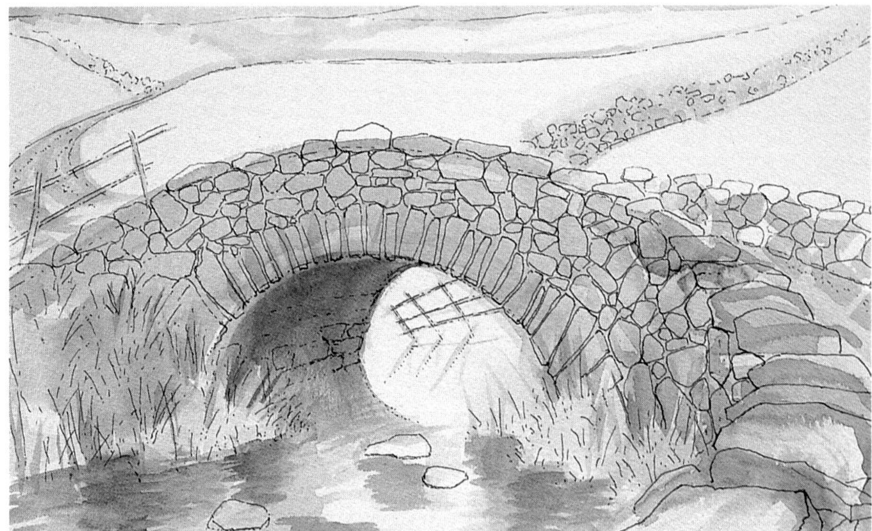

Working on the dried wash with pen, I drew in the chief features, aware of different textures and allowing for this in the chosen strokes. Continuous lines were used for the stones, and broken lines for the grasses. The background is lightly indicated.

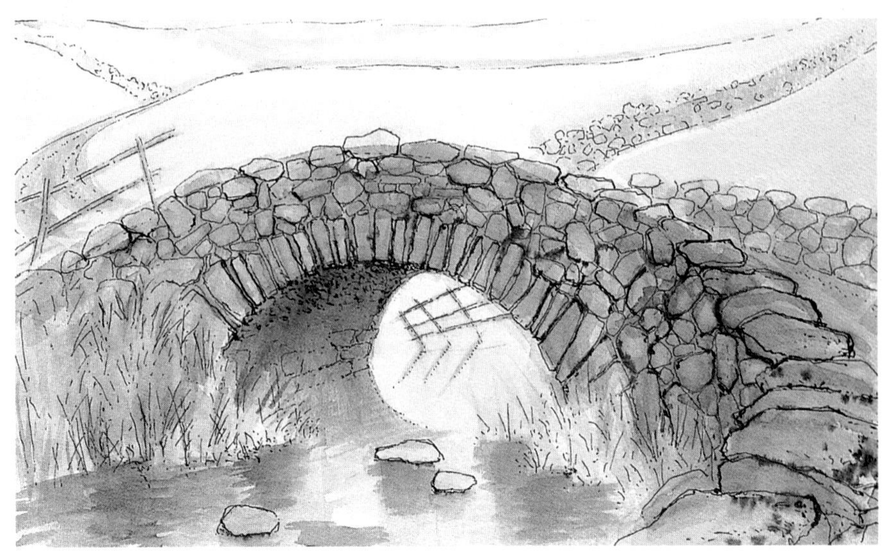

More non-waterproof ink wash has been added, blending with the underlying lines to give a smudgy effect.

To suggest the atmosphere of water, damp stones and springy grass, pale washes of Raw Sienna and Indigo are added. These are brushed on quickly to avoid picking up too much of the underlying ink wash and becoming too grey. It is crucial to get the right balance between ink and watercolour washes. The colour should not be too intrusive.

The final drawing builds up the detail of the different surfaces, with a variety of pen strokes to bring out the textures, some added to wet wash, others to dry wash. The bridge shows a combination of stipples and lines, to suggest weathering and the growth of lichen and moss. This is most marked on the larger stones in the foreground, where the pen marks have spread on the wet wash. The grasses, too, show different lines: long and fine; short and stubby.

The shadows and reflections in the water are made by a series of wiggly lines, tapering towards the end, with some more heavily drawn than others for tonal contrast.

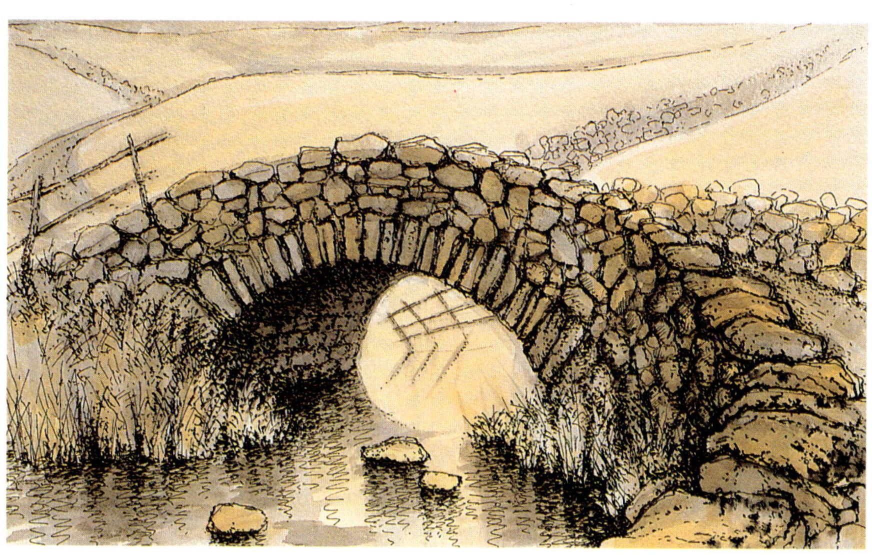

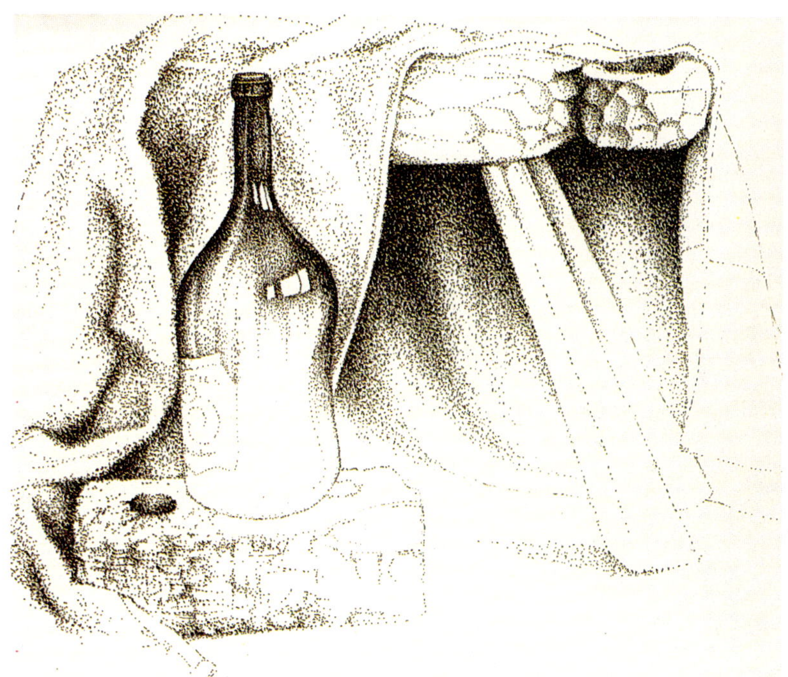

Bottle with Fabric *Pen work alone produced the textures in this drawing.*

Compare the bottle with the fabric. The technique on the bottle shows small, regular marks, with clearly defined tonal changes. On the fabric, the marks are longer, looser and less regular.

The picture has been left incomplete to show the progress from the first lines to the final phase.

Symmetry

You will probably have noticed that the bottle in my drawing is not symmetrical, that it has a decided bulge on one side. This is not a result of carelessness on my part! The bottle really was wonky, which made it much more fun to draw. This raises an interesting point: how many things that appear symmetrical really *are* symmetrical?

Take the human face for example, and the positioning of the eyes or the ears. One is usually slightly higher or lower than the other. This should teach us to look more carefully at things, and not assume the symmetry that we think we see. It will encourage us to draw the particular and not the general, and cultivate sensitivity in our work.

Next time you draw a bottle, take another look. Is it really the same on both sides?

TONAL EFFECTS

MATERIALS & EQUIPMENT

- Paper
- Pen holder
- Nibs
- Brushes
- Inks
- Watercolour paints
- Water
- Palette
- Drawing board
- Paper tissue

Earlier in the book, you were shown tonal techniques to help make your drawings look solid and three-dimensional. In this chapter, I want to show how tone can be used to heighten atmosphere and drama in a picture, and sometimes add a touch of mystery.

Dramatic lighting effects have captured the artist's imagination from the time of the Renaissance onwards, producing powerful and compelling images. Visit any major art gallery and you will find pictures that are evidence of this. Caravaggio, Rembrandt, Goya and Turner are all names that come to mind in this context. Van Gogh's ink studies of peasants and Henry Moore's shelter drawings make strong use of tone to convey their emotional impact.

Now that you have become acquainted with and practised the techniques covered in this book, you will want to exploit these achievements and open up new areas of expression. One way is to consider the mood you wish to establish in a picture and the tonal range that will help to attain it. Is your picture to be one of contrasts between sun and shadow, or an interior with a single source of light? Perhaps your choice is for a night scene, or one lit by candle-light? For their effect, all these subjects will rely upon the atmosphere you are able to conjure up through your use of tone.

Whatever you decide upon, the actual selection of techniques will depend upon a number of factors: whether the full scope of colour would be more appropriate than the austerity of black and white; whether pen alone would produce the desired effect or be better used in conjunction with brush. Sometimes a choice is made simply because of the challenge it offers, and at other times the technique spontaneously suggests itself as part of the overall inspiration.

The illustrations on the opposite page show how different treatments of the same subject can change the character of a drawing. This is owed not only to the change of lighting on the group but also to the variety of techniques used: pen and wash, pen and watercolour, and pen with Sepia and black ink on a tinted paper.

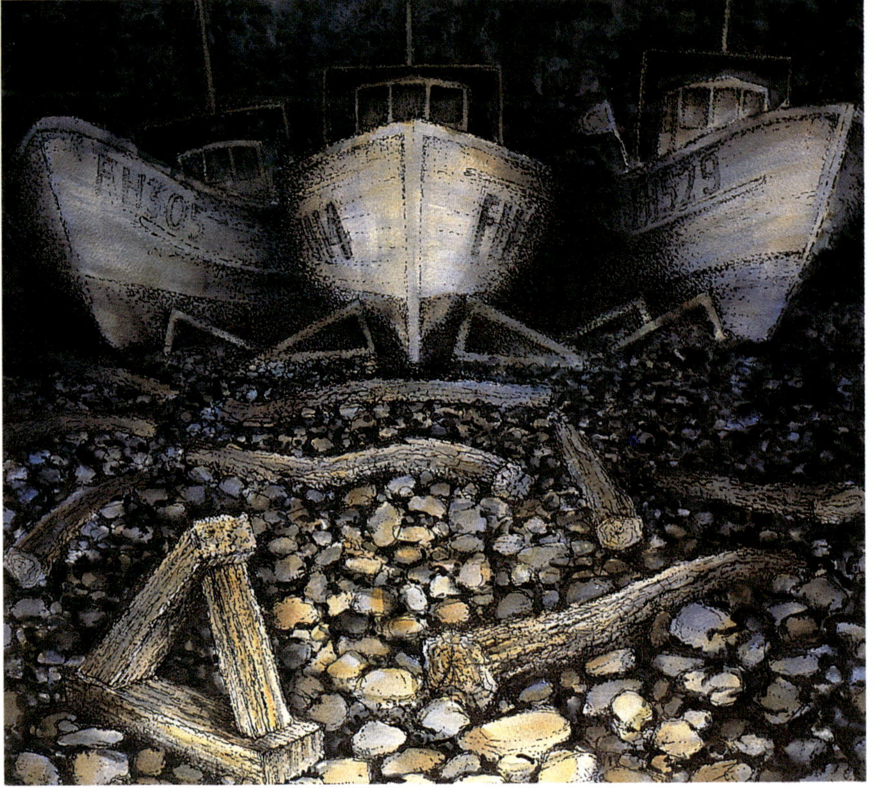

Night Boats *The effects of light at night have fascinating possibilities. These fishing boats were lit by the light coming from a doorway throwing its beam across the pebbles and on to the ghostly hulls. It was a romantic subject with an aura of mystery. I chose to do it in pen and watercolour, building up successive layers of drawing and colour until it had the atmosphere I wanted.*

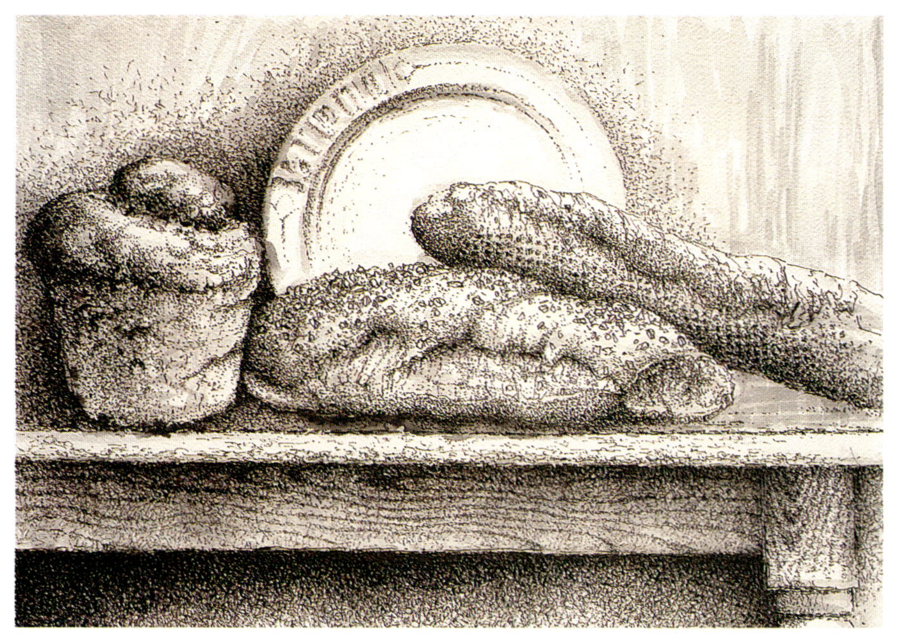

Loaves of Bread (Daylight)
A pen and wash drawing, using non-waterproof ink, showing some loaves of bread seen in daylight.

A pale wash is used first to block in the main shapes, and then a darker wash introduces tone. Next the drawing is added, using both thick and medium nibs. The whole picture is worked over to suggest diffused light, which has some tonal variety but not the strong contrasts evident in the following two pictures. A vigorous pen stroke is used to build up mass quickly and to bring out the rough textures of the loaves.

Notice the low viewpoint, bringing everything to the front of the picture.

Loaves of Bread (Artificial Light) *In this second version of the group, the loaves of bread are seen under artificial light and from a more usual viewpoint.*

Here watercolour is used with pen and ink. The colours bring out the warmth that is characteristic of normal artificial light. Raw and Burnt Sienna were used predominantly, with Raw Umber and Indigo to add balance.

This lighting produces strong shadows and greater contrasts than in the previous picture. The pen work echoes this, with considerable build-up in the dark passages. A thick nib is used first, to keep the work bold and open, and then a finer one is worked on top to give added density.

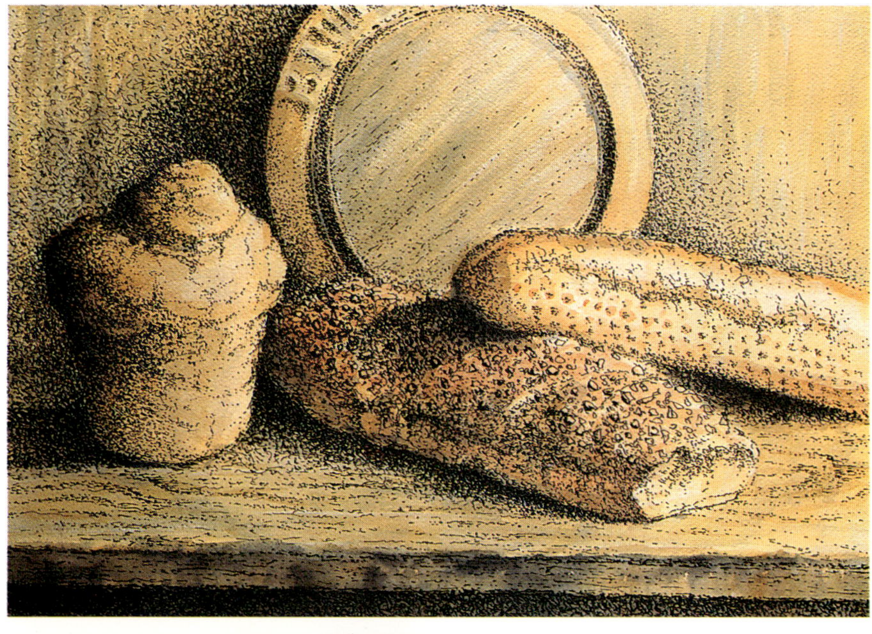

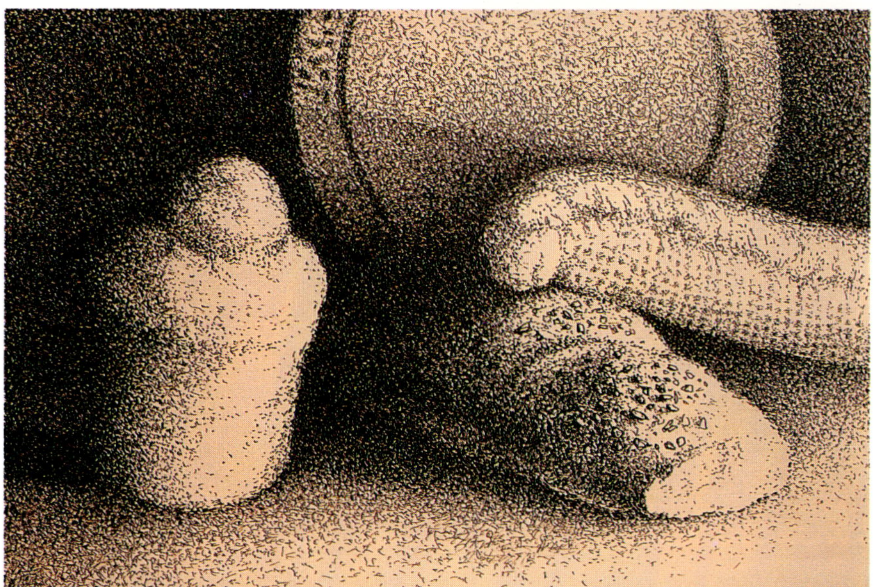

Loaves of Bread (Candlelight)
This drawing shows the group by candlelight.

The shapes are seen as areas of intense light or dark. Forms dissolve into shadow and merge with the background, the lighted parts contrasting sharply against it.

Sepia and black Indian inks were used on buff paper. The sparkle of tiny specks of paper showing through the pen strokes gives luminosity to the shadows.

Candlelight – Step-by-Step

MATERIALS
A Group by Candlelight

- Stretched paper or Drawing block
- Pen and nibs
- Brush
- Watercolours
- Black Indian ink
- Sepia ink
- Water

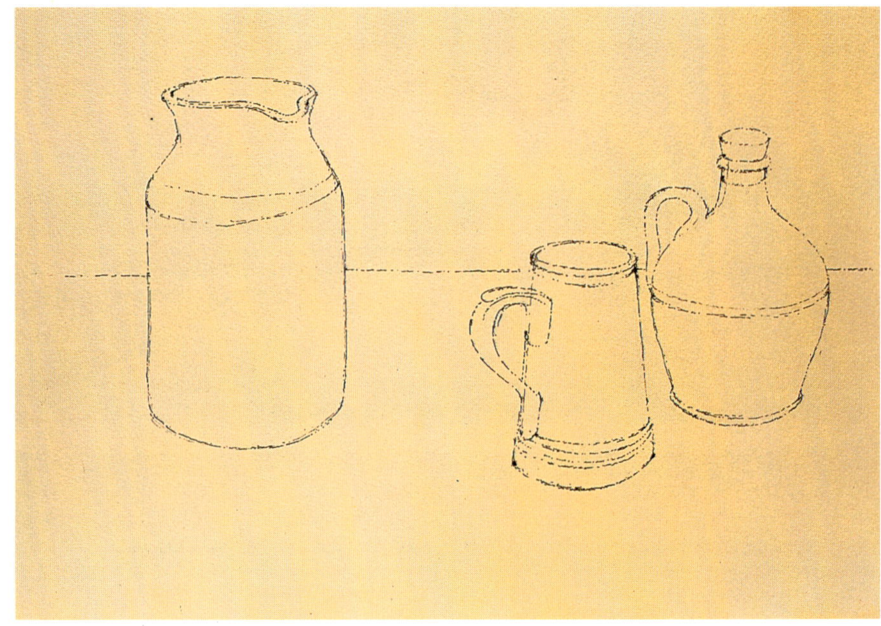

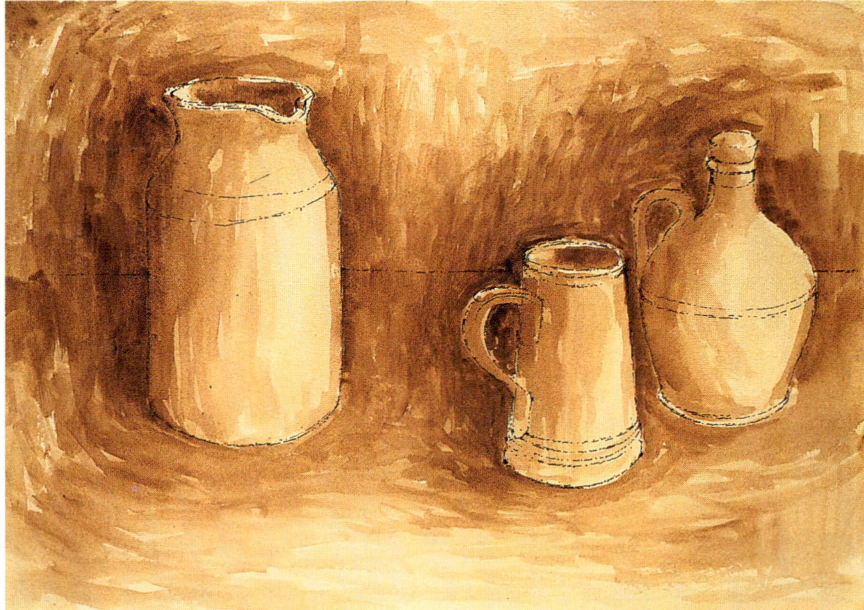

In the warm and mellow light of a candle, local colours become subdued and appear almost monochromatic.

I started by brushing a pale wash of Raw Sienna watercolour over the whole area of paper, using a flat 2cm (¾in) brush. Then I drew in the outlines of the group with pen and black Indian ink.

As the tonal range is dominant in this picture it needed to be established early on.

Changing to a round No. 12 brush, I mixed up a wash of Burnt Umber watercolour and put in the dark areas of the background, linking the vessels together and fixing their spatial relationship.

The direction of the picture now is to thrust the light areas forward and the shadowy areas back. Later, some outlines will be swallowed up by the darker tones.

I added an orange wash to the vessels and then concentrated on the pen drawing. To bring out the warmth in this dark picture, I started the drawing in Sepia, piling up a density of stippled and scribbled strokes.

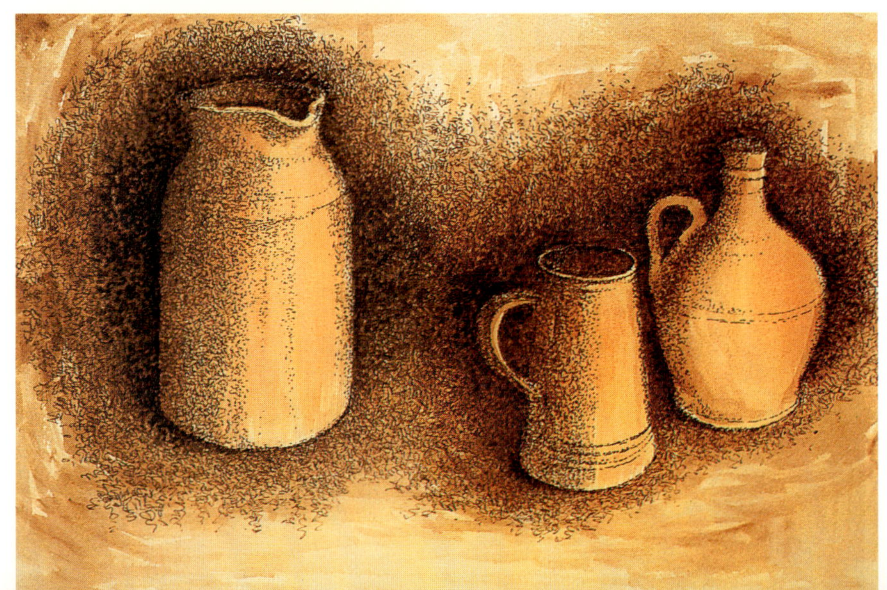

Tonal Effects

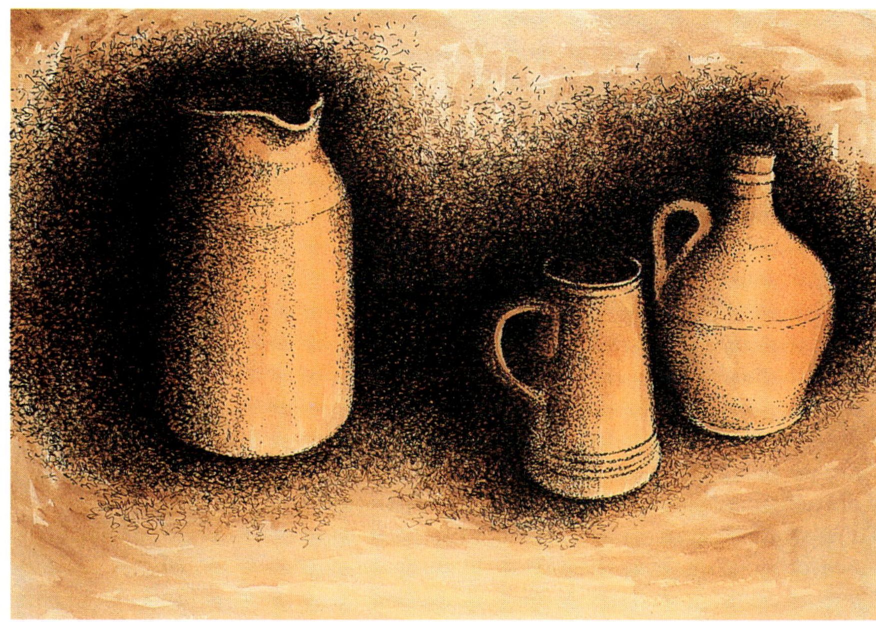

Having built up a profusion of brown strokes, I finished by working on top of them with black Indian ink, using the same technique of scribbles and stipples. These, I find, allow little chinks of colour and wash to show through, which gives a sense of movement, preventing the dark mass becoming too solid looking. I want to imply depth even where it cannot be seen.

Now you can see how some of the forms have been absorbed by the surrounding darkness, heightening the dramatic effect of the subject.

The mixture of black and Sepia made the depth of colour and tone that was needed – dark yet vibrant, appropriate for the atmosphere of candlelight.

A room of a house in Burgundy that has been lovingly restored by its owners without losing its original country character. It was a cool place of refuge from the fierce heat of the sun outside.

I have tried to convey these aspects in my drawing, and to communicate a sense of a place that is lived in and welcoming: the homely touches of the things on the shelves; the bottle lamp on the rickety small table; the back of the sturdy wooden chair.

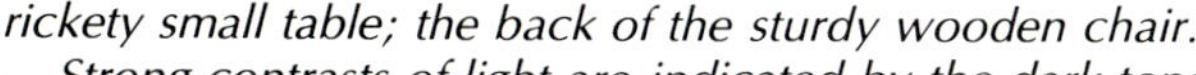

Strong contrasts of light are indicated by the dark tones on the stone walls against the light areas of door and window.

The drawing on the right of the picture has been left incomplete, so that you may see how it developed.

Back-Up Exercise – Interiors

Interiors can be fascinating subjects offering atmosphere and a diversity of tonal contrasts. A room by day looks quite different at night under artificial light. Even daylight has its own infinite variations according to the season, the weather and the hour, which produce corresponding interior variations.

At night, the intense pools of light will contrast with deep shadows absorbing the forms; areas of mystery under chairs and tables, behind doors and in unlit corners.

As a back-up exercise, make several drawings of a room under different lighting, in both colour and black and white. They need not be finished – they could be just sketches – but concentrate on capturing the mood and lighting of the room.

An interior is like a portrait; its character reflects a sense of the people who live there.

Viewpoints

How often do you really consider the viewpoint of a picture? Having spent time organizing the subject, you probably sit down and get on with the drawing. But stop for a moment! How will your arrangement look from the other side, or from an oblique position? Sit on a low stool and see how that alters the perspective; or sit on a table and put the group on the floor.

These different angles will show you familiar things in a new way; ordinary shapes will seem suddenly strange and unusual, igniting a spark of excitement that your drawing might not have had from a more conventional position.

Drawing is about seeing and expressing images in an individual way; a less obvious viewpoint can help to achieve this.

WORKING OUT OF DOORS

MATERIALS & EQUIPMENT

- Sketchbook
- Sketchblock
- Pen holder
- Nibs
- Brushes
- Art pens
- Ball-point pens
- Watercolour pens
- Inks
- Watercolour paints
- Water
- Sketching stool
- Easel

Sketching *An artist at work out of doors. A sketch in pen and Indian ink on cartridge paper.*

Blots do sometimes occur, especially when working quickly, as can be seen here!

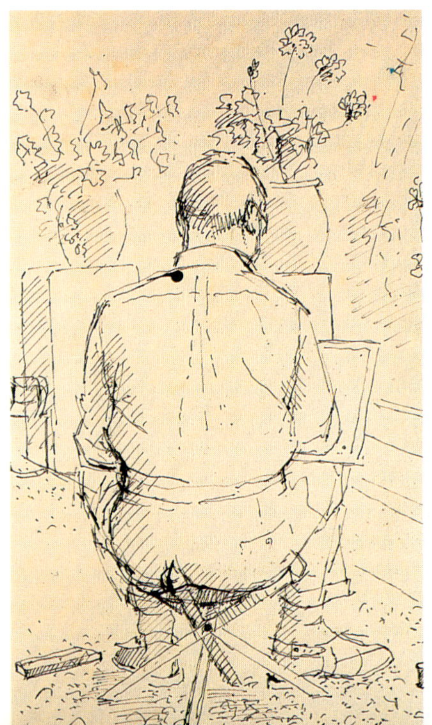

Setting up an intractable easel in a field while the wind plays games with your paper and inquisitive cows gather round, is not everybody's idea of a blissful afternoon's drawing.

Working out of doors can be unpredictable, but at its best it is a most pleasurable experience. On a calm day, with the sun warming your back and a beautiful landscape around you, with insects droning busily in the flowers and scents of pine and wild thyme filling your nostrils, outdoor drawing can be enjoyed to the full.

A small sketchbook and a clutch of ball-point pens may be all that is needed. Thick and thin drawing points will accommodate quick sketches and more detailed studies. This is paring the equipment down to the minimum, but if time is limited it will be adequate.

However, if you intend to make a day of it, you will want a wider choice of materials at your disposal, including some form of colour.

Watercolour paints are convenient, more so than coloured inks, which can easily get spilt and the tops mislaid. Watercolour pens are useful too, but no good if colour washes are required.

All this should fit into a sketching bag or small knapsack with shoulder straps, leaving your hands free to carry a sketchbook or block and a lightweight folding stool.

I have always regarded a sketching easel as unnecessary, preferring to rest my sketchbook on my lap, but you may prefer to work at an easel. There are several available in wood or metal, which fold up for ease of carrying.

Having made yourself ready for a good day's work, all that is wanted is kind weather and a subject. Landscapes, seascapes, buildings, plants, people and animals – the choice can be bewildering.

Let us start with a popular subject: landscape. After selecting your spot, take a long look around while making up your mind which particular part to draw. One difficulty with landscape is that, not having a beginning or end, it is a continuous sequence of features, a vast panorama, unlike a still life with its compact grouping of

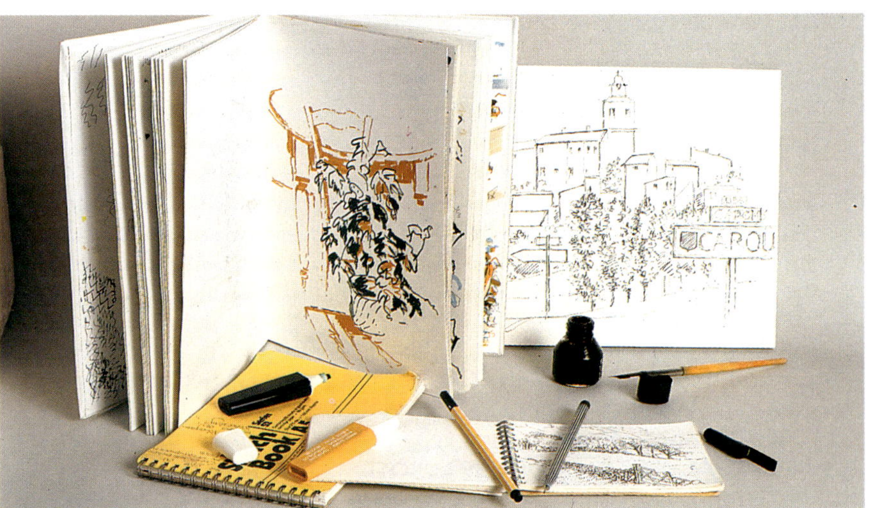

Pens and Paper *A collection of sketchbooks, block and pens suitable for drawing outside with minimum fuss. The foreground sketchbook would fit easily into a pocket or handbag.*

objects. Cupping the hands to form a frame and thus isolating certain areas may help you to make up your mind. If there is a dominant focal point – a house, tree or other feature – then the picture can be built around it. Once your decision is made, block in the main shapes with pen or brush. Keep it light and open at this early stage to allow for possible alterations. Try to finish the drawing at one sitting to retain the freshness and immediacy typical of outdoor work.

One advantage of landscape is that it does not usually move about! Drawing moving objects, like people and animals, raises new problems. How do you tackle something that only keeps still for a few seconds? A pen that travels quickly over the paper is essential; ball-points and fibre-tips are perfect for this. The actual drawing is a combination of seeing and remembering. Each time the subject moves, begin a new drawing. Your paper will soon be covered with lots of incomplete sketches; sometimes the subject will revert to an earlier position and more can be added to that sketch. Concentrate on the line of the pose – there is no time for detail. After a while, you will get your eye in and capture the essentials more rapidly.

This is excellent training for co-ordination of eye and hand. It takes practice but encourages fluent drawing.

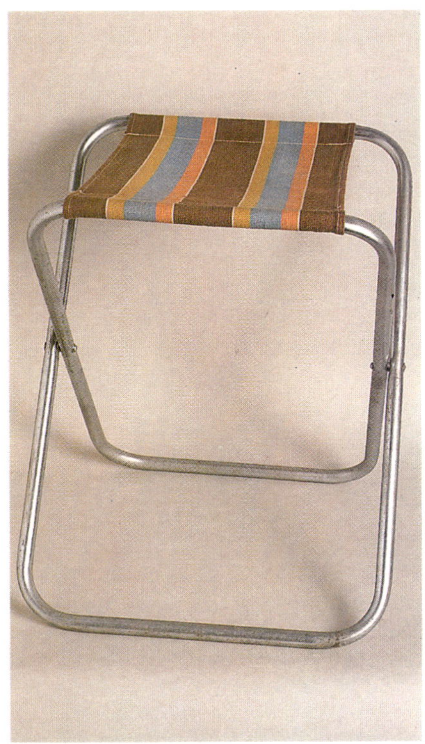

Sketching Stool *A lightweight sketching stool that folds flat for convenience of carrying. Its disadvantage is that, having no back rest, it can become uncomfortable if you are sitting on it for a long time.*

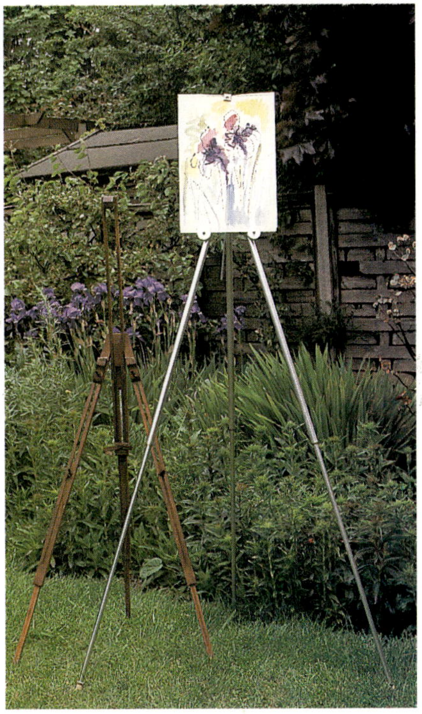

Sketching Easels *Two sketching easels, one made of aluminium and the other of wood. They both fold up compactly, the metal one being the lighter of the two to carry.*

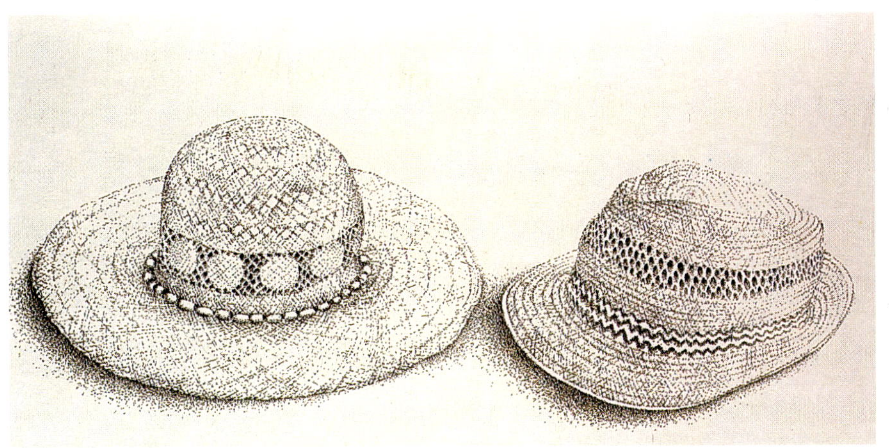

Hats *Hats may be necessary if you intend working in the full sun. They prevent sunstroke and will also provide shade for your eyes. The two shown here, made of straw, are both cool and protective. It is easy to forget just how strong the sun can be, beating down on your head when you are engrossed in a drawing.*

Working Out of Doors

Sketching

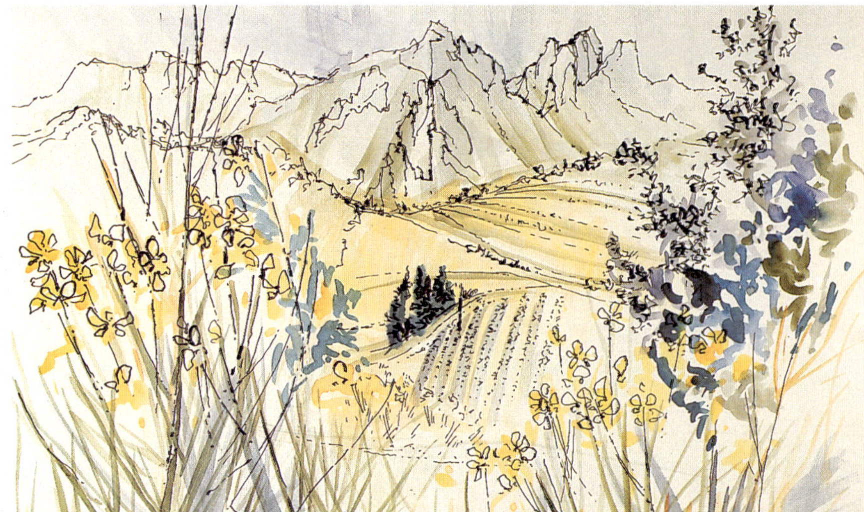

Dentelles and Gorse *In this panoramic view, the foreground gorse bushes make a framework. They hold the composition together, directing the eye towards the middle-distance trees, and the mountain beyond.*

Scale is important too. The size of the flowers, seen against other features, conveys a sense of space.

The technique here is watercolour with pen and Indian ink, a favourite method of mine, allowing for the freedom of brush and colour, applied first, with the control of pen drawing. Different nibs were used: a thick one to add weight to the foreground, and a finer one for the distance.

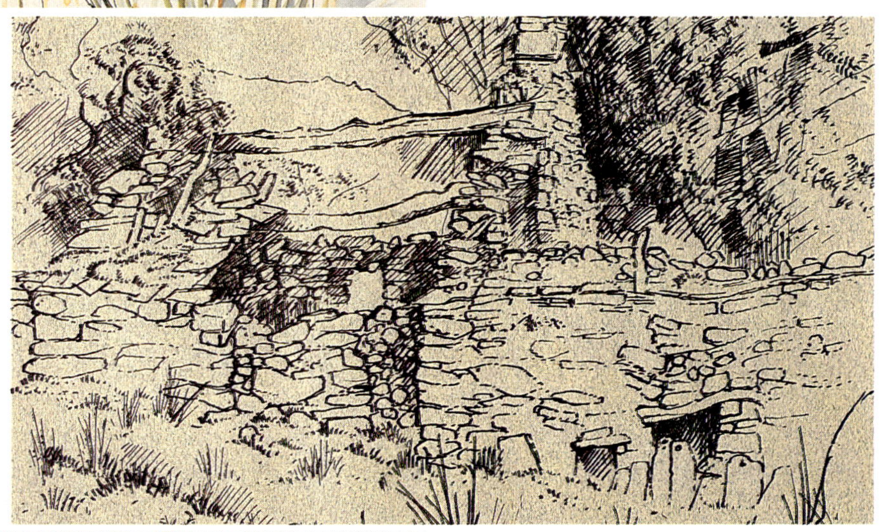

Grimecrags *Ruins in a landscape have much romantic appeal and have inspired artists through the ages.*

The illustration here was done in pen and Indian ink on a flecked, tinted paper. Because of the detailed information it contains, it could be used as a study for a painting or another drawing in a different medium.

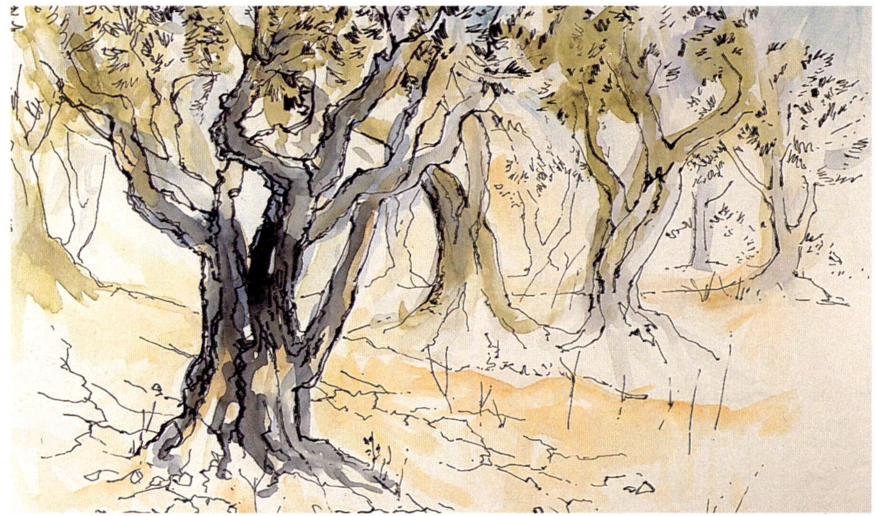

Olive Trees *Trees are lovely to draw, with their sculptural shape and varied patterns. Olive trees come high on my arboreal list.*

Their rugged textures provide many possibilities for pen and ink techniques. The drawing here was made late one evening, so had to be done quickly before the daylight faded. Again, pen and watercolour were used, the drawing being applied on top of the colour. I was intrigued by the angular cracks of the parched soil, which echoed the convoluted structure of the branches.

Crab Pots and Gull *The seashore provides a wealth of subjects for drawing. Not only are the shapes interesting and inspiring, but the colours, too, are enticing. The weathering in the salt water and air bleaches and subdues colours to subtle shades.*

This drawing of crab pots was done in a small fishing village. Because it was difficult to settle anywhere for long – not wishing to obstruct the fishermen as they moved the boats – I drew standing up, making swift sketches with a fine ball-point pen. Written colour notes were added, in case I wanted to make a more finished drawing from the sketch later on.

Never be reluctant to make written notes on your sketches. They can be helpful in several ways: to remind you of colours, if it is inconvenient to use them on the spot; to describe textures and patterns; or, indeed, anything that will expand on the drawn image.

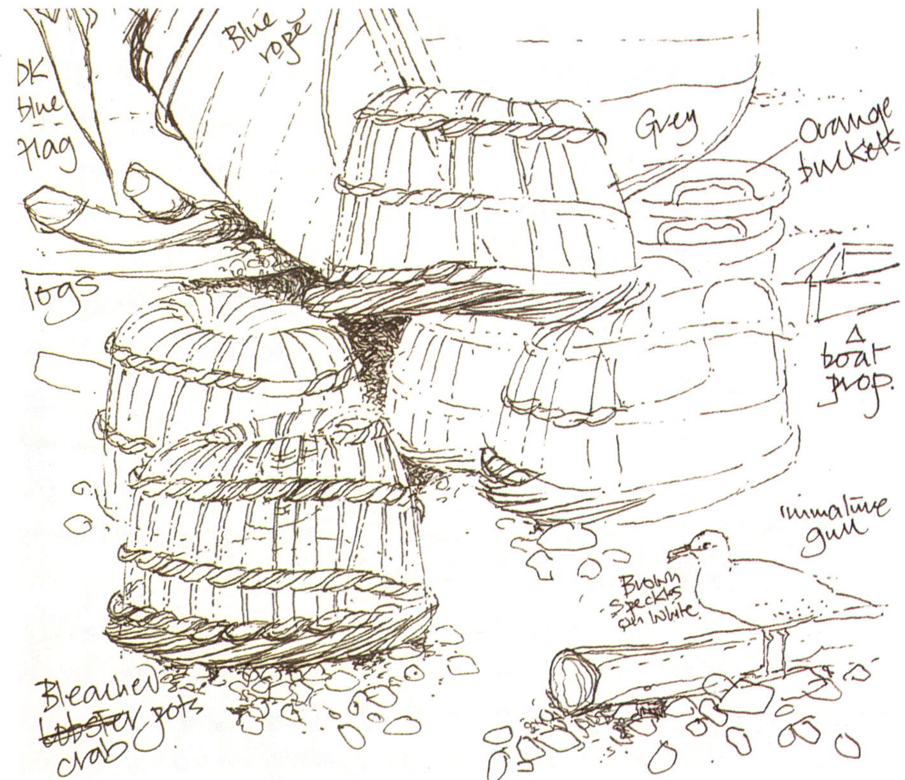

The Greenhouse *If your sketchbook is not very big, try using the whole double spread to give more room. That has been done here in the drawing of a greenhouse.*

Watercolour pens were used with a fine ball-point pen. I liked the combination of thick, chunky lines with the thin, spidery ones. The colour has been interpreted in a personal way, with a gentler blue being substituted for the rather raw green that was actually there.

This is one advantage of drawing. Things can be altered to accommodate individual expression; there is no need for you always to feel bound to record the subject literally.

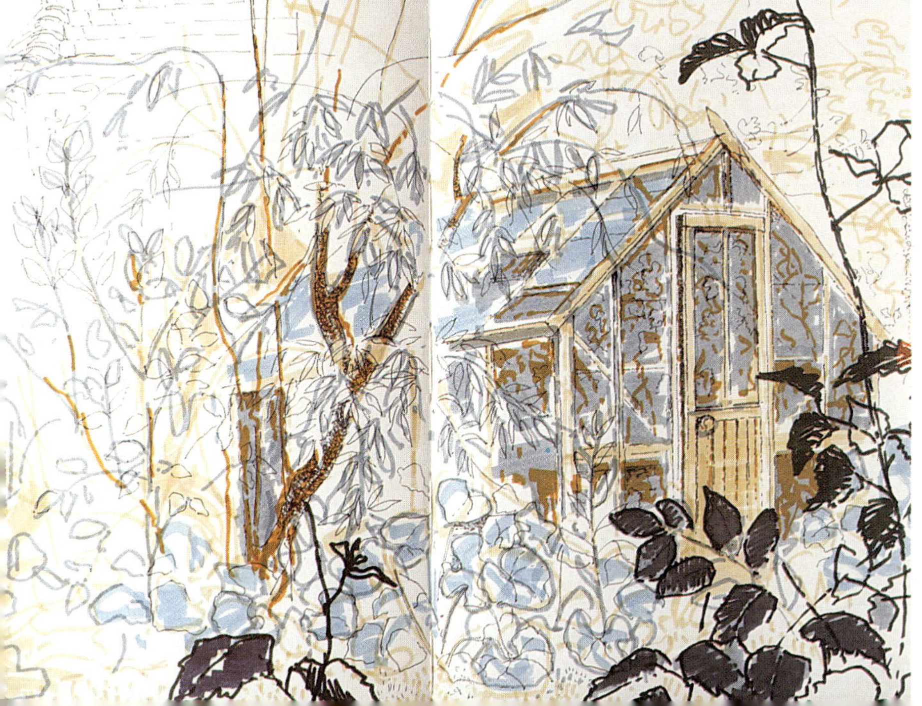

Using Photographs

The use of photography is a controversial issue among artists. My own view is that the camera can be useful in providing information and back-up material if it is used with discretion.

Your sketchbook should always be your primary means of recording images. Each drawing that you make will record not only what you saw but also a sense of time, place and how you felt. It is a unique visual diary, which captures a special atmosphere that will be missing if you rely upon a snapshot.

Sadly, far too many people copy from photographs found in books and magazines, producing uncreative pictures that are dull and lifeless.

I would encourage you always to do original work, which will have much more value than any copy, however technically proficient.

Moving Subjects

Dorothy's Pigs *These sketches were made with a fibre-tip pen.*

Pigs are fascinating creatures: intelligent, curious, full of character and expression, especially when 'talking' with their ears. This is common to many animals, and is an important factor to notice when drawing them. Get the ears right and you are well on the way to capturing their quintessential quality.

Drawing animals is not without its hazards! Busily sketching, with drawing pad propped against the sty door, I became aware that my foot was getting wet. Hastily I moved my position. Did I detect a malevolent gleam in the eye of a young porker standing nearby? Whether this was a comment upon my presence, or the drawing, I can only guess.

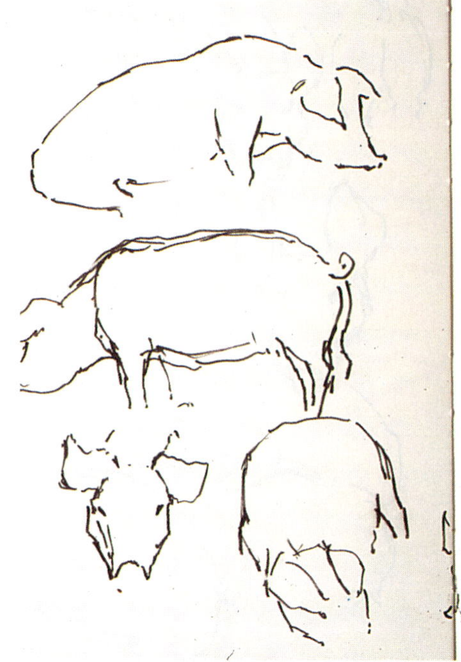

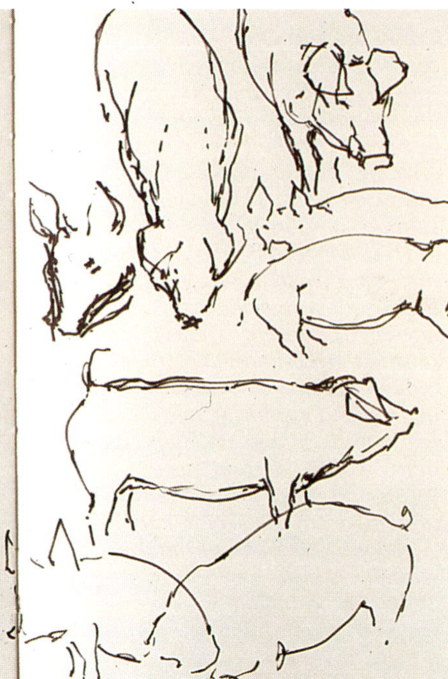

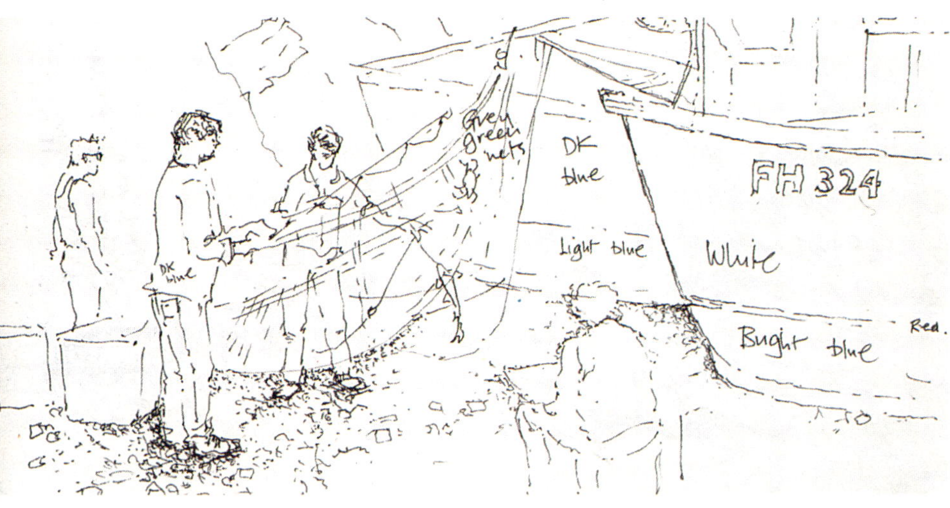

Cornish Fishermen *A rapid drawing, with ball-point pen, of fishermen at work. Because of their movement I found that a direct linear technique was best.*

I was not the only one drawing. Notice the artist in the foreground – the sketcher sketched!

Ducks' Heads *A study in pen and Indian ink on cartridge paper. I was interested in the pattern and texture of the feathers, and used varying pen strokes to capture them.*

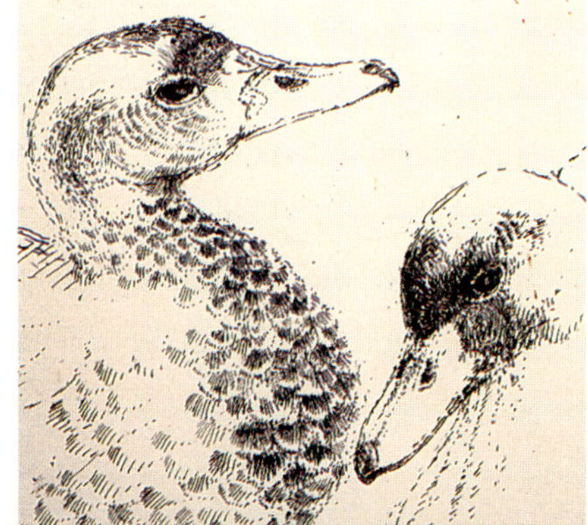

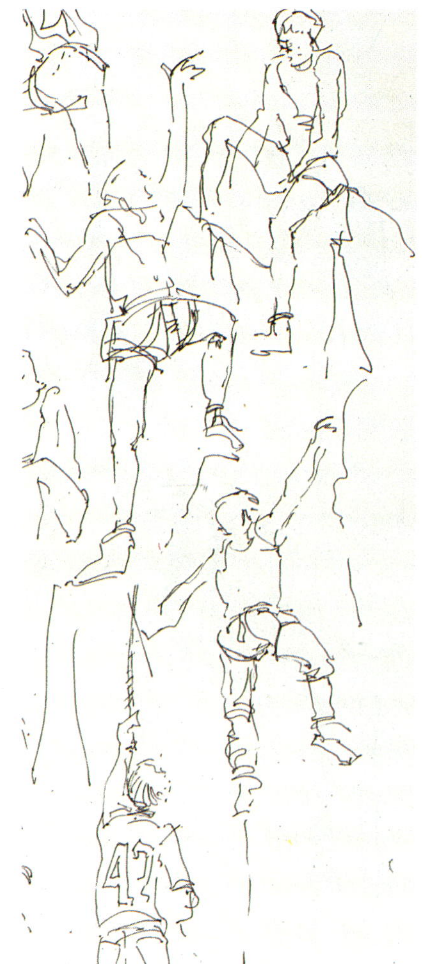

Rock Climbers *More quick sketches, using ball-point pen, of people in action. Climbing produces tremendous tensions but also relaxed moments.*

I have tried to show this contrast in these drawings.

Working Out of Doors

Plants *in situ*

Apple Blossom *Whenever possible I prefer to draw plants* in situ. *The slight movement that is there, even on the stillest of days, avoids that frozen look that can beset the cut flower in a vase.*

In this pen and watercolour of apple blossom, first the pink and then the green were brushed on with a round No. 10 brush. Having established the main flow of the picture through colour, the pen drawing was added, defining the structure. Because of the fragile nature of the subject, strokes were kept light and understated.

The 'hit-and-miss' approach of this technique – colour first then pen, with the two not quite matching – gives greater mobility and conveys better a sense of newly opened blossom. The tonal working around the petals thrusts them forward and suggests the dark spaces found in foliage. The background is kept low key, with forms merely indicated and colours fused together with a wash of pale Indigo.

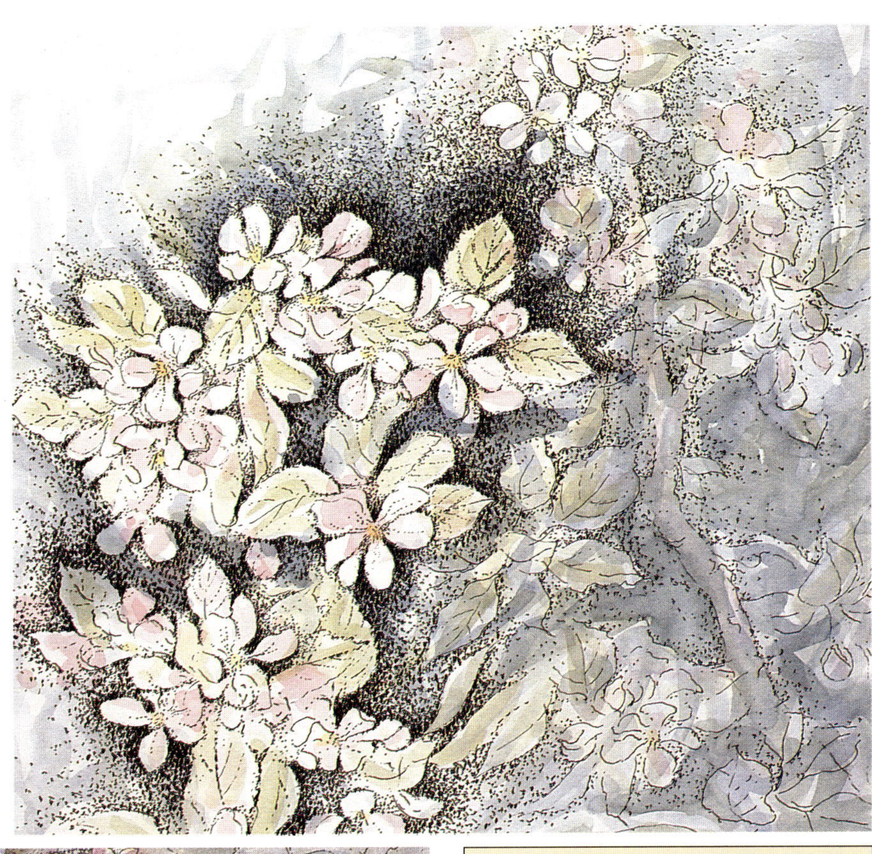

Sketchbooks and Notebooks

Your sketchbooks and notebooks will be among your most precious possessions, artistically speaking. They are the source of ideas and information that will nurture your pictures. Never part with them as they form a valuable collection of images which are irreplaceable. Most artists are happy enough to sell their finished drawings and paintings, but not their sketchbooks, which are their seed corn.

Honesty *Another picture done in a similar way to the one above, but on blue/grey paper. This pulls the colours together, suggesting shade. Dark tones imply depth through and beyond the plants.*

A View from the Window – Step-by-Step

MATERIALS
A View from the Window

- Stretched paper or Drawing block
- Pen and nibs
- Ball-point pen
- Brushes
- Black Indian ink
- Watercolour paints
- Water
- Mixing palette

Working from a Window

Drawing from a window allows the artist to work in comfort, undisturbed by passers-by or inclement weather. It also offers a wide choice of subject. In a town there are vistas of roof tops and chimney pots, streets, traffic and people; in the country there are gardens, fields, farmyards, trees and possibly animals.

Varied window heights will alter appearances. A tree seen from ground level will look different when viewed from above, and have you ever noticed the extraordinary foreshortening produced when looking down on a crowd of people? Drawing them like this could give unexpected results.

Adverse weather can be used to advantage. Rain beating against windows, mingling shapes and colours, could be the inspiration for an abstract. Patterned glass produces similar distortions.

Winter, too, produces compelling images: landscapes and cityscapes seen in the grip of blustery wind, enshrouding snow or even the occasional pale sunshine. It would be difficult, if not impossible, to draw these out in the open, but from the sanctuary of a window you can.

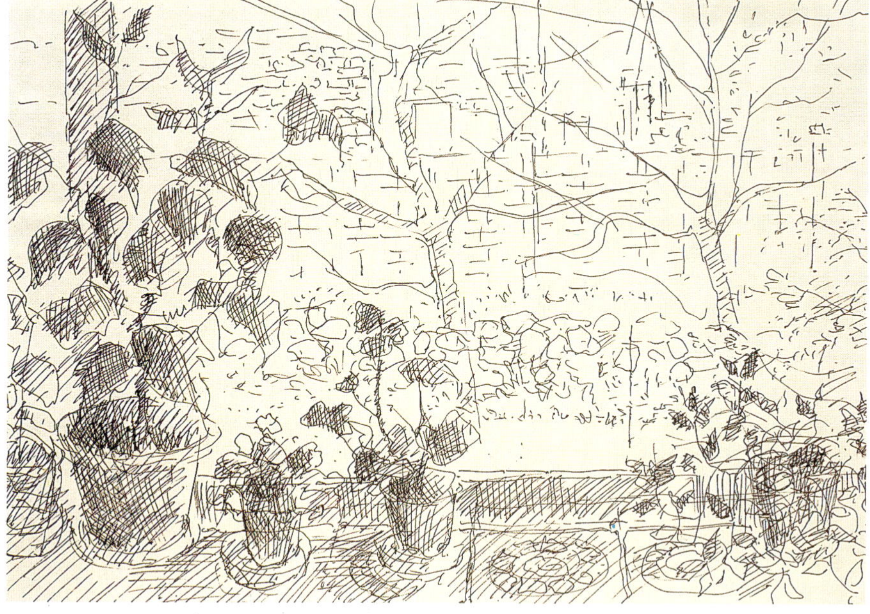

Making a preliminary sketch can be a helpful way of sorting out a composition, which is what I decided to do here.

I was interested in the different scale between the plants on the window sill and the view of the garden, but the real life scene was longer in proportion and would have made an awkward shape on the paper. Tonal contrasts were also an important feature.

These problems were resolved in this quick drawing, done in ball-point pen. By eliminating and condensing shapes, I arrived at a more suitable composition and blocked in the tones with cross-hatching to establish the pattern of light and dark that I wanted.

Working from the preliminary sketch, but also referring constantly to the real scene, I drew in the picture in a pale-blue wash, using a round No. 10 brush. The light colour allows plenty of flexibility in case of later alterations. Once the composition had been decided, I started to build up with a darker blue. Because the plants inside the window are seen almost as silhouettes I wanted to establish this contrast early on.

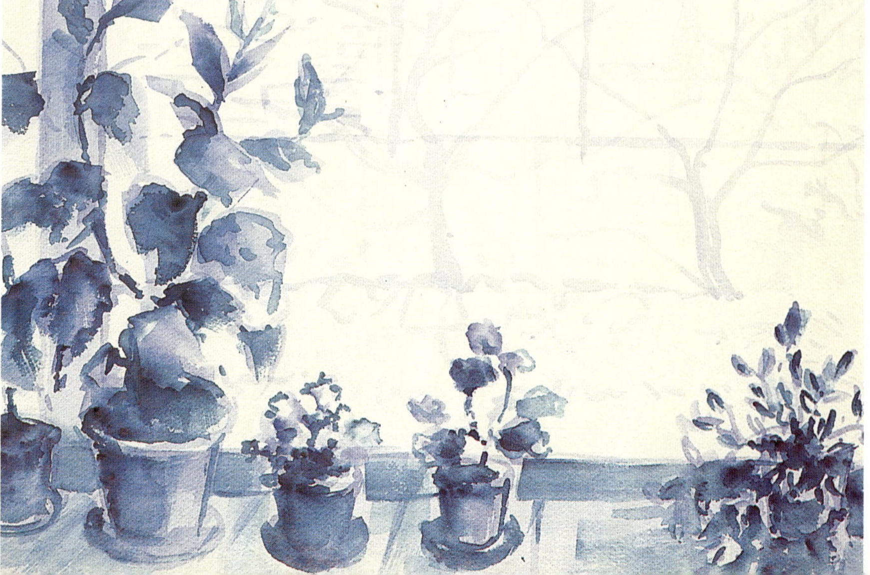

At this stage the picture appears unbalanced with all the weight on the foreground plants. It also needs some warmer colour to offset the cool blues. This is provided by a wash of Raw Sienna on the garden, which immediately helps to co-ordinate the whole drawing.

Further colours are added: Raw Umber to the trees, stones, fence and church; Yellow Ochre to the window frame and sill, and touches here and there on the stones; Olive Green to the foreground plants and trees; and, lastly, a hint of Payne's Grey to the church.

Now I start to draw in the shapes with pen.

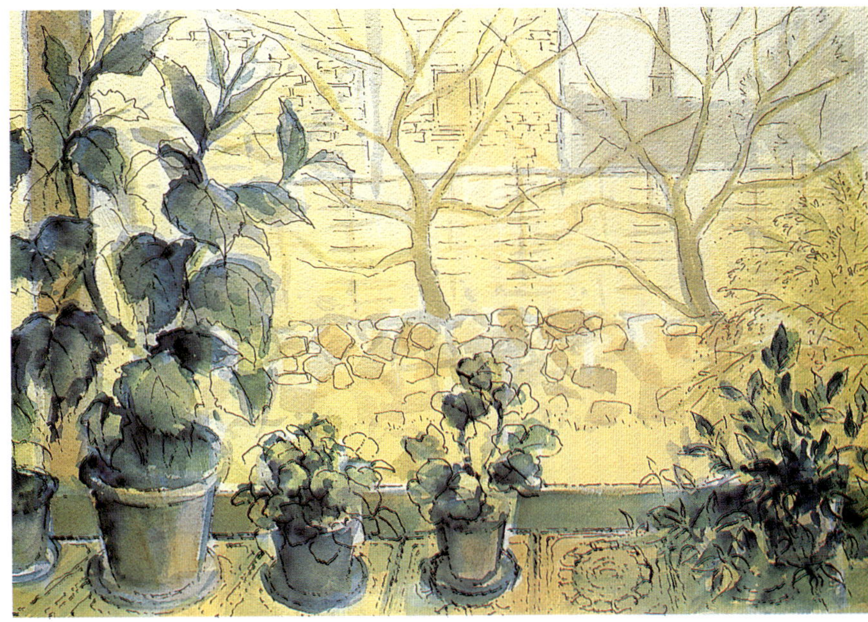

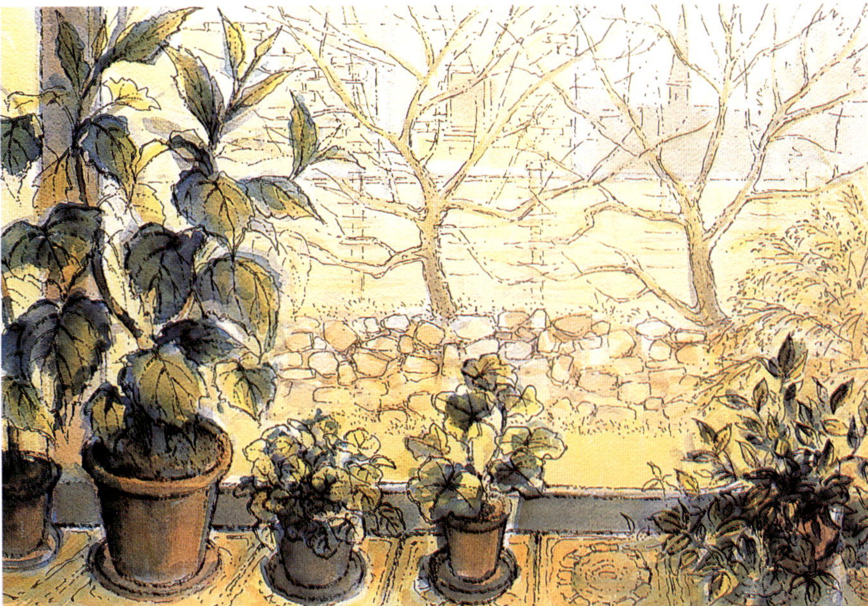

The build-up of colour and drawing continues. Yellows are brought in to make greens on the houseplants, and a pale lemon wash is used in the middle distance.

Browns and orange are used on the flower pots and window sill. A light brushing of Cobalt Blue is put on in places: the wall, apple trees, and the feathery plant outside on the extreme right.

This has produced a more mellow colour key generally, but I will have to moderate the dominant yellow/green on the houseplants in the final step.

The drawing has been strengthened in the foreground and kept lighter in the background.

More colour added in this final sequence, but attention is focused mainly on drawing. Extensive work on the window-sill plants brings them out, accentuating characteristics of leaf and structure. Texture also plays a part.

Darkening the window frame points up the difference between inside and outside. More drawing has been put on the garden, but detail has been underplayed to avoid confusion.

Pen techniques have included stippling, hatching and a variety of lines, using thick and fine nibs.

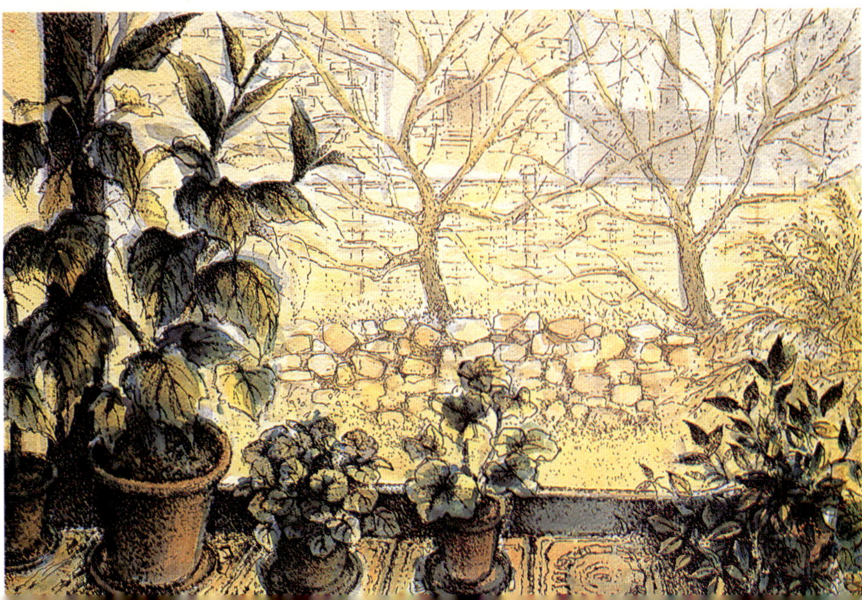

PAPERS

Papers *A collage illustrating different surface textures.*

The grey papers are both Ingres, and the orange background and yellow papers are coloured cartridge.

The word paper comes from papyrus, used by the ancient Egyptians for making scrolls, although its invention is attributed to the Chinese in 105AD. Paper became known to the Arabs in the eighth century and the Moors introduced it to Europe in 1150, through Spain. Paper making was first recorded in Britain about 1490. It was made by hand until the end of the eighteenth century, when two machines were invented – the Foudrinier and the Cylinder Moulds – and it is these machines which dominate paper production today.

The range of available papers for artists is enormous and too extensive for this book to cover comprehensively. However, a few facts should help you make an appropriate selection for your particular needs.

Handmade papers are the best and most expensive. Made largely from cotton fibres, they have deckle edges on all sides, which is the effect produced naturally in the making process. Originally they would have been made from linen rags. The term 'rag' is still retained today to denote all quality papers made from cotton, including those made by machine.

Machine-made papers fall into two categories. The best are mould made from cotton or a combination of cotton and woodpulp. The higher the ratio of cotton, the better the quality. These papers have only two natural deckle edges, the other two being torn to simulate the effect. Economy machine-made papers are produced from wood-pulp or extracted cellulose and have straight-cut edges. Their quality is still highly acceptable.

Although these are generally considered to be watercolour papers, do not be put off by this but try them with pen and ink. You will find many of them lovely to use.

The most commonly used papers for drawing in any medium are Cartridge and Ingres paper. Cartridge is so named from its original use of wrapping powder and ball for guns. It is a smooth, general-purpose paper, often used in sketchbooks. It varies in quality and the content of the paper is rarely specified. Ingres paper is also smooth, usually tinted, and frequently flecked. It provides a stimulating change from a plain, white surface.

There are a number of art boards and papers produced specially for graphic artists, which are smooth and excellent for fine pen and ink work.

Paper surfaces are of three types: 'hot pressed', which is smooth; 'not', abbreviated from 'not hot pressed', which is medium; and 'rough' which is the coarsest texture. These gradings may vary with different makes.

You will discover that paper surface has a marked effect upon your pen strokes, depending also upon the size and type of nib or pen, and the technique used. Some surfaces will give a line that is sharp and clear, while others, more absorbent, will cause the line to spread slightly. Some examples of different techniques and their effects on papers are illustrated on the opposite page.

Weights of paper have already been dealt with in 'Materials and Equipment' (*see* page 6).

It is wise to start with economical ranges while you are learning. Nevertheless, the occasional treat of an expensive paper, even in the early stages, can be invigorating and spur you on.

Find out what suits you and do not be too bound by conventions that stipulate particular papers for certain purposes. Challenging these things is stimulating and will encourage exploitation of new techniques. Sometimes, simply choosing intuitively, just liking the look and feel of a paper, can in the end be the easiest and perhaps the best way.

Examples of machine-made papers. From the top: CS10 – a designer's paper with a very smooth, durable finish; Rough – medium-weight, 100 per cent rag, mould-made paper; Hot-Pressed – lightweight, 100 per cent rag, mould-made; Not – lightweight, 100 per cent rag, mould-made; CS2-HP – Hot-Pressed, less smooth than CS10.

'White' paper varies from cold chalk to warm, creamy tones.

An illustration depicting relative paper thickness. From the left: thick – 425 gsm [200 lbs]; medium – 300 gsm [140 lbs]; light – 185 gsm [90 lbs]. All these examples are Not surface, and will take pen and ink very well.

If buying single sheets of these papers, it may be necessary to stretch the 185 gsm for use with wash, to prevent cockling.

Papers in sketchblocks will not need stretching.

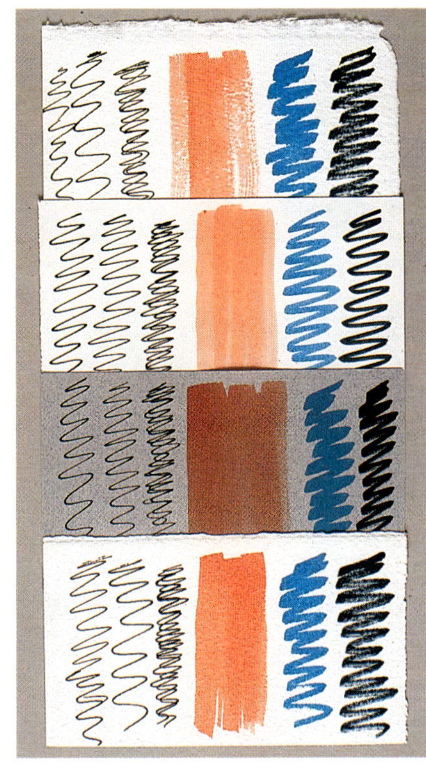

Effects of different techniques on paper surfaces, made by pen and Indian ink; brush and coloured ink wash; watercolour pens. From the top the papers are: Rough – 300 gsm [140 lbs]; Hot-Pressed – 185 gsm [90lbs]; Ingres tinted – smooth surface; Not – 300 gsm [140 lbs].

The character of the paper affects the appearance of the result, most apparent in the brush and ink wash samples. Compare also the quality of pen line on the rough and smooth surfaces.

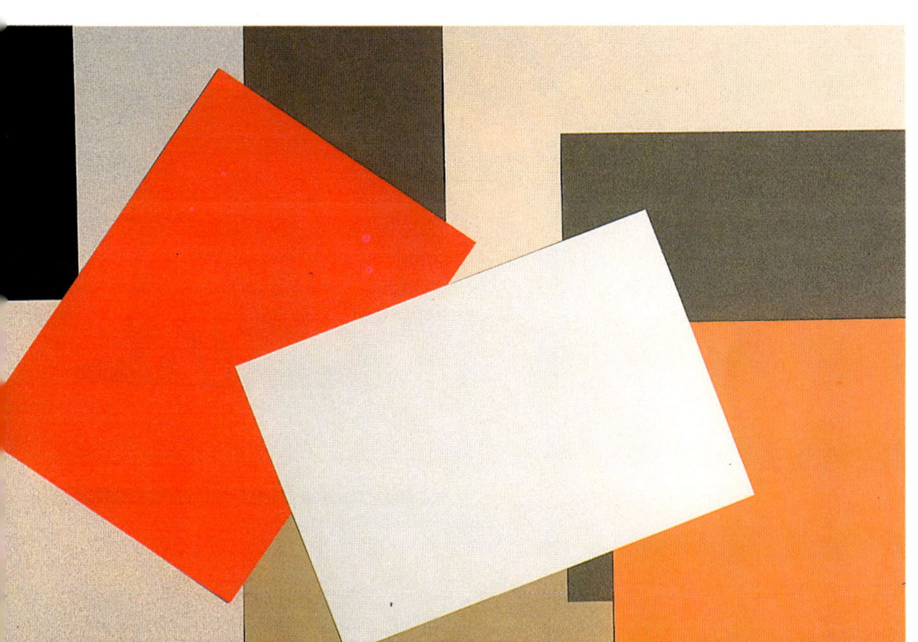

A kaleidoscope of colour! These papers respond well to pen and ink, and will take colour washes if they are not too wet. Some are smooth on one side and textured on the other.

It is not always possible to judge how a colour wash will appear until it is on the paper. Unusual effects can be achieved with these colour combinations.

Coloured cartridge papers are good for use in design and experimental work.

PRESENTATION OF WORK

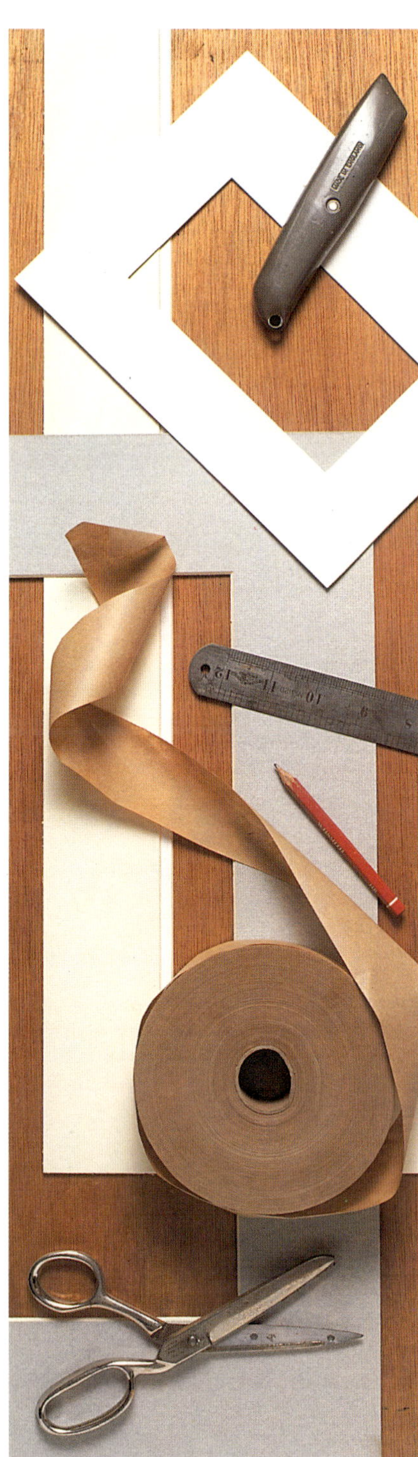

Examples of mounts and the equipment for making them. The largest is a double mount; the others are single.

Having spent time and effort on a drawing, you may want to know how best to present it. Many a picture has been spoiled by an unsuitable frame, whereas a picture well framed will be enhanced. Even here, though, be careful. An attractive frame may catch the eye at the expense of the drawing, and elicit that dreaded comment, 'I *do* like the frame'!

The purpose of framing drawings is to protect them and present them to their best advantage. It is the finishing touch that pulls the picture together and isolates it from surrounding distractions. This is especially relevant in an exhibition, with competition from other pictures.

Presentation can be a very simple mount, or a professional purpose-built frame. Between these two, there are several variations. Reasonably priced, mass-produced frames can be purchased, including the popular clip frames. An alternative is to make your own. Lengths of frame moulding can be bought, cut, and fixed together. The drawback to this is that it does need to be done skilfully, with mitred corners fitting properly, otherwise it can look very tatty, and will not help your picture at all.

A frame suitable for a drawing will usually consist of an inner mount, glass, backing and a wood, metal or synthetic surround holding it together. Surround mouldings range from the plain to the elaborate. The question of colour will arise: too dark a mount can overpower a drawing; too light, and everything may look anaemic. So careful judgment is required.

If you are inexperienced and find choosing difficult, go to a local artists' exhibition and see how other people frame their pictures. This is less costly than the trial-and-error approach, and will enable you to form opinions, which can then be applied to the presentation of your own work.

Making a Mount – Step-by-Step

These illustrations demonstrate how to make a simple mount. I used white card 1.5mm (1/16in) thick. This is a medium card, easy to cut with a sharp craft knife. When cutting the corners of the aperture, press down with the knife tip until the card lifts out cleanly; never pull it or you will leave a tag.

MATERIALS
Making a Mount

- Card 1.5mm (1/16in)
- Craft knife
- Steel rule
- Pencil
- Sticky tape
- Cutting board

Place picture on card, making the lower border deeper than the sides and top. Using pencil, mark the card 6mm (1/4in) in from the edge of the picture on all sides.

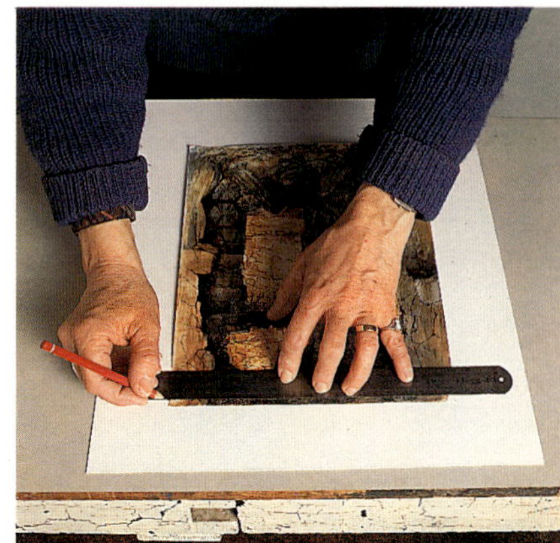

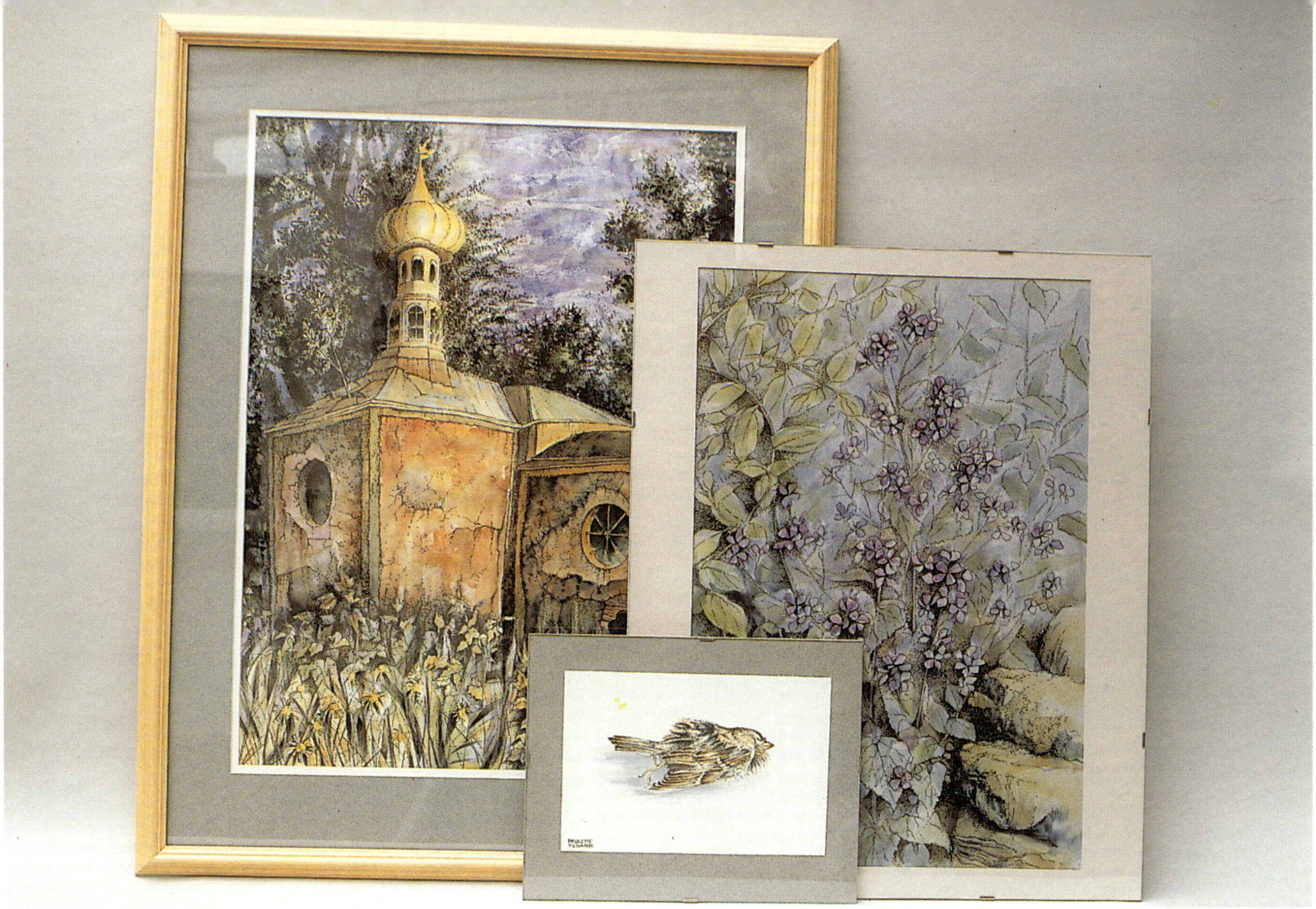

Frames *A group of purchased frames.*

The largest frame was made by a specialist frame-maker. It demonstrates double mounting: two mounts cut and positioned, one on top of the other. In the photograph, the bigger aperture on the top, dark mount allows the white undermount to show through, forming a narrow band around the picture. This type of frame is expensive but it does give a really professional finish.

The other two frames are the clip variety, and consist of a sheet of glass, hardboard backing, and metal clips to hold them together. Their main advantage is economy.

Join the marks up lightly with a pencil. Using a steel rule and a craft knife, cut out the rectangle. Make sure you have a thick board underneath to cut on.

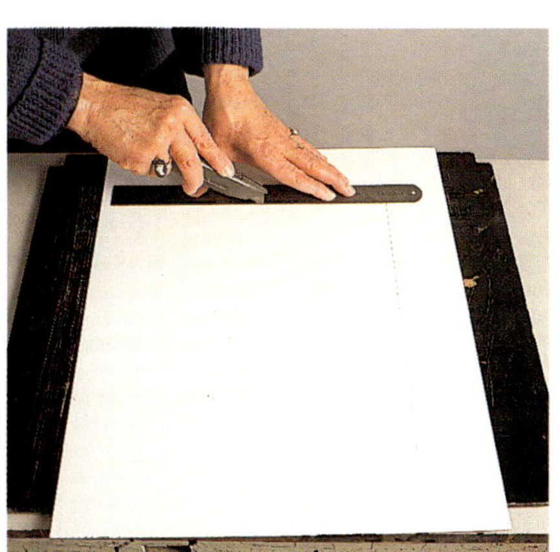

Turn the mount over and attach the picture to the back with sticky tape. Larger pictures will need to be fixed along the sides as well as the corners.

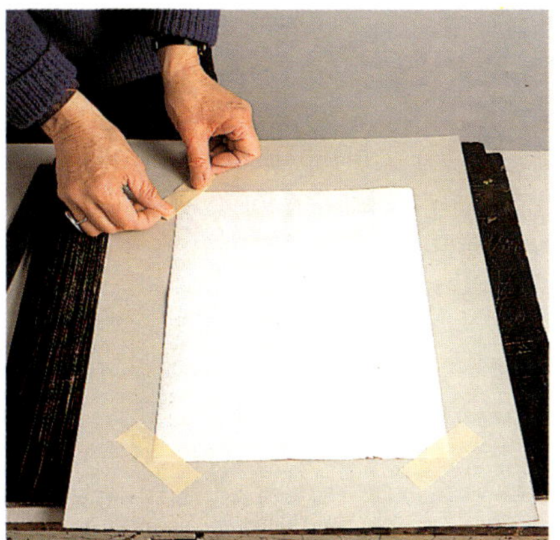

Remove all pencil marks and the mount is finished. The mounted picture is ready to be put into a clip-frame if you want to hang it on a wall.

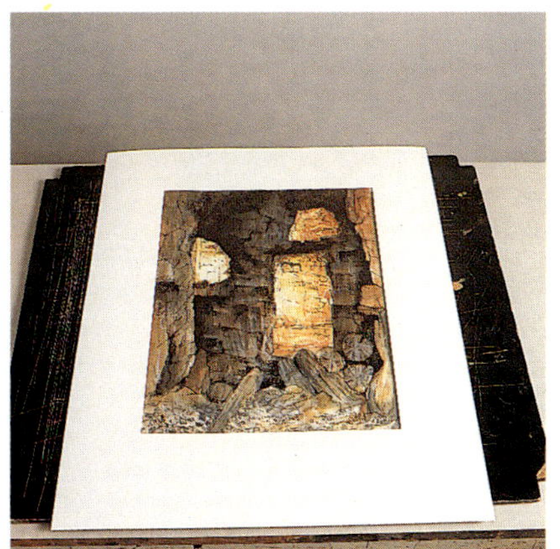

CONCLUSION

Opossum *A pen and black Indian ink drawing of an opossum. Several types of pen stroke have been used: small, varied short lines on the animal to suggest fur; stippling in the background, which merges to form a dark tone against the opossum and the leaves; longer lines on the foliage, branch and details of paws.*

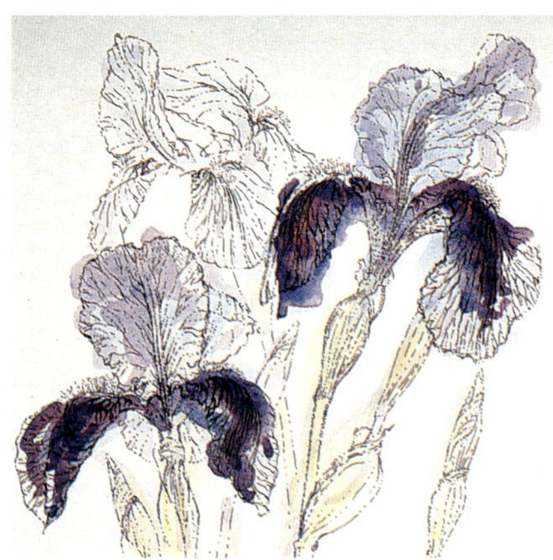

Irises *A study of irises done in pen, black Indian ink and watercolour.*

The watercolour was used first, the brush being dipped into Alizarin Crimson, then Ultramarine, and applied fairly wet to the paper. The colour mixtures were produced by the spontaneous merging of the wet paint. The pen drawing was added after the watercolour had dried.

Part 1

As this book comes towards its end, it is, perhaps, an appropriate time to take stock of what you can hope to have achieved.

Throughout, it has been my concern to put before you as comprehensive a concept of pen and ink drawing as I could; to equip you with the necessary skills to carry out the different methods demonstrated; and ultimately, by helping you build up your expertise, knowledge and confidence, enable you to express yourself through drawing.

To this end, illustrations and guides have been provided, showing how the techniques are produced and what materials are required in their execution. Opportunities have been given to study a range of subjects, from still life, landscape and buildings, to people, plants and animals. You have worked, not only with pen and inks, but with brush, watercolour and less conventional materials, and been encouraged to find inspiration both out of doors and inside. Innovation has also been an important element at times.

If, before reading this book, you were under the impression that pen and ink work was a rather limited branch of art, restricted to making black lines on white paper, then I hope these chapters have convinced you otherwise. Now you should be more aware of the enormous potential of this exciting medium. By this I do not wish to imply that straightforward pen and ink drawing is dull or unadventurous. Far from it! In its richness and diversity, it has been responsible for some of the loveliest and most sensitive drawings in the world. For two very different examples, take a look at the plant studies of Leonardo da Vinci, or the fluid line drawings of Matisse.

While working your way through the book, you may have realized that the boundaries of art are not clear cut; that the various media tend to encroach on each other; that the tools are interchangeable (the brush is used by the pen and ink artist, just as the pen or pencil is used by the painter). A book on pen and ink techniques is likely to contain passages on using watercolour, while a comprehensive survey of watercolour painting will almost certainly include references to pen and ink. This interrelating of the various art techniques is particularly noticeable today. Go to almost any exhibition of pictures or craftwork and you will usually find several items described as mixed media. This opens up all sorts of possibilities, some of which have been touched upon in the experimental sections.

One advantage of working from a book is that you can pick and choose at will, selecting those chapters which you believe are relevant to your needs. There is no sense of being pressurized into tackling subjects that are less appealing to you. You are free to decide when to work and for how long. However, this can be a two-edged sword! Without the physical presence of a tutor to encourage and persuade you to try the unfamiliar, you could be tempted to keep only to those methods with which you feel safe, and to eschew areas with any hint of risk.

This would be a pity because often, a jolt of something new can be just the stimulus you need to make your drawing blossom and develop. It can become very mechanical if it is allowed to run on and on in the same track. If you have disregarded certain parts for this reason, believing they would be uncongenial to you, I would urge you to have another look; they may well prove to be more beneficial than you think.

Conclusion

Part 2

In addition to demonstrating techniques, I have also tried to provide you with as much information as possible about the equipment you require to implement these methods. Most materials I have mentioned should be obtainable at a good art shop in a reasonable sized town. The one difficulty you could experience is in getting hold of a sufficient choice of suitable pen nibs. Most shops seem to stock the finer drawing nibs; it is the medium sizes that are harder to get. Be careful about being fobbed off with the usual calligraphic or lettering pen nibs. These are the ones that have a broad, straight end to the tip, rather than a point as the true drawing nib has.

Conversely, there is no reason why you should not try using a calligrapher's nib for drawing if you would like to; indeed, this echoes the spirit of inventiveness I have sought to encourage! What they lack is the flexibility and sensitivity of the drawing pen, and you may find this makes them unsympathetic to work with.

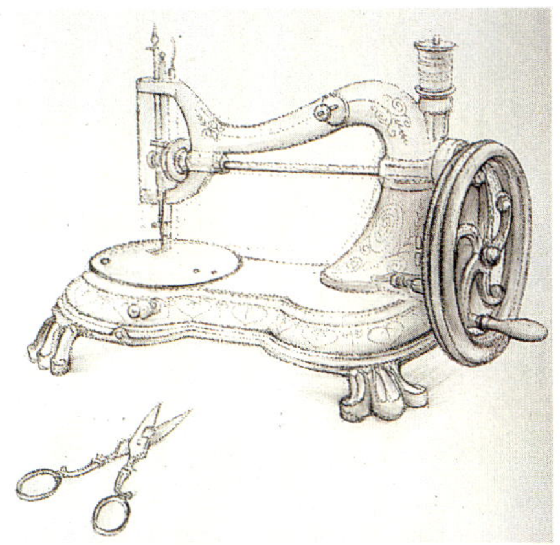

Sewing Machine *A pen and wash drawing of an early sewing machine, using non-waterproof ink. The pen drawing was done first, then a wet brush was pulled along the lines to produce tone.*

If you continue to have problems getting proper nibs locally, get in touch with one of the nationally advertised specialist firms. It is usually possible to find one of those excellent – often long-established – firms who take a pride in supplying this sort of thing, and will probably send you an informative catalogue and offer a mail-order service. There are also some firms who deal exclusively by mail order. Admittedly you will have to pay the extra cost of postage in addition to the cost of the materials, but this is often justified by the ease and convenience of getting a good supply of what you need. It is frustrating and time-wasting to make journeys, only to find that the materials you want are out of stock, or not even stocked at all.

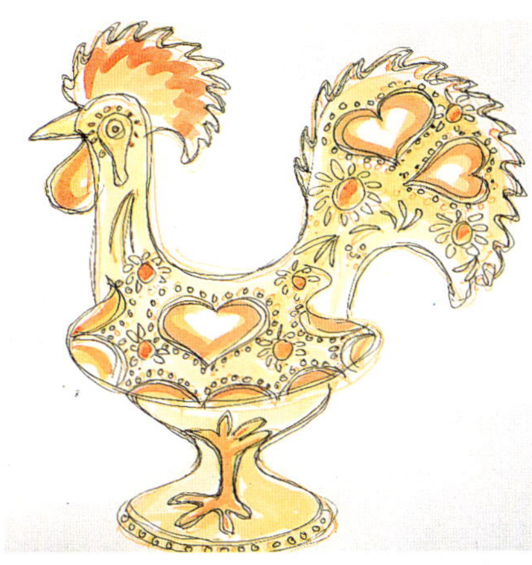

Cock *A decorative drawing of a cock, carried out in coloured ink washes of yellow and orange, with freely added lines in black Indian ink.*

Some of the specialist papers, particularly the handmade variety, may have to be bought in the same way. A good selection of names and addresses can be found in most national art magazines and periodicals.

Part 3

When you first started reading this book, you may possibly have wondered whether you would ever be able to make the fluent lines that appear to come so effortlessly from the practised exponent. Many of us feel similarly at the beginning of a study course; the goal can seem very far away. Looking back from this end of the book, I hope you feel your perseverance has been justified, not only by greater competence but by greater enjoyment, too.

Most pursuits, if they are worth while, will merit application and a lot of practice. Drawing is no exception: in fact, because of all it encompasses, it will require a great deal of your attention. There will never be a time when you can sit back and declare 'There, that's it. I can draw, there's nothing more to be learnt!' It may be that you *can* draw, and very well too, but it is an ongoing activity that must always be allowed to change

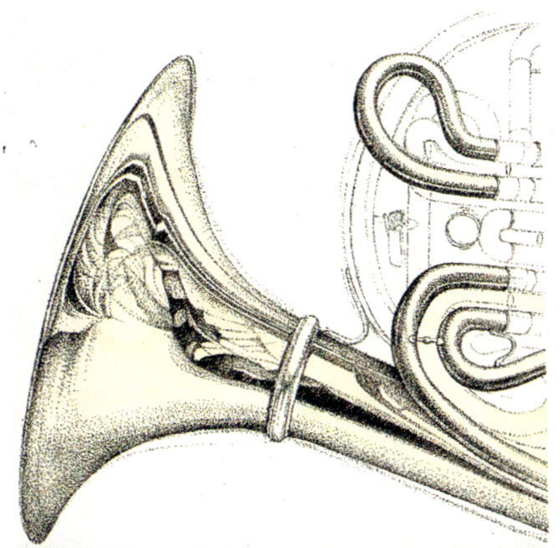

French Horn *A French horn drawn in detail to capture the fascinating shapes of the reflections. This type of study necessitates careful observation. Pen and Indian ink were used with a light wash of watercolour.*

Conclusion

and grow, however proficient you become.

This book has been about technique, but the underlying theme has been drawing, the ability to give visual shape on paper to things seen and things imagined.

Occasionally, I have brought your attention to the fact that technique is only a means to an end, and not the end itself. It is what you have to *say* in your drawing that matters, the special quality that identifies it as being by you and nobody else. Technical skill is necessary to *serve* these aims, not to be the master of them. It can be taught in classes and learnt from books, but the quintessence of drawing must come from within yourself and be tempered by experience and observation.

Now that you have finished this book, I hope you feel confident enough to continue on your own. Search out new subjects and scrutinize the work of other artists, not to copy, but to inspire your own ideas. Tune up your skills and cultivate an awareness of the world around you. This will be rewarded in the extension of both your drawing and sensibility.

I set out to make a book that would be attractive, informative and stimulating. I hope it fulfils at least some of these objectives and makes you want to draw for ever.

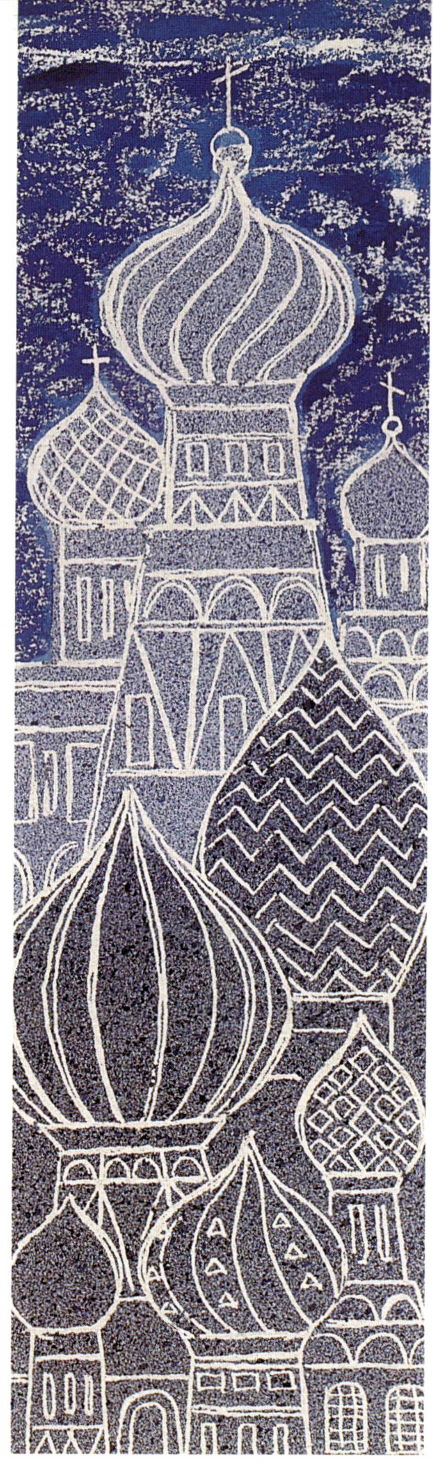

In this design, inks were sprayed over lines drawn with masking fluid, and brushed over wax in the sky. Other effects were achieved by using masking film.

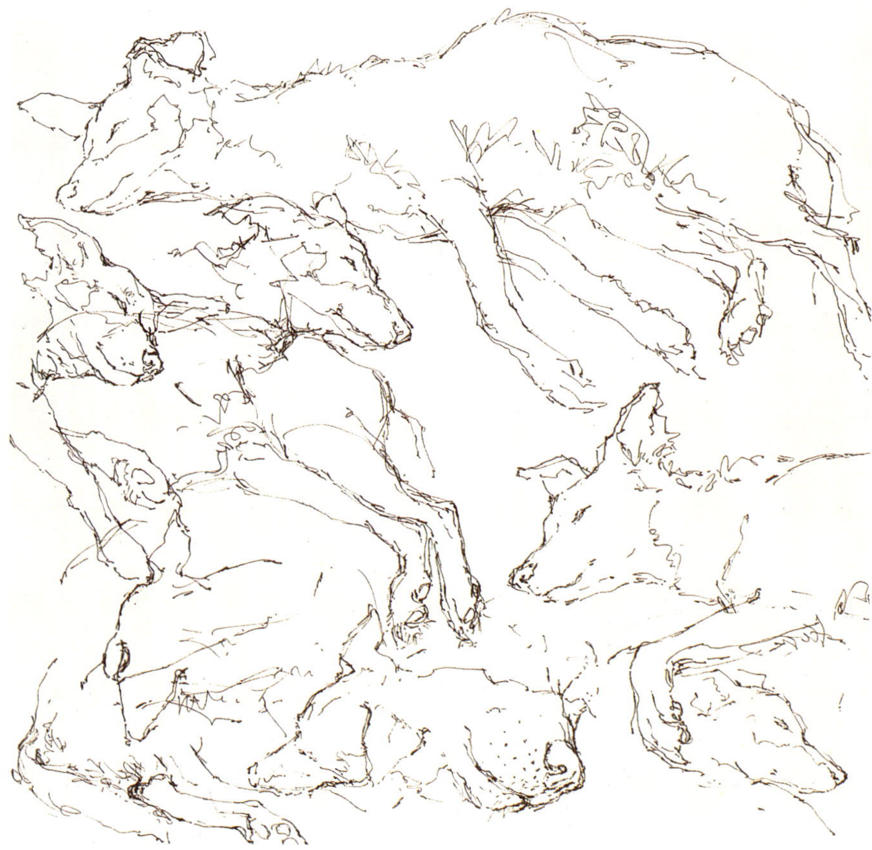

Sketches of a sleeping dog who frequently altered position. A fibre-tip pen captures the essential pose without bothering about the finer details.

ARTISTS' TIPS

As a final adjunct to the book, I have compiled a few tips which may be useful.

Pens and Inks

New nibs make the crispest and finest lines. As they wear, they thicken. Instead of discarding them when this happens, keep one or two. They will produce a thick, rugged line which can be an interesting addition to your repertoire of pen strokes. The older the better, I find!

When you are drawing, wipe the nib periodically with a tissue to prevent it clogging. Occasionally, give it a more thorough cleaning by dipping it in water.

Always clean all implements properly at the end of each drawing session. They will perform better and last longer. Make sure nibs are thoroughly dry or they may rust.

Ensure you have enough separate dishes for mixing inks and for diluting them to make washes. The 'nests' of dishes are good for this.

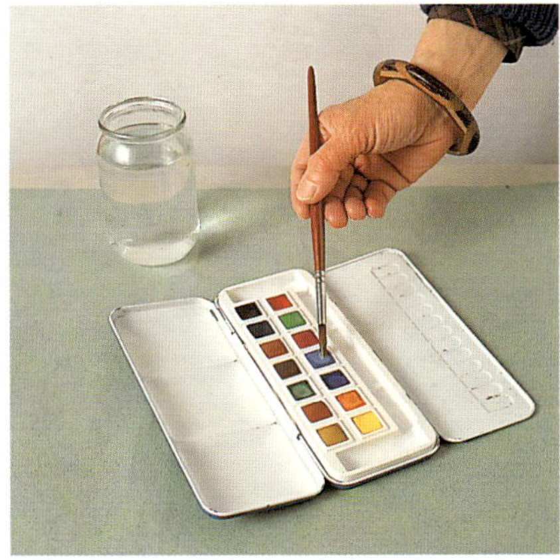

To keep watercolour pans in good condition, make sure they are slightly moist. If they have become dry and cracked, add a brushful of clean water and leave them overnight. This should restore them.

Ink bottles sometimes get encrusted round the neck. Wipe them to prevent particles falling into the ink and interfering with drawing.

If the tops are difficult to undo, immerse the bottle upside down in a bowl of hot water. This will usually loosen them.

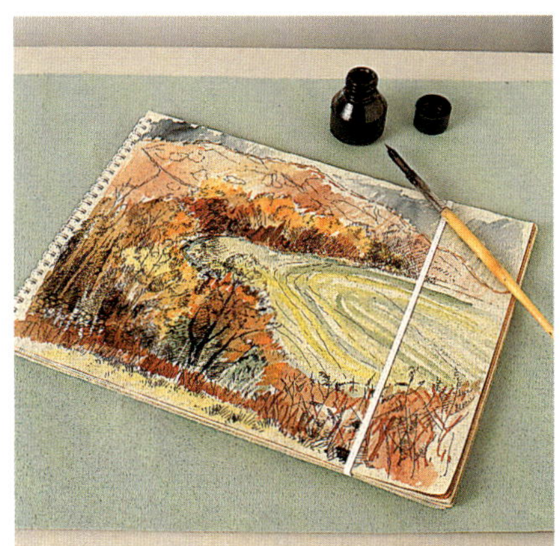

A piece of elastic around a sketchbook is invaluable. It keeps the pages firmly together while you are carrying it, and stops the pages flapping if you are drawing in a breeze.

Sketching Out of Doors

To prevent brushes getting damaged in a sketch bag, fix them to a stout piece of card with elastic bands. The card should be longer than the brushes to protect the hairs. Several brushes can be kept together in this way.

If you happen to have no water but you do have wine, it makes an excellent substitute! I was in this situation once and found the wine gave a beautifully delicate, pinkish tint to my sketch.

General

To help you see if a picture looks 'right', try turning it upside down. It then becomes a series of shapes and tones which can be judged more objectively, with less distraction from the subject matter. Looking at the reverse image in a mirror is another way; you see it with fresh eyes. Both these 'dodges' are often used by artists.

Have a spare mount available to place round your drawing occasionally while you are working. It pulls the picture together, isolating it from surrounding objects, and again aids judgement.

If you work closely at your drawing, look at it from a distance now and again. Not only will it rest your eyes, but you may notice new things about it.

When you are using water for colour washes, change it frequently to keep the colours clean.

Save the cardboard backing from used-up sketchblocks. It makes a good cutting board when you are using a craft knife.

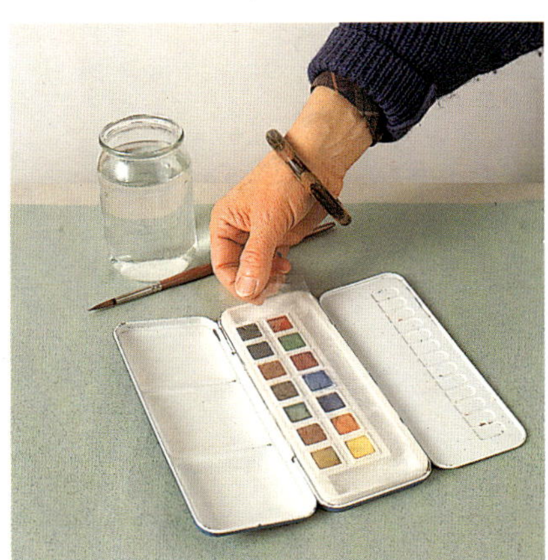

Once your watercolours are nicely moist, a piece of plastic laid over them will prevent drying out and have them always ready for use. Scrubbing at wizened paints to produce a modicum of colour makes an unpropitious start. They should be succulent and inviting!

First published in 1992 by
The Crowood Press Ltd
Ramsbury, Marlborough
Wiltshire SN8 2HR

British Library Cataloguing in Publication Data

A catalogue record for this book is available from the British Library

ISBN 1 85223 668 X

Acknowledgements

I should like to express my gratitude to the following people: my husband, Michael, for his encouragement, advice and invaluable help with the text; Sue Atkinson for the photographs and for making our working days together such a pleasure; Diane Wright for her patience and hard work in producing the final typescript; JBM Ltd and Michelle Bates for their help; and all my family for their support and forbearance.

Typeset by Acūté, Stroud, Gloucestershire.
Printed and bound in Great Britain by BPCC Hazells Ltd
Member of BPCC Ltd